CAMBRIDGE Advanced Level Mathematics

Mechanics 1

Douglas Quadling

Series editor Hugh Neill

CAMBRIDGE
UNIVERSITY PRESS

PUBLISHED BY THE PRESS SYNDICATE OF THE UNIVERSITY OF CAMBRIDGE
The Pitt Building, Trumpington Street, Cambridge, United Kingdom

CAMBRIDGE UNIVERSITY PRESS
The Edinburgh Building, Cambridge CB2 2RU, UK   http://www.cup.cam.ac.uk
40 West 20th Street, New York, NY 10011-4211, USA   http://www.cup.org
10 Stamford Road, Oakleigh, Melbourne 3166, Australia
Ruiz de Alarcón 13, 28014 Madrid, Spain

First published 2000

Printed in the United Kingdom at the University Press, Cambridge

Typefaces Times, Helvetica   *Systems* Microsoft® Word, MathType™

A catalogue record for this book is available from the British Library

ISBN 0 521 78600 2 paperback

Cover image: Images Colour Library

Contents

Introduction   v

1   Velocity and acceleration   1

2   Force and motion   19

3   Vertical motion   31

4   Resolving forces   43

5   Friction   60

6   Motion due to gravity   77

Revision exercise 1   91

7   Newton's third law   94

8   Momentum   117

9   Combining and splitting forces   126

10   Forces in equilibrium   143

11   General motion in a straight line   158

Revision exercise 2   175

Mock examinations   178

Answers   182

Index   192

Introduction

Cambridge Advanced Level Mathematics has been written especially for the OCR modular examination. It consists of one book or half-book corresponding to each module. This book is the first Mechanics module, M1.

The books are divided into chapters roughly corresponding to syllabus headings. Occasionally a section includes an important result that is difficult to prove or outside the syllabus. These sections are marked with an asterisk (*) in the section heading, and there is usually a sentence early on explaining precisely what it is that the student needs to know.

Occasionally within the text paragraphs appear in *this type style*. These paragraphs are usually outside the main stream of the mathematical argument, but may help to give insight, or suggest extra work or different approaches.

Numerical work is presented in a form intended to discourage premature approximation. In ongoing calculations inexact numbers appear in decimal form like 3.456..., signifying that the number is held in a calculator to more places than are given. Numbers are not rounded at this stage; the full display could be either 3.456 123 or 3.456 789. Final answers are then stated with some indication that they are approximate, for example '1.23 correct to 3 significant figures'.

The value of g is taken as 9.8 m s^{-2}.

Some chapters contain practical experiments, which are intended to reinforce the theory. There may be some safety issues to think about where you see *[Safety!]*. There are plenty of exercises, and each chapter contains a Miscellaneous exercise which includes some questions of examination standard. Questions which go beyond examination requirements are marked by an asterisk. In the middle and at the end of the book there is a set of Revision exercises and two practice examination papers. The authors thank Maurice Godfrey, David A. Lee and Geoff Staley, the OCR examiners who contributed to these exercises, and also Peter Thomas, who read the books very carefully and made many extremely useful and constructive comments.

The author thanks OCR and Cambridge University Press for their help in producing this book. However, the responsibility for the text, and for any errors, remains with the author.

1 Velocity and acceleration

This chapter introduces kinematics, which is about the connections between displacement, velocity and acceleration. When you have completed it, you should

- know the terms 'displacement', 'velocity', 'acceleration' and 'deceleration' for motion in a straight line
- be familiar with displacement–time and velocity–time graphs
- be able to express speeds in different systems of units
- know formulae for constant velocity and constant acceleration
- be able to solve problems on motion with constant velocity and constant acceleration, including problems involving several such stages.

1.1 Motion with constant velocity

A Roman legion marched out of Lincoln along a straight road, with a velocity of 100 paces per minute due north. Where was the legion 90 minutes later?

Notice the word **velocity**, rather than speed. This is because you are told not only how fast the legion marched, but also in which direction. Velocity is speed in a particular direction.

Two cars travelling in opposite directions on an east–west motorway may have the same speed of 70 miles per hour, but they have different velocities. One has a velocity of 70 m.p.h. east, the other a velocity of 70 m.p.h. west.

The answer to the question in the first paragraph is, of course, that the legion was 9000 paces (9 Roman miles) north of Lincoln. The legion made a **displacement** of 9000 paces north. Displacement is distance in a particular direction.

This calculation, involving the multiplication $100 \times 90 = 9000$, is a special case of a general rule.

> An object moving with constant velocity u units in a particular direction for a time t units makes a displacement s units in that direction, where $s = ut$.

The word 'units' is used three times in this statement, and it has a different sense each time. For the Roman legion the units are paces per minute, minutes and paces respectively. You can use any suitable units for velocity, time and displacement provided that they are consistent.

The equation $s = ut$ can be rearranged into the forms $u = \dfrac{s}{t}$ or $t = \dfrac{s}{u}$. You decide which form to use according to which quantities you know and which you want to find.

Example 1.1.1

An airliner flies from Heathrow to Accra, a displacement of 3175 miles south, at a speed of 500 m.p.h. How long does the flight last?

You know that $s = 3175$ and $u = 500$, and want to find t. So use

$$t = \frac{s}{u} = \frac{3175}{500} = 6.35.$$

For the units to be consistent, the unit of time must be hours. The flight lasts 6.35 hours, or 6 hours and 21 minutes.

This is not a sensible way of giving the answer. In a real flight the aircraft will travel more slowly while climbing and descending. It is also unlikely to travel in a straight line, and the figure of 500 m.p.h. for the speed looks like a convenient approximation. The solution is based on a **mathematical model**, in which such complications are ignored so that the data can be put into a simple mathematical equation. But when you have finished using the model, you should then take account of the approximations and give a less precise answer, such as 'about $6\frac{1}{2}$ hours'.

The units almost always used in mechanics are metres (m) for displacement, seconds (s) for time and metres per second (written as $m\,s^{-1}$) for velocity. These are called **SI units** (SI stands for *Système Internationale*), and scientists all over the world have agreed to use them.

Example 1.1.2

Express a speed of 90 m.p.h. in $m\,s^{-1}$.

If you travel 90 miles in an hour at a constant speed, you go $\dfrac{90}{60 \times 60}$ miles in each second, which is $\frac{1}{40}$ of a mile in each second. A mile is just over 1600 metres, so you go approximately $\frac{1}{40}$ of 1600 metres in a second. Thus a speed of 90 m.p.h. is approximately $40\ m\,s^{-1}$.

You can extend this result to give a general rule: to convert any speed in m.p.h. to $m\,s^{-1}$, you multiply by $\frac{40}{90}$, which is $\frac{4}{9}$. But remember that this is only approximate.

1.2 Graphs for constant velocity

You do not always have to use equations to describe mathematical models. Another method is to use graphs. There are two kinds of graph which are often useful in kinematics.

The first kind is a **displacement–time graph**, as shown in Fig. 1.1. The coordinates of any

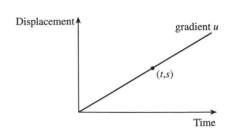

Fig. 1.1

point on the graph are (t, s), where s is the displacement of the moving object after a time t (both in appropriate units). Notice that $s = 0$ when $t = 0$, so the graph passes through the origin. If the velocity is constant, then $\dfrac{s}{t} = u$, and the gradient of the line joining (t, s) to the origin has the constant value u. So the graph is a straight line with gradient u.

> For an object moving along a straight line with constant velocity u,
> the displacement–time graph is a straight line with gradient u.

The second kind of graph is a **velocity–time graph** (see Fig. 1.2). The coordinates of any point on this graph are (t, v), where v is the velocity of the moving object at time t. If the velocity has a constant value u, then the graph has equation $v = u$, and it is a straight line parallel to the time-axis.

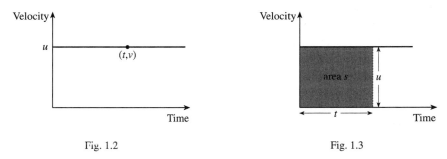

Fig. 1.2   Fig. 1.3

How is displacement shown on the velocity–time graph? Fig. 1.3 answers this question for motion with constant velocity. The coordinates of any point on the graph are (t, u), and you know that $s = ut$. This product is the area of the shaded rectangle in the figure, which has width t and height u.

> For an object moving along a straight line with constant velocity, the
> displacement from the start up to any time t is represented by the area of the
> region under the velocity–time graph for values of the time from 0 to t.

Exercise 1A

1   How long will an athlete take to run 1500 metres at 7.5 m s^{-1}?

2   A train maintains a constant velocity of 60 m s^{-1} due south for 20 minutes. What is its displacement in that time? Give the distance in kilometres.

3   How long will it take for a cruise liner to sail a distance of 530 nautical miles at a speed of 25 knots? (A knot is a speed of 1 nautical mile per hour.)

4   Some Antarctic explorers walking towards the South Pole expect to average 1.2 miles per hour. What is their expected displacement in a day in which they walk for 14 hours?

5   On the Ml motorway Junction 15 (Northampton South) is 13 miles north-west of Junction
    14 (Milton Keynes). A coach travels from Junction 14 to Junction 15 in 15 minutes, and a
    car travels from Junction 15 to Junction 14 in 12 minutes. Both travel at constant speed.
    Find the approximate velocities of the coach and the car

    (a) in miles per hour,   (b) in metres per second.

6   Here is an extract from the diary of Samuel Pepys for 4 June 1666.

    'We find the Duke at St James's, whither he is lately gone to lodge. So walking through the
    Parke we saw hundreds of people listening to hear the guns.'

    These guns were at the battle of the English fleet against the Dutch in the Downs off Deal
    in Kent, a distance of between 110 and 120 km away. The speed of sound in air is
    344 m s^{-1}. How long did it take the sound of the gunfire to reach London?

7   Light travels at a speed of $3.00 \times 10^{8} \text{ m s}^{-1}$. Light from the star Sirius takes 8.65 years to
    reach the earth. What is the distance of Sirius from the earth in kilometres?

8   The speed limit on a Belgian motorway is 120 km per hour. What is this in SI units?

9   A train travels from Newcastle to London, a displacement of 440 km south, in $2\frac{1}{2}$ hours.
    Model the journey by drawing

    (a) a velocity–time graph,   (b) a displacement–time graph.

    Label your graphs to show the numbers 440 and $2\frac{1}{2}$ and to indicate the units used.
    Suggest some ways in which your models may not match the actual journey.

10 An aircraft flies at 800 km per hour from Birmingham to Berlin, a displacement of
    1000 km due east. Model the flight by drawing

    (a) a displacement–time graph,   (b) a velocity–time graph.

    Label your graphs to show the numbers 800 and 1000 and to indicate the units used. Can
    you suggest ways in which your models could be improved to describe the actual flight
    more accurately?

1.3 Acceleration

A vehicle at rest cannot suddenly start to move with constant velocity. There has to be a
period when the velocity increases. The rate at which the velocity increases is called the
acceleration.

In the simplest case the velocity increases at a constant rate. For example, suppose that a
train accelerates from 0 to 90 m.p.h. in 100 seconds at a constant rate. You know from
Example 1.1.2 that 90 m.p.h. is about 40 m s^{-1}, so the speed is increasing by 0.4 m s^{-1}
in each second.

The SI unit of acceleration is 'm s^{-1} per second', or $\left(\text{m s}^{-1}\right)\text{s}^{-1}$; this is always simplified
to m s^{-2} and read as 'metres per second squared'. Thus in the example above the train has

a constant acceleration of $\frac{40}{100}$ m s^{-2}, which is 0.4 m s^{-2}.

Consider the period of acceleration. After t seconds the train will have reached a speed of 0.4t m s^{-1}. So the velocity–time graph has equation $v = 0.4t$. This is a straight line segment with gradient 0.4, joining $(0,0)$ to $(100,40)$. It is shown in Fig. 1.4.

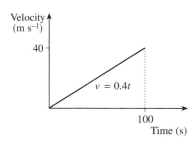

Fig. 1.4

This is a special case of a general rule.

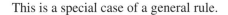

> The velocity–time graph for an object moving with constant acceleration a is a straight line segment with gradient a.

Now suppose that at a later time the train has to stop at a signal. The brakes are applied, and the train is brought to rest in 50 seconds. If the velocity drops at a constant rate, this is $\frac{40}{50}$ m s^{-2}, or 0.8 m s^{-2}. The word for this is **deceleration** (some people use **retardation**).

Fig. 1.5 shows the velocity–time graph for the braking train. If time is measured from the instant when the brakes are applied, the graph has equation $v = 40 - 0.8t$.

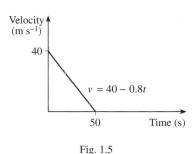

Fig. 1.5

There are two new points to notice about this graph. First, it doesn't pass through the origin, since at time $t = 0$ the train has a velocity of 40 m s^{-1}. The velocity when $t = 0$ is called the **initial velocity**.

Secondly, the graph has negative gradient, because the velocity is decreasing. This means that the acceleration is negative. You can either say that the acceleration is -0.8 m s^{-2}, or that the deceleration is 0.8 m s^{-2}.

The displacement is still given by the area of the region between the velocity–time graph and the t-axis, even though the velocity is not constant. In Fig. 1.4 this region is a triangle with base 100 and height 40, so the area is $\frac{1}{2} \times 100 \times 40 = 2000$. This means that the train covers a distance of 2000 m, or 2 km, while gaining speed.

In Fig. 1.5 the region is again a triangle, with width 50 and height 40, so the train comes to a standstill in 1000 m, or 1 km.

A justification that the displacement is given by the area will be found in Section 11.3.

1.4   Equations for constant acceleration

You will often have to do calculations like those in the last section. It is worth having algebraic formulae to solve problems about objects moving with constant acceleration.

Fig. 1.6 shows a velocity–time graph which could apply to any problem of this type. The initial velocity is u, and the velocity at time t is denoted by v. If the acceleration has the constant value a, then between time 0 and time t the velocity increases by at. It follows that, after time t,

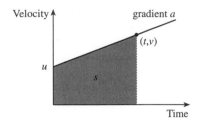

Fig. 1.6

$$v = u + at.$$

Remember that in this equation u and a are constants, but t and v can vary. In fact, this equation is just like $y = mx + c$ (or, for a closer comparison, $y = c + mx$). The acceleration a is the gradient, like m, and the initial velocity u is the intercept, like c. So $v = u + at$ is just the equation of the velocity–time graph.

There is, though, one important difference. This equation only applies so long as the constant acceleration lasts, so the graph is just part of the line.

There are no units in the equation $v = u + at$. You can use it with any units you like, provided that they are consistent.

To find a formula for the displacement, you need to find the area of the shaded region under the graph between $(0, u)$ and (t, v) in Fig. 1.6. You can work this out in either of two ways, illustrated in Figs. 1.7 and 1.8. In Fig. 1.7 the region is shown as a trapezium, with parallel vertical sides of length u and v, and width t. The formula for the area of a trapezium gives

$$s = \tfrac{1}{2}(u + v)t.$$

Fig. 1.8 shows the region split into a rectangle, whose area is ut, and a triangle with base t and height at, whose area is $\tfrac{1}{2} \times t \times at$. These combine to give the formula

$$s = ut + \tfrac{1}{2}at^2.$$

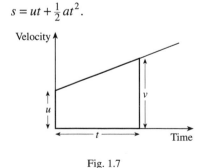

Fig. 1.7

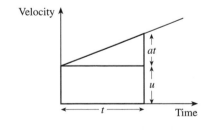

Fig. 1.8

Example 1.4.1

A racing car enters the final straight travelling at 35 m s^{-1}, and covers the 600 m to the finishing line in 12 s. Assuming constant acceleration, find its speed as it crosses the finishing line.

Measuring the displacement from the start of the final straight, and using SI units, you know that $u = 35$. You are told that when $t = 12$, $s = 600$, and you want to know v at that time. So use the formula connecting u, t, s and v.

Substituting in the formula $s = \frac{1}{2}(u + v)t$,

$$600 = \tfrac{1}{2}(35 + v) \times 12.$$

This gives $35 + v = \dfrac{600 \times 2}{12} = 100$, so $v = 65$.

Assuming constant acceleration, the car crosses the finishing line at 65 m s^{-1}.

Example 1.4.2

A skier pushes off from the top of a slope with a speed of 1.5 m s^{-1}, and accelerates at 2 m s^{-2}. The slope is 22 m long. How long does she take to reach the bottom of the slope, and how fast is she moving then?

You are given that $u = 1.5$ and $a = 2$, and want to find t when $s = 22$. The formula which connects these four quantities is $s = ut + \frac{1}{2}at^2$, so displacement and time are connected by the equation

$$s = 1.5t + t^2.$$

When $s = 22$, t satisfies the quadratic equation $t^2 + 1.5t - 22 = 0$. Solving this by the formula, $t = \dfrac{-1.5 \pm \sqrt{1.5^2 + 4 \times 1 \times 22}}{2}$, giving $t = -5.5$ or 4. In this model t must be positive, so $t = 4$. The skier takes 4 seconds to reach the bottom of the slope.

To find how fast she is then moving, you have to calculate v when $t = 4$. Since you now know u, a, t and s, you can use either of the formulae involving v. The algebra is simpler using $v = u + at$, which gives

$$v = 1.5 + 2 \times 4 = 9.5.$$

The skier's speed at the bottom of the slope is 9.5 m s^{-1}.

Exercise 1B

1   A police car accelerates from 15 m s^{-1} to 35 m s^{-1} in 5 seconds. The acceleration is constant. Illustrate this with a velocity–time graph. Use the equation $v = u + at$ to calculate the acceleration. Find also the distance travelled by the car in that time.

2   A marathon competitor running at 5 m s^{-1} puts on a sprint when she is 100 metres from the finish, and covers this distance in 16 seconds. Assuming that her acceleration is constant, use the equation $s = \frac{1}{2}(u + v)t$ to find how fast she is running as she crosses the finishing line.

3 A train travelling at 20 m s^{-1} starts to accelerate with constant acceleration. It covers the next kilometre in 25 seconds. Use the equation $s = ut + \frac{1}{2}at^2$ to calculate the acceleration. Find also how fast the train is moving at the end of this time. Illustrate the motion of the train with a velocity–time graph.

How long does the train take to cover the first half kilometre?

4 A long-jumper takes a run of 30 metres to accelerate to a speed of 10 m s^{-1} from a standing start. Find the time he takes to reach this speed, and hence calculate his acceleration. Illustrate his run-up with a velocity–time graph.

5 Starting from rest, an aircraft accelerates to its take-off speed of 60 m s^{-1} in a distance of 900 metres. Assuming constant acceleration, find how long the take-off run lasts. Hence calculate the acceleration.

6 A train is travelling at 80 m s^{-1} when the driver applies the brakes, producing a deceleration of 2 m s^{-2} for 30 seconds. How fast is the train then travelling, and how far does it travel while the brakes are on?

7 A balloon at a height of 300 m is descending at 10 m s^{-1} and decelerating at a rate of 0.4 m s^{-2}. How long will it take for the balloon to stop descending, and what will its height be then?

1.5 More constant acceleration equations

All the three formulae in Section 1.4 involve four of the five quantities u, a, t, v and s. The first leaves out s, the second a and the third v. It is also useful to have formulae which leave out t and u, and you can find these by combining the formulae you already know.

To find a formula which omits t, rearrange the formula $v = u + at$ to give $at = v - u$, so $t = \dfrac{v-u}{a}$. If you now substitute this in $s = \frac{1}{2}(u+v)t$, you get

$$s = \tfrac{1}{2}(u+v) \times \frac{v-u}{a},$$

which is $2as = (u+v)(v-u)$. The right side of this is $(v+u)(v-u) = v^2 - u^2$, so that finally $2as = v^2 - u^2$, or

$$v^2 = u^2 + 2as.$$

The fifth formula, which omits u, is less useful than the others. Turn the formula $v = u + at$ round to get $u = v - at$. Then, substituting this in $s = ut + \frac{1}{2}at^2$, you get $s = (v - at)t + \frac{1}{2}at^2$, which simplifies to

$$s = vt - \tfrac{1}{2}at^2.$$

> For an object moving with constant acceleration a and initial velocity u, the following equations connect the displacement s and the velocity v after a time t.
>
> $$v = u + at \qquad s = ut + \tfrac{1}{2}at^2 \qquad v^2 = u^2 + 2as$$
> $$s = \tfrac{1}{2}(u+v)t \qquad s = vt - \tfrac{1}{2}at^2$$

You should learn these formulae, because you will use them frequently throughout this mechanics course.

Example 1.5.1

The barrel of a shotgun is 0.9 m long, and the shot emerges from the muzzle with a speed of 240 m s^{-1}. Find the acceleration of the shot in the barrel, and the length of time the shot is in the barrel after firing.

In practice the constant acceleration model is likely to be only an approximation, but it will give some idea of the quantities involved.

The shot is initially at rest, so $u = 0$. You are given that $v = 240$ when $s = 0.9$, and you want to find the acceleration, so use $v^2 = u^2 + 2as$.

$$240^2 = 0^2 + 2 \times a \times 0.9.$$

This gives $a = \dfrac{240^2}{2 \times 0.9} = 32\,000$.

You can now use any of the other formulae to find the time. The simplest is probably $v = u + at$, which gives $240 = 0 + 32\,000t$, so $t = 0.0075$.

Taking account of the approximations in the model and the data, you can say that the acceleration of the shot is about $30\,000$ m s^{-2}, and that the shot is in the barrel for a little less than one-hundredth of a second.

Example 1.5.2

The driver of a car travelling at 60 m.p.h. in mist suddenly sees a stationary bus 100 metres ahead. With the brakes full on, the car can decelerate at 4 m s^{-2} in the prevailing road conditions. Can the driver stop in time?

You know from Example 1.1.2 that 60 m.p.h. is about $60 \times \tfrac{4}{9}$ m s^{-1}, or $\tfrac{80}{3}$ m s^{-1}. This suggests writing $u = \tfrac{80}{3}$ and $a = -4$ in the formula $v^2 = u^2 + 2as$ to find v when $s = 100$. Notice that a is negative because the car is decelerating.

When you do this, you get $v^2 = \left(\tfrac{80}{3}\right)^2 - 2 \times 4 \times 100 = -\tfrac{800}{9}$. This is clearly a ridiculous answer, since a square cannot be negative.

The reason for the absurdity is that the equation only holds so long as the constant acceleration model applies. In fact the car stops before s reaches the value 100, and after that it simply stays still.

To avoid this, it is better to begin by substituting only the constants in the equation, leaving v and s as variables. The equation is then

$$v^2 = \tfrac{6400}{9} - 8s.$$

This model holds so long as $v^2 \geqslant 0$. The equation gives $v = 0$ when $s = \dfrac{6400}{9 \times 8} = \dfrac{800}{9}$, which is less than 100. So the driver can stop in time.

This example could be criticised because it assumes that the driver puts the brakes on as soon as he sees the bus. In practice there would be some 'thinking time', perhaps 0.3 seconds, while the driver reacts. At $\frac{80}{3}$ m s^{-1}, the car would travel 8 metres in this time, so you should add 8 metres to the distance calculated in the example. You can see that he will still avoid an accident, but only just.

Exercise 1C

1   Interpret each of the following in terms of the motion of a particle along a line, and select the appropriate constant acceleration formula to find the answer. The quantities u, v, s and t are all positive or zero, but a may be positive or negative.

(a) $u = 9$, $a = 4$, $s = 5$, find v

(b) $u = 10$, $v = 14$, $a = 3$, find s

(c) $u = 17$, $v = 11$, $s = 56$, find a

(d) $u = 14$, $a = -2$, $t = 5$, find s

(e) $v = 20$, $a = 1$, $t = 6$, find s

(f) $u = 10$, $s = 65$, $t = 5$, find a

(g) $u = 18$, $v = 12$, $s = 210$, find t

(h) $u = 9$, $a = 4$, $s = 35$, find t

(i) $u = 20$, $s = 110$, $t = 5$, find v

(j) $s = 93$, $v = 42$, $t = \frac{3}{2}$, find a

(k) $u = 24$, $v = 10$, $a = -0.7$, find t

(1) $s = 35$, $v = 12$, $a = 2$, find u

(m) $v = 27$, $s = 40$, $a = -4\frac{1}{2}$, find t

(n) $a = 7$, $s = 100$, $v - u = 20$, find u

2   A train goes into a tunnel at 20 m s^{-1} and emerges from it at 55 m s^{-1}. The tunnel is 1500 m long. Assuming constant acceleration, find how long the train is in the tunnel for, and the acceleration of the train.

3   A milk float moves from rest with acceleration 0.1 m s^{-2}. Find an expression for its speed, v m s^{-1}, after it has gone s metres. Illustrate your answer by sketching an (s, v) graph.

4   A cyclist riding at 5 m s^{-1} starts to accelerate, and 200 metres later she is riding at 7 m s^{-1}. Find her acceleration, assumed constant.

5   A train travelling at 55 m s^{-1} has to reduce speed to 35 m s^{-1} to pass through a junction. If the deceleration is not to exceed 0.6 m s^{-2}, how far ahead of the junction should the train begin to slow down?

6   A liner leaves the harbour entrance travelling at 3 m s^{-1}, and accelerates at 0.04 m s^{-2} until it reaches its cruising speed of 15 m s^{-1}.

(a)   How far does it travel in accelerating to its cruising speed?

(b)   How long does it take to travel 2 km from the harbour entrance?

7 A downhill skier crosses the finishing line at a speed of 30 m s^{-1} and immediately starts to decelerate at 10 m s^{-2}. There is a barrier 50 metres beyond the finishing line.

   (a) Find an expression for the skier's speed when she is s metres beyond the finishing line.

   (b) How fast is she travelling when she is 40 m beyond the finishing line?

   (c) How far short of the barrier does she come to a stop?

   (d) Display an (s, v) graph to illustrate the motion.

8 A boy kicks a football up a slope with a speed of 6 m s^{-1}. The ball decelerates at 0.3 m s^{-2}. How far up the slope does it roll?

9 A cyclist comes to the top of a hill 165 metres long travelling at 5 m s^{-1}, and free-wheels down it with an acceleration of 0.8 m s^{-2}. Write expressions for his speed and the distance he has travelled after t seconds. Hence find how long he takes to reach the bottom of the hill, and how fast he is then travelling.

10 A car travelling at 10 m s^{-1} is 25 metres from a pedestrian crossing when the traffic light changes from green to amber. The light remains at amber for 2 seconds before it changes to red. The driver has two choices: to accelerate so as to reach the crossing before the light changes to red, or to try to stop at the light. What is the least acceleration which would be necessary in the first case, and the least deceleration which would be necessary in the second?

11 A freight train $\frac{1}{4}$ mile long takes 20 seconds to pass a signal. The train is decelerating at a constant rate, and by the time the rear truck has passed the signal it is moving 10 miles per hour slower than it was when the engine reached it. Find the deceleration in mile–hour units, and the speed at which the train is moving when the rear truck has just passed the signal.

12 A cheetah is pursuing an impala. The impala is running in a straight line at a constant speed of 16 m s^{-1}. The cheetah is 10 m behind the impala, running at 20 m s^{-1} but tiring, so that it is decelerating at 1 m s^{-2}. Find an expression for the gap between the cheetah and the impala t seconds later. Will the impala get away?

1.6 Multi-stage problems

A journey can often be broken down into several stages, in each of which there is constant velocity, or constant acceleration or deceleration. For example, a car might accelerate at different rates in different gears, or it might slow down to go through a village and then speed up again. You can analyse situations like these by applying the formulae to each stage separately, or you can use a velocity–time graph.

Example 1.6.1

A sprinter in a 100-metre race pushes off the starting block with a speed of 6 m s^{-1}, and accelerates at a constant rate. He attains his maximum speed of 10 m s^{-1} after 40 metres, and then continues at that speed for the rest of the race. What is his time for the whole race?

For the accelerating stage you know that $u = 6$, $v = 10$ and $s = 40$. The equation $s = \frac{1}{2}(u+v)t$ gives $40 = 8t$, so $t = 5$.

The remaining 60 metres are run at a constant speed of 10 m s^{-1}. You can now measure s and t from the time when the sprinter reaches his maximum speed, and use the formula $s = ut$ to find that $t = \dfrac{s}{u} = \dfrac{60}{10} = 6$.

So the sprinter takes 5 seconds to accelerate and then a further 6 seconds at maximum speed, a total of 11 seconds.

Fig. 1.9 shows the velocity–time graph for the run. You could use this to find the time, but the calculation is essentially no different.

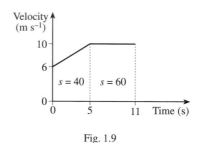

Fig. 1.9

Example 1.6.2

Two stations on an underground railway are 960 metres apart. A train starts from one station, accelerates at a constant rate to its maximum speed of 15 m s^{-1}, maintains this speed for some time and then decelerates at a constant rate to stop at the other station. The total time between the stations is 84 seconds.

(a) For how many seconds does the train travel at its maximum speed?

(b) If the train accelerates at 0.5 m s^{-2}, at what rate does it decelerate?

You can draw a single velocity–time graph (Fig. 1.10) for the whole journey. This is made up of three line segments: the first with positive gradient, the second parallel to the t-axis, and the third with negative gradient.

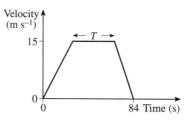

Fig. 1.10

(a) The region between the velocity–time graph and the t-axis has the shape of a trapezium. The area of this trapezium represents the distance between the two stations.

If the train travels at its maximum speed for T seconds, this trapezium has parallel sides 84 and T, height 15 and area 960. So

$$960 = \tfrac{1}{2}(84+T)\times 15,$$

which gives $84 + T = \dfrac{2 \times 960}{15}$, and $T = 44$.

(b) To reach a speed of 15 m s^{-1} from rest with an acceleration of 0.5 m s^{-2} takes $\dfrac{15}{0.5}$ seconds, which is 30 seconds. So the train takes 30 seconds accelerating and

44 seconds at maximum speed , and this leaves 10 seconds in which to come to a stop. The deceleration is therefore $\dfrac{15}{10}$ m s^{-2}, which is 1.5 m s^{-2}.

The train travels at its maximum speed for 44 seconds, and then decelerates at a rate of 1.5 m s^{-2}.

Example 1.6.3

A truck is travelling at a constant speed of 60 m.p.h. The driver of a car, also going at 60 m.p.h., decides to overtake it. The car accelerates up to 75 m.p.h., then immediately starts to decelerate until its speed has again dropped to 60 m.p.h. The whole manoeuvre takes half a minute. If the gap between the car and the truck was originally 40 yards, the truck is 10 yards long and the car is 4 yards long, what will be the gap between the truck and the car afterwards?

You are not told the acceleration and deceleration, or when the car reaches its greatest speed, so if you try to use algebra there will be several unknowns. It is much simpler to use velocity–time graphs.

Fig. 1.11 shows the velocity–time graphs for both the truck and the car over the half minute. The distance travelled by the truck is the area of the region between the horizontal line segment AB and the time-axis, and the distance travelled by the car is the area between the two-part graph AMB and the time-axis. So the difference in the distances travelled is given by the area of the triangle AMB.

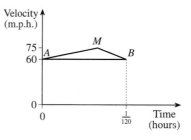

Fig. 1.11

To do the calculation you must use a consistent system of units, and mile–hour units is the obvious choice. Since half a minute is $\frac{1}{120}$ hours, the difference in the distances is $\frac{1}{2} \times \frac{1}{120} \times (75 - 60)$ miles, which is $\frac{1}{16}$ miles, or 110 yards.

Fig. 1.12 shows the relative positions of the car and the truck before and afterwards. The front of the car was originally $40 + 10$, or 50 yards behind the front of the truck, so it ends up $(110 - 50)$ yards, or 60 yards in front. The gap afterwards is therefore $(60 - 4)$ yards, or 56 yards.

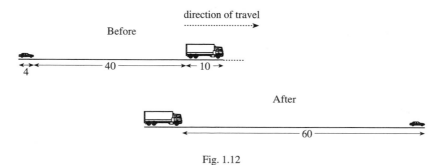

Fig. 1.12

1.7 Average velocity

You can if you like omit this section for a first reading, and come back to it later.

The constant acceleration formula $s = \frac{1}{2}(u+v)t$ can be rearranged as

$$\frac{s}{t} = \frac{1}{2}(u+v).$$

The fraction on the left, the displacement divided by the time, is called the **average velocity**. So what this equation states is that, for an object moving with constant acceleration, the average velocity is equal to the mean of the initial and final velocities.

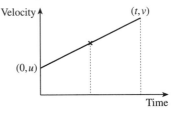

Notice also that, in Fig. 1.13, the mid-point of the line-segment which represents the motion has coordinates $\left(\frac{1}{2}t, \frac{1}{2}(u+v)\right)$. So $\frac{1}{2}(u+v)$ is also the velocity of the object when half the time has passed.

Fig. 1.13

For an object moving with constant acceleration over a period of time, these three averages are equal:

- the average velocity,
- the mean of the initial and final velocities,
- the velocity when half the time has passed.

But Fig. 1.13 shows that, if the acceleration is positive, the area under the graph for the first half of the period is less than the area for the second half. So when half the time has passed, less than half the distance has been covered.

The idea of average velocity is sometimes useful in solving problems.

Example 1.7.1

A passenger notices that a train covers 4 km in 3 minutes, and 2 km in the next minute. Assuming that the acceleration is constant, find how fast the train is travelling at the end of the fourth minute.

Method 1   In the first 3 minutes the average velocity is $\frac{4}{3}$ km min^{-1}, so this is the velocity of the train after $1\frac{1}{2}$ minutes. In the last minute the average velocity is 2 km min^{-1}, so this is the velocity after $3\frac{1}{2}$ minutes. It follows that in $\left(3\frac{1}{2} - 1\frac{1}{2}\right)$ minutes the velocity increases by $\left(2 - \frac{4}{3}\right)$ km min^{-1}. So the velocity increases at a rate of $\frac{2}{3}$ km min^{-1} in 2 minutes. This is an acceleration of $\frac{1}{3}$ km min^{-2}.

The velocity after $3\frac{1}{2}$ minutes is 2 km min^{-1} and in a further $\frac{1}{2}$ minute it increases by $\frac{1}{2} \times \frac{1}{3}$ km min^{-1}, which is $\frac{1}{6}$ km min^{-1}.

So after 4 minutes the velocity is $2\frac{1}{6}$ km min^{-1}.

Method 2   Suppose that the velocity after 4 minutes is v km min^{-1}, and that the acceleration is a km min^{-2}. The train travels 6 km in the whole 4 minutes, and 2 km in the last minute. Using the equation $s = vt - \frac{1}{2}at^2$ for each of these periods,

$$6 = v \times 4 - \frac{1}{2}a \times 16 \quad \text{and} \quad 2 = v \times 1 - \frac{1}{2}a \times 1,$$

giving $\quad 6 = 4v - 8a \quad$ and $\quad 2 = v - \frac{1}{2}a$.

From these equations,

$$16 \times 2 - 6 = 16\left(v - \frac{1}{2}a\right) - (4v - 8a), \quad \text{which gives} \quad 26 = 12v.$$

Therefore $v = \frac{26}{12} = 2\frac{1}{6}$.

The train is travelling at $2\frac{1}{6}$ km min^{-1}, which is 130 km per hour, at the end of the fourth minute.

Exercise 1D

1   A cyclist travels from A to B, a distance of 240 metres. He passes A at 12 m s^{-1}, maintains this speed for as long as he can, and then brakes so that he comes to a stop at B. If the maximum deceleration he can achieve when braking is 3 m s^{-2}, what is the least time in which he can get from A to B?

2

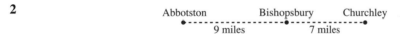

Abbotston   Bishopsbury   Churchley
              9 miles   7 miles

The figure shows a map of the branch line from Abbotston to Churchley. The timetable is based on the assumption that the top speed of a train is 60 miles per hour; that it takes 3 minutes to reach this speed from rest, and 1 minute to bring the train to a stop, both at a constant rate; and that at an intermediate station 1 minute must be allowed to set down and pick up passengers. How long must the timetable allow for the whole journey

(a)   for trains which don't stop at Bishopsbury,

(b)   for trains which do stop at Bishopsbury?

3   Two villages are 900 metres apart. A car leaves the first village travelling at 15 m s^{-1} and accelerates at $\frac{1}{2}$ m s^{-2} for 30 seconds. How fast is it then travelling, and what distance has it covered in this time?

The driver now sees the next village ahead, and decelerates so as to enter it at 15 m s^{-1}. What constant deceleration is needed to achieve this? How much time does the driver save by accelerating and decelerating, rather than covering the whole distance at 15 m s^{-1}?

4   A car rounds a bend at 10 m s^{-1}, and then accelerates at $\frac{1}{2}$ m s^{-2} along a straight stretch of road. There is a T-junction 400 m from the bend. When the car is 100 m from the T-junction, the driver brakes and brings the car to rest at the junction with constant deceleration. Draw a (t, v) graph to illustrate the motion of the car. Find how fast the car is moving when the brakes are applied, and the deceleration needed for the car to stop at the junction.

5 A car comes to a stop from a speed of 30 m s^{-1} in a distance of 804 m. The driver brakes so as to produce a deceleration of $\frac{1}{2} \text{ m s}^{-2}$ to begin with, and then brakes harder to produce a deceleration of $\frac{3}{2} \text{ m s}^{-2}$. Find the speed of the car at the instant when the deceleration is increased, and the total time the car takes to stop.

6 A motorbike and a car are waiting side by side at traffic lights. When the lights turn to green, the motorbike accelerates at $2\frac{1}{2} \text{ m s}^{-2}$ up to a top speed of 20 m s^{-1}, and the car accelerates at $1\frac{1}{2} \text{ m s}^{-2}$ up to a top speed of 30 m s^{-1}. Both then continue to move at constant speed. Draw (t, v) graphs for each vehicle, using the same axes, and sketch the (t, s) graphs.

(a) After what time will the motorbike and the car again be side by side?

(b) What is the greatest distance that the motorbike is in front of the car?

7 An ice-skater increases speed from 4 m s^{-1} to 10 m s^{-1} in 10 seconds at a constant rate.

(a) What is her average velocity over this period?

(b) For what proportion of the time is she moving at less than her average velocity?

(c) For what proportion of the distance is she moving at less than her average velocity?

8 A cyclist is free-wheeling down a long straight hill. The times between passing successive kilometre posts are 100 seconds and 80 seconds. Assuming her acceleration is constant, find this acceleration.

9 A train is slowing down with constant deceleration. It passes a signal at A, and after successive intervals of 40 seconds it passes points B and C, where $AB = 1800 \text{ m}$ and $BC = 1400 \text{ m}$.

(a) How fast is the train moving when it passes A?

(b) How far from A does it come to a stop?

10 A particle is moving along a straight line with constant acceleration. In an interval of T seconds it moves D metres; in the next interval of $3T$ seconds it moves $9D$ metres. How far does it move in a further interval of T seconds?

Miscellaneous exercise 1

1 A car starts from rest at the point A and moves in a straight line with constant acceleration for 20 seconds until it reaches the point B. The speed of the car at B is 30 m s^{-1}. Calculate

(a) the acceleration of the car,

(b) the speed of the car as it passes the point C, where C is between A and B and $AC = 40 \text{ m}$.   (OCR)

2 A motorist travelling at $u \text{ m s}^{-1}$ joins a straight motorway. On the motorway she travels with a constant acceleration of 0.07 m s^{-2} until her speed has increased by 2.8 m s^{-1}.

(a) Calculate the time taken for this increase in speed.

(b) Given that the distance travelled while this increase takes place is 1050 m, find u.   (OCR)

3 A cyclist, travelling with constant acceleration along a straight road, passes three points A, B and C, where $AB = BC = 20$ m. The speed of the cyclist at A is 8 m s^{-1} and at B is 12 m s^{-1}. Find the speed of the cyclist at C. (OCR)

4 As a car passes the point A on a straight road, its speed is 10 m s^{-1}. The car moves with constant acceleration a m s^{-2} along the road for T seconds until it reaches the point B, where its speed is V m s^{-1}. The car travels at this speed for a further 10 seconds, when it reaches the point C. From C it travels for a further T seconds with constant acceleration $3a$ m s^{-2} until it reaches a speed of 20 m s^{-1} at the point D. Sketch the (t, v) graph for the motion, and show that $V = 12.5$.

Given that the distance between A and D is 675 m, find the values of a and T. (OCR)

5 The figure shows the (t, v) graph for the motion of a cyclist; the graph consists of three straight line segments. Use the information given on the graph to find the acceleration of the cyclist when $t = 2$ and the total distance travelled by the cyclist for $0 \leqslant t \leqslant 30$.

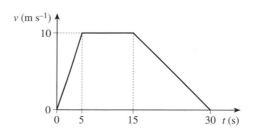

Without making any detailed calculations, sketch the displacement–time graph for this motion. (OCR)

6 A car is waiting at traffic lights with a van behind it. There is a 1 metre gap between them. When the lights turn green, the car accelerates at 1.5 m s^{-2} until it reaches a speed of 15 m s^{-1}; it then proceeds at this speed. The van does the same, starting when the gap between the vehicles is 4 metres.

Find a formula for the distance travelled by the car in the first t seconds $(0 \leqslant t \leqslant 10)$, and hence the time interval between the car starting and the van starting. Find also the distance between the vehicles when they are both going at 15 m s^{-1}. (OCR)

7 Two runners, Alice and Belle, are leading the field in a long-distance race. They are both running at 5 m s^{-1}, with Alice 10 m behind Belle. When Belle is 50 m from the tape, Alice accelerates but Belle doesn't. What is the least acceleration Alice must produce to overtake Belle?

If instead Belle accelerates at 0.1 m s^{-2} up to the tape, what is the least acceleration Alice must produce?

8 A woman stands on the bank of a frozen lake with a dog by her side. She skims a bone across the ice at a speed of 3 m s^{-1}. The bone slows down with deceleration 0.4 m s^{-2}, and the dog chases it with acceleration 0.6 m s^{-2}. How far out from the bank does the dog catch up with the bone?

9 A man is running for a bus at 3 m s^{-1}. When he is 100 m from the bus stop, the bus passes him going at 8 m s^{-1}. If the deceleration of the bus is constant, at what constant rate should the man accelerate so as to arrive at the bus stop at the same instant as the bus?

10 (a) A train travels from a station P to the next station Q, arriving at Q exactly 5 minutes after leaving P. The (t, v) graph for the train's journey is approximated by three straight line segments, as shown in the figure.

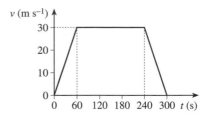

(i) Write down the acceleration of the train during the first minute of the journey.

(ii) Find the distance from P to Q.

(b) On one occasion, when the track is being repaired, the train is restricted to a maximum speed of 10 m s^{-1} for the 2000 m length of track lying midway between P and Q. The train always accelerates and decelerates at the rate shown in the figure. When not accelerating or decelerating or moving at the restricted speed of 10 m s^{-1}, the train travels at 30 m s^{-1}. Sketch the (t, v) graph for the train's journey from P to Q when the speed restriction is in force, and hence find how long the train takes to travel from P to Q on this occasion.

(c) The second figure shows the (t, v) graph for the train accelerating from rest up to a maximum speed of $V \text{ m s}^{-1}$ and then immediately decelerating to a speed of 10 m s^{-1}. The acceleration and deceleration have the same value as shown in the first figure. Show that the distance travelled is $(2V^2 - 100)$ metres.

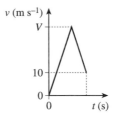

Determine whether the train in (b) could, by exceeding the normal speed of 30 m s^{-1} when possible, make up the time lost due to the speed restriction when travelling from P to Q. Assume that the acceleration and deceleration must remain as before.   (OCR)

11 If a ball is placed on a straight sloping track and then released from rest, the distances that it moves in successive equal intervals of time are found to be in the ratio $1:3:5:7:\ldots$. Show that this is consistent with the theory that the ball rolls down the track with constant acceleration.

2 Force and motion

This chapter introduces the idea of force, and shows how forces affect the motion of an object. When you have completed it, you should

- understand Newton's first law of motion
- know some different types of force
- know and be able to apply Newton's second law to simple examples of objects moving in a straight line
- understand the idea of equilibrium.

2.1 Newton's first law

Chapter 1 showed how you can use mathematics to describe how objects move. The English scientist Isaac Newton (1643–1727) went on from there to try to answer the question 'how can mathematics be used to explain why objects move in the way they do?' In his book *Principia*, he put his findings in the form of three laws, called **Newton's laws of motion**. It is a remarkable fact that the whole of mechanics results from applying these three laws in different situations.

In 1977 the United States launched the Voyager space probe to send back pictures of the outer planets of the solar system and their moons. By clever timing and programming it was possible for Voyager to pass close to Jupiter, Saturn, Uranus and Neptune in turn. Then it headed out into space, getting further and further from the sun. By now the effect of the sun's attraction is almost negligible, and the probe continues to travel into outer space with constant velocity.

This is an instance of what is called 'Newton's first law', although in fact this law was already known to Galileo, who died in the year that Newton was born.

> **Newton's first law**   Every object remains in a state of rest or of uniform motion in a straight line unless forces act on it to change that state.

It is difficult to demonstrate this law on or near the earth's surface because you can't eliminate all the forces. Many inventors have tried to make a permanent motion machine, but none has succeeded.

But you can make some approximations. When you are riding a bicycle on a level path and start to free-wheel, you can keep up an almost constant velocity for some time. But eventually you will slow down, partly because of air resistance. This is shown in Fig. 2.1, where the resistance is indicated by an arrow.

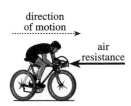

Fig. 2.1

Another example is when a stone is sent sliding
across the frozen surface of a lake. However
smooth the ice appears, the stone eventually
slows down because of friction between the
two surfaces (see Fig. 2.2).

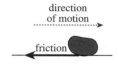

Fig. 2.2

What Newton's first law states is that, if an object is seen to speed up (accelerate) or
slow down (decelerate), there must be some agent causing the change. Newton called
this agent a **force**. Air resistance and friction are two types of force.

2.2 Force and acceleration

Newton's first law is a purely qualitative statement, that force is the agent which
produces a change in the velocity of an object. It says nothing about the size of the
force, or the amount of acceleration or deceleration that it produces. That is the subject
of Newton's second law.

Suppose that the car you are driving runs out of
petrol within sight of a filling station. You may
persuade your passenger to get out and push.
The effect of this is shown in Fig. 2.3. The car
is stationary at first, and the result of the push
is to give the car a velocity, so that the car
accelerates. The figure uses arrows to show
both the force and the acceleration, which are in the same direction. It is sensible to use
one kind of arrow for force, and a different kind of arrow for acceleration.

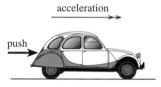

Fig. 2.3

It is intuitively obvious that the harder the push, the greater the acceleration of the car.
You would expect that two people pushing with equal force would produce twice the
acceleration that one would achieve. This is summarised in the second of Newton's laws
of motion, in which he stated that

> change of motion is proportional to the applied force, and in the same direction.

However, by 'change of motion' Newton meant more than simply acceleration. It takes
much more force to push a limousine than a Mini with the same acceleration, because a
limousine is much heavier. So the full statement of the law must also take into account the
heaviness of the object being accelerated. This is measured by a quantity called **mass**.

In SI the unit of mass is the **kilogram**, usually abbreviated to kg. You will be familiar
with this from buying vegetables or posting parcels. For heavy objects it is sometimes
more convenient to give the mass in tonnes, where 1 tonne $= 1000 \, \text{kg}$. For light objects
the mass can be given in grams, where 1 gram $= \frac{1}{1000} \, \text{kg}$. For example, the mass of a
small family car is about a tonne, and the mass of a drawing pin is about a gram.

The full statement of Newton's second law is that the force acting on an object is
proportional to the product of its mass and the acceleration produced. Denoting the force
by F, the mass of the object by m, and the acceleration by a, the law can be written as
an equation

$$F = cma,$$

where c is a constant.

How do you deal with the constant c? The answer is to use a very neat trick, and to choose the unit of force so that c has the value 1. You can do this because, although you know that in SI the units of mass and acceleration are kg and m s^{-2} respectively, nothing has yet been said about the unit of force.

So define the unit of force, the **newton**, as the force needed to give a mass of 1 kg an acceleration of 1 m s^{-2}. Then, substituting in the equation $F = cma$, you get

$$1 = c \times 1 \times 1, \quad \text{giving} \quad c = 1.$$

The abbreviation for newton is N. A newton is approximately the force you need to hold a medium-sized apple. In a tug-of-war, a fit person might be able to exert a pull of about 200 N.

You can now summarise Newton's second law as a simple equation.

> When a force of F newtons acts on an object of mass m kg, the acceleration a m s^{-2} is given by $F = ma$.

Example 2.2.1
A car of mass 1200 kg is pushed with a force of 150 N. Calculate the acceleration of the car, and find how long it will take to reach a speed of $1\frac{1}{2}$ m s^{-1} from rest.

Substituting $F = 150$ and $m = 1200$ in the equation $F = ma$ gives $150 = 1200a$, so $a = \frac{15}{120} = \frac{1}{8}$.

To find the time, use the equation $v = u + at$ with $u = 0$ and $a = \frac{1}{8}$. This gives $v = \frac{1}{8}t$. When $v = 1\frac{1}{2}$, $t = \frac{3\frac{1}{2}}{\frac{1}{8}} = 12$.

The acceleration of the car is $\frac{1}{8}$ m s^{-2}, and the car takes 12 seconds to reach a speed of $1\frac{1}{2}$ m s^{-1} from rest.

Example 2.2.2
A curling stone of mass 18 kg is launched across ice with a speed of 2 m s^{-1}, and goes a distance of 30 metres before coming to rest. Calculate the deceleration, and find the frictional force between the stone and the ice.

You know that $u = 2$ and that $v = 0$ when $s = 30$. So use the equation $v^2 = u^2 + 2as$ to get $0 = 2^2 + 2 \times a \times 30$, which gives $a = -\frac{4}{60} = -\frac{1}{15}$. The negative value of a indicates that it is a deceleration.

In Fig. 2.4 the friction is shown as R newtons opposite to the direction of motion. So the equation $F = ma$ takes the form

$$-R = 18 \times \left(-\tfrac{1}{15}\right),$$

which gives $R = 1.2$.

The deceleration is $\tfrac{1}{15}$ m s^{-2}, and the frictional force is 1.2 newtons.

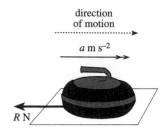

direction
of motion

a m s^{-2}

R N

Fig. 2.4

2.3 Some other types of force

There would be other ways of getting the car in Section 2.2 to the filling station. You might stop a passing car and get a tow. The force accelerating the car is then provided through the towing rope. A force like this is called a **tension**. It is represented by the force T newtons in Fig. 2.5.

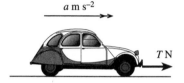

a m s^{-2}

T N

Fig. 2.5

Another possibility would be to walk to the filling station and buy a can of petrol. The car could then be driven to the filling station. Although the motive force has its origin in the engine, the force which actually moves the car forward is provided by the grip between the tyres and the road. It is therefore shown by the force D N at road level in Fig. 2.6. This is called the **driving force**.

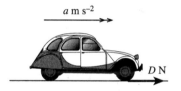

a m s^{-2}

D N

Fig. 2.6

Example 2.3.1

The World's Strongest Man has a cable attached to a harness round his shoulders. The cable is horizontal, and the other end is attached to a 20 tonne truck. The man starts to pull so that the tension in the cable is 800 N. How long will it take for the truck to move 1 metre from rest?

In SI units, the mass of the truck is $20\,000$ kg. If the acceleration is a m s^{-2}, the equation $F = ma$ gives

$$800 = 20\,000 \times a, \quad \text{so} \quad a = 0.04.$$

You now want to find the time, t seconds, given that $u = 0$ and $a = 0.04$.

The equation $s = ut + \tfrac{1}{2}at^2$ gives $s = 0.02t^2$. So when $s = 1$,

$$t = \sqrt{\frac{1}{0.02}} = \sqrt{50} = 7.07\ldots .$$

The truck will take just over 7 seconds to move 1 metre from rest.

Exercise 2A

1 The engine of a car of mass 800 kg which is travelling along a straight horizontal road, is producing a driving force of 1200 N. Assuming that there are no forces resisting the motion, calculate the acceleration of the car.

2 A van is pulling a broken-down car of mass 1200 kg along a straight horizontal road. The only force acting on the car which affects the motion of the car is the tension in the horizontal towbar. Calculate the acceleration of the car when the tension is 750 N.

3 For the first stage of its motion on the runway, before take-off, an aircraft of mass 2200 kg has a constant acceleration of 4.2 m s^{-2}. Calculate the magnitude of the force necessary to provide this acceleration.

4 A novice skier is being pulled along a horizontal section of a nursery slope. Given that her acceleration of 0.8 m s^{-2} is provided by a force of 52 N, calculate her mass.

5 A wooden block of mass m kg is at rest on a table, 1.6 metres from an edge. The block is pulled directly towards the edge by a horizontal string. The tension in the string has magnitude $0.2m$ N. Calculate the time taken for the block to reach the edge of the table.

6 Two children are sliding a puck to each other on a frozen lake. The puck, of mass 0.4 kg, leaves one child with speed 5 m s^{-1} and reaches the other, who is 8 m away, after 2.5 s. Calculate the deceleration of the puck, and find the frictional force resisting the motion of the puck.

7 A particle P of mass m kg is moving in a straight line with constant deceleration. It passes point A with speed 6 m s^{-1} and point B with speed 3.6 m s^{-1}. Given that the distance between A and B is 12 m, calculate, in terms of m, the magnitude of the force resisting the motion of P.

8 A man pushes a car with a force of 127.5 N along a straight horizontal road. He manages to increase the speed of the car from 1 m s^{-1} to 2.8 m s^{-1} in 12 s. Find the mass of the car.

• 9 A runaway sledge of mass 10 kg travelling at 15 m s^{-1} reaches a horizontal snow field. It travels in a straight line before it comes to rest. Given that the force of friction slowing the sledge down has magnitude 60 N, calculate how far the sledge travels in the snow field.

10 A hockey player hits a stationary ball, of mass 0.2 kg. The contact time between the stick and the ball is 0.3 s and the force exerted on the ball by the stick is 60 N. Find the speed with which the ball leaves the stick.

11 A boy slides a box of mass 2 kg across the floor of the stage in the school theatre. The initial speed of the box is 8 m s^{-1} and it comes to rest in 5 m. Calculate the deceleration of the box and find the frictional force between the box and the floor.

• 12 A boat of mass 3000 kg, travelling at a speed of $u \text{ m s}^{-1}$, is brought to rest in 20 s by water resistance of 370 N. Find the value of u.

13 A car of mass of 1000 kg runs out of petrol and comes to rest just 30 m from a garage.
    The car is pushed, with a force of 120 N, along the horizontal road towards the garage.
    Calculate the acceleration of the car and find the time it takes to reach the garage.

· 14 A bullet of mass 0.12 kg is travelling horizontally at 150 m s^{-1} when it enters a fixed
     block of wood. Assuming that the bullet's motion remains horizontal and that the force
     resisting motion has constant magnitude 10 kN, calculate how far the bullet penetrates the
     block.

. 15 A jet plane of mass 30 tonnes touches down with a speed of 55 m s^{-1} and comes to rest
     after moving for 560 m in a straight line on the runway. Assuming that the only forces
     stopping the plane are provided by the reverse thrust of its two engines, and that these
     forces are equal and directed in the direction of motion, calculate the magnitude of the
     thrust in each engine.

2.4   Forces acting together

Often there is more than one force acting on an object. For example, think again about
the car being pushed to the filling station. It takes quite a large force to accelerate the car
up to walking speed, as in Example 2.2.1. But after that you just want to keep it moving
with constant velocity.

Newton's first law suggests that no force is needed to do this, but in practice a small
push is still required. When the car is moving there is some resistance, which would
slow it down if it were left to run by itself. So the pusher has to exert enough force to
balance the resistance.

This is shown in Fig. 2.7. The push is denoted by
F newtons, and the resistance by R newtons.
Since there is no acceleration, $F = R$, which can
be written as

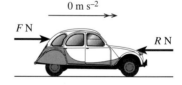

$$F - R = 0.$$

Fig. 2.7

The quantity $F - R$ is sometimes called the 'net force' on the car in the forward direction.
You can use the idea of net force to write Newton's laws in a more general form.

> If several forces act on an object parallel to a given direction, then
> the **net force** is the sum of the forces in that direction minus the
> sum of the forces in the opposite direction.
>
> If the net force is zero, the forces on the object are said to be in
> **equilibrium**. The object then remains at rest, or moves with
> constant velocity. (Newton's first law.)
>
> The net force is equal to the product of the mass of the object and
> its acceleration in the given direction. (Newton's second law.)

You will meet the word 'equilibrium' in two slightly different senses in mechanics. If an object is not moving, so that the net force on it is zero, then the object itself is said to be 'in equilibrium'. But if the net force is zero and the object is moving, then the definition says that the forces are in equilibrium, but you would not usually say that the object is in equilibrium.

Example 2.4.1

A heavy box of mass 32 kg has a handle on one side. Two children try to move it across the floor. One pulls horizontally on the handle with a force of 20 N, the other pushes from the other side of the box with a force of 25 N, but the box does not move. Find the frictional force resisting the motion.

Fig. 2.8 shows the forces on the box in diagrammatic form. (Don't try to draw the children.) If the frictional force is R newtons, the net force on the box is $(20 + 25 - R)$ newtons. Since the box remains at rest,

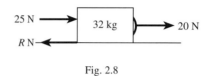

Fig. 2.8

$$20 + 25 - R = 0,$$

so $R = 45$.

The frictional force is 45 newtons.

Notice that one item of data, that the mass is 32 kg, is never used in solving this example. The frictional force is the same whatever the mass of the box, so long as the box remains stationary.

Example 2.4.2

Two builders push a skip of mass 300 kg across the ground. They both push horizontally, one with a force of 200 N, the other with 240 N. Motion is resisted by a frictional force of 380 N. Find the acceleration of the skip.

Fig. 2.9 shows the forces on the skip producing an acceleration of a m s^{-2}. Applying Newton's second law,

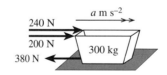

Fig. 2.9

$$200 + 240 - 380 = 300a,$$

which gives

$$60 = 300a, \quad \text{so} \quad a = 0.2.$$

The acceleration of the skip is 0.2 m s^{-2}.

Example 2.4.3

A wagon of mass 250 kg is pulled by a horizontal cable along a straight level track against a resisting force of 150 N. The wagon starts from rest. After 10 seconds it has covered a distance of 60 m. Find the tension in the cable.

If the tension in the cable is T newtons, and
the acceleration of the wagon is a m s^{-2}
(see Fig. 2.10), Newton's second law gives

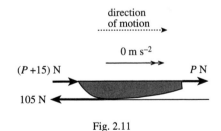

$$T - 150 = 250a.$$

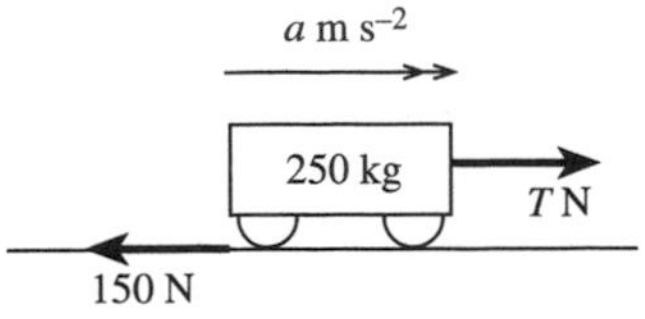

Fig. 2.10

You can't find T from this equation until
you know a. To calculate this, use the
equation $s = ut + \frac{1}{2}at^2$ with $u = 0$, which is $s = \frac{1}{2}at^2$. You are given that $s = 60$
when $t = 10$, so

$$60 = \frac{1}{2}a \times 100, \quad \text{which gives} \quad a = 1.2.$$

Substituting 1.2 for a in the first equation,

$$T - 150 = 250 \times 1.2, \quad \text{so} \quad T = 150 + 300 = 450.$$

The tension in the cable is 450 newtons.

*You will notice that in Fig. 2.10 the resisting force has been drawn at ground level. In
fact, it is probably a mixture of air resistance and a frictional force, but in this example
you don't need to know how it is split between the two.*

Example 2.4.4

A dinghy of mass 90 kg is moved across a horizontal beach at a steady speed of
2 m s^{-1}. One of the crew pulls with a force of P newtons, the other pushes with a force
of $(P+15)$ newtons. The frictional force resisting the motion is 105 newtons. Find P.

The forces are shown in Fig. 2.11. There is
no need to show the velocity in the figure,
since it doesn't come into the equation.

As the boat is moving with constant
velocity, you know from Newton's first law
that the net force is zero, so

$$P + (P+15) - 105 = 0.$$

This gives $2P = 90$, so $P = 45$.

Fig. 2.11

In solving this example you don't use the mass of the dinghy. In practice, this might
well affect the size of the frictional force, but since that force is part of the data you have
all the information you need to apply Newton's first law.

2.5 The particle model

In this chapter Newton's laws have been applied to objects as various as stones, cars,
boats, boxes, skips and space vehicles. These are very different in size, but what they
have in common is that the forces acting on them may cause a change in velocity, but do
not make them rotate. In such cases, the object is being modelled as a **particle**.

In ordinary language a particle is something very small, but this need not be the case when the word 'particle' is used in a modelling sense. In all the examples it would have been sufficient to picture the situation by a figure such as Fig. 2.12, without trying to draw something that looks like the particular object.

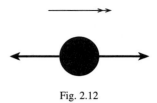

Fig. 2.12

You could even describe an object such as the earth as a particle, so long as you are only interested in its motion through space rather than what makes it spin on its axis.

Exercise 2B

1 Three men are trying to move a skip. Two of the men are pushing horizontally with forces of magnitude 120 N and 150 N and one man is pulling with a horizontal force of magnitude X N. The frictional force resisting the motion is 385 N. Given that the box does not move, find the value of X.

2 A boy is pushing one side of a box, of mass m kg, with a force of 25 N. His sister is pushing from the opposite side of the box with a force of 13 N. The box does not move. Given that the frictional force resisting the motion has magnitude $3m$ N, calculate the value of m. The boy now pushes with an increased force of 35 N. Assuming that the frictional force remains as before, show that the box accelerates at 2.5 m s^{-2}.

3 A motorcyclist moves with an acceleration of 5 m s^{-2} along a horizontal road against a total resistance of 120 N. The total mass of the rider and his machine is 400 kg. Find the driving force provided by the engine.

4 A car of mass 1200 kg is moving with a constant speed of 20 m s^{-1} in a horizontal straight line, against a resisting force of 300 N. What driving force is being provided to sustain this motion? The driver speeds up uniformly over the next 30 s to reach a speed of 30 m s^{-1}. Assuming that the resisting force remains at 300 N, calculate the extra driving force produced.

5 A student is dragging his luggage trunk of mass 85 kg along the corridor of his hall of residence with an acceleration of 0.18 m s^{-2}. The horizontal force he exerts is 180 N. Find the frictional force between the floor and the trunk.

6 A boy is pushing, horizontally, a box of old newspapers of mass 8 kg along a straight path, against a frictional force of 16 N. Calculate the force with which the boy is pushing when he is moving

(a) with constant speed, (b) with a constant acceleration of 1.2 m s^{-2}.

7 A particle of mass 5 kg is pulled, with constant speed, along a rough surface by a horizontal force of magnitude 45 N. Calculate the magnitude of the frictional force. Assuming that this force remains constant, calculate the acceleration of the particle when the magnitude of the horizontal force is increased to 55 N.

8 A water-skier of mass 80 kg is towed over a straight 100-metre run of water. The tension in the horizontal towline is constant and of magnitude 300 N. The resistance to motion of the skier has magnitude 140 N. Given that the skier takes 6.8 seconds to complete the run, calculate her speed at the start of the run.

9 A railway engine of mass 5000 kg is moving at 0.25 m s^{-1} when it strikes the buffers in a siding. Given that the engine is brought to rest in 0.4 s, find the force, assumed constant, exerted on the engine by the buffers.

10 A barge of mass 2×10^5 kg is being towed, with a force of 2.5×10^4 N, in a straight line with an acceleration of 0.06 m s^{-2}. Calculate the magnitude of the resisting force provided by the water.

11 A particle of mass 2.5 kg is pulled along a horizontal surface by a string parallel to the surface with an acceleration of 2.7 m s^{-2}. Given that the frictional force resisting motion has magnitude 4 N, calculate the tension in the string. At the instant that the particle is moving with speed 3 m s^{-1}, the string breaks. Calculate how much further the particle moves before coming to rest.

12 At a particular instant a cabin cruiser, which is driven by a force of magnitude 5400 N, is accelerating at 1.6 m s^{-2} against a resistance of 1200 N. Calculate the mass of the cabin cruiser.

13 A porter is pushing a heavy crate of mass M kg along a horizontal floor with a horizontal force of 180 N. The resistance to motion has magnitude $3M$ newtons. Given that the acceleration of the crate is 0.45 m s^{-2}, find the value of M.

14 A motor-boat of mass 8 tonnes is travelling along a straight course with a constant speed of 28 km h^{-1}. The constant force driving the boat forward has magnitude 780 N. Find the force resisting motion, assumed constant. The engine is now shut off. Calculate, to the nearest second, the time it takes the motor-boat to stop, assuming that the resistance remains the same as before.

15 One horse pulls, with a force of X N, a cart of mass 800 kg along a horizontal road at constant speed. Three horses, each pulling with a force of X N, give the cart an acceleration of 0.8 m s^{-2}. Find the time it would take two horses to increase the speed of the cart from 2 m s^{-1} to 5 m s^{-1}, given that each horse pulls with a force of X N, and that the resistance to motion has the same constant value at all times.

Miscellaneous exercise 2

1 A car of mass 850 kg is moving, with an acceleration of 1.4 m s^{-2}, along a straight horizontal road. The engine of the car produces a total forward force of magnitude X newtons and there is a horizontal resisting force of magnitude 450 N. Find X.   (OCR)

2 A toy car of mass m kg is pulled along a horizontal playground by a horizontal string. The tension in the string has magnitude $4.5m$ N and the frictional force resisting the motion has magnitude $4m$ N. How long does it take for the car to move 30 m from rest?

3 At a particular instant the engine of a motor launch of mass 2300 kg is producing a driving force of magnitude 6000 N and the launch is accelerating at 2 m s^{-1}. Find the magnitude of the force opposing the motion of the launch.

4 A child is pulling a toy animal of mass 1.8 kg, with constant speed 0.6 m s^{-1}, along a horizontal path by means of a horizontal string. She then increases the pulling force by 0.36 N. Calculate the time taken for the toy to move 16 m, from the instant that the pulling force is increased, given that the resistance to motion remains constant throughout the whole motion.

5 Three men, each providing a horizontal force of 250 N, cannot move a skip of mass 280 kg. Find the magnitude of the frictional force opposing the motion. When a fourth man pushes with a horizontal of force 300 N, the skip moves with acceleration of 0.4 m s^{-2}. Find the force resisting the motion in this case.

6 A laundry basket, which is initially at rest on a horizontal surface, is pulled along the surface with a horizontal force of magnitude 6 N for 8 seconds. At the end of the period the speed of the basket is 2.4 m s^{-1}. Assuming that the surface may be modelled as frictionless, find the mass of the basket.

7 A twin-engined aircraft of mass 12 000 kg is flying horizontally at a steady speed of 75 m s^{-1}, against air resistance of magnitude 9000 N. Calculate the thrust provided by each engine.

8 A driver is carrying a large box, of total mass 45 kg, in the boot of his car. The box will begin to slip if a force of more than 90 N is applied to it. When the car is travelling at 12 m s^{-1} the driver brakes uniformly until the car comes to rest in a distance of 35 m. Does the box slip?

9 The total mass of a cyclist and his bicycle is 100 kg. He is travelling along a straight horizontal road with speed 15 m s^{-1} when he stops pedalling and free-wheels until coming to rest in 1 minute. Calculate the deceleration of the cyclist and find the force resisting motion (assuming this to be constant).

10 When a missile launcher of mass 2000 kg fires a missile horizontally, the launcher recoils horizontally with an initial speed of 3 m s^{-1}. Find the minimum force, assumed constant, that needs to be applied to the launcher to bring it to rest within 2 m.

11 On a particular journey the resistance to motion of a car of mass 1000 kg is proportional to its speed. The car is travelling at a constant speed of 15 m s^{-1} with a driving force of 870 N. The driving force is instantaneously increased to 1200 N.

(a) Find the instantaneous acceleration produced.

(b) Find the resistance to motion and the acceleration when the car is moving at 20 m s^{-1}.

12 A van of mass 800 kg, moving in a straight line along a horizontal road, is brought to rest in 5 seconds from a speed of 12 m s^{-1}. Given that there is a constant resisting force of magnitude 200 N, find the braking force, assumed constant.

13 A particle of mass 2 kg is acted upon by a horizontal force of magnitude 10 N for 8 seconds, in which time it moves from rest until it is travelling with speed v m s^{-1}. Show that $v = 40$. The particle continues to move with this speed for the next 10 seconds. It is then brought to rest by the application of a constant resisting force of magnitude X newtons. The total distance travelled is 800 m. Find the time for which the particle is decelerating, and the value of X.

14 The diagram shows the (t, v) graph for the motion of a car of mass 600 kg which slows down uniformly from a speed of 20 m s^{-1} to rest in 4 s. The car is moving on a straight level road.

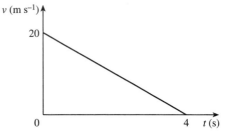

(a) Calculate the magnitude of the braking force that is applied to the car.

(b) Sketch a (t, v) graph for the motion of the car when the braking force applied is initially less than the value calculated in part (a) but increases in magnitude as the car slows down. Assume that the initial speed of the car and the time for the car to stop are the same as before.   (OCR)

15 Pat and Nicholas are controlling the movement of a canal barge by means of long ropes attached to each end. The tension in the ropes may be assumed to be horizontal and parallel to the line and direction of motion of the barge, as shown in the diagrams.

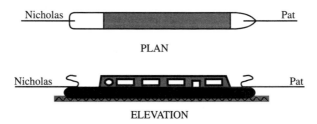

The mass of the barge is 12 tonnes and the total resistance to forward motion may be taken to be 250 N at all times.

Initially Pat pulls the barge forwards from rest with a force of 400 N and Nicholas leaves his rope slack.

(a) Write down the equation of motion for the barge and hence calculate its acceleration.

Pat continues to pull with the same force until the barge has moved 10 m.

(b) What is the speed of the barge at this time and for what length of time did Pat pull?

Pat now lets her rope go slack and Nicholas brings the barge to rest by pulling with a constant force of 150 N.

(c) Calculate

(i) how long it takes the barge to come to rest,

(ii) the total distance travelled by the barge from when it first moved,

(iii) the total time taken for the motion.   (MEI, adapted)

3 Vertical motion

This chapter continues the topic of force and motion, and applies Newton's laws to objects moving in a vertical line. When you have completed it, you should

- know that, if there is no air resistance, objects fall with constant acceleration g
- know the meaning of weight, and be able to distinguish weight from mass
- know that an object of mass m has weight mg
- be able to write equations for motion and equilibrium in a vertical direction
- understand the normal contact force
- understand the function of scales and balances for measuring mass.

3.1 Acceleration due to gravity

Newton wrote 'if I have seen further than other men it is because I stood on the shoulders of giants'. Most important of these giants was Galileo (1564–1642).

By combining experimental observation with mathematical argument Galileo showed that, when an object is dropped, it falls with constant acceleration. This now seems a very simple idea, but at the time it was so novel that Galileo only published it near the end of his life.

Other experiments compared the motion of spheres of different masses. When these were dropped from a height, they took the same time to fall; and if swung on a string like a pendulum they kept time with each other. From this it follows that all objects fall with the same constant acceleration. This assumes that air resistance is neglected.

> All objects, when dropped, fall towards the earth in a vertical line with the same constant acceleration, provided that there is no air resistance.

This acceleration is called the **acceleration due to gravity**, and it is always denoted by the letter g. Another name for it is the **acceleration of free fall**.

But the value of g is not quite the same at all points of the earth's surface. This is because the earth is not a perfect sphere, and because it spins on its axis. The acceleration is about $9.78 \, \mathrm{m\,s^{-2}}$ at points on the equator and $9.83 \, \mathrm{m\,s^{-2}}$ at the poles. It also varies a little with height; at the top of Everest it is about $\frac{1}{4}\%$ less than at sea-level. But everywhere on earth its value is $9.8 \, \mathrm{m\,s^{-2}}$, correct to 2 significant figures. This is the value used in this book.

Solving mechanics problems usually involves setting up a mathematical model to represent a real situation, and this already introduces some simplification. So you need not worry that using an approximation for g will make your solutions too inaccurate.

3.2 Weight

If an object has an acceleration, then Newton's second law states that there is a force which causes it.

For an object falling with acceleration g, that force must act vertically downwards. It is a force of attraction on the object from the earth, called the **force of gravity**. For a particular object it is called the 'weight' of the object.

> The **weight** of an object on or near the surface of the earth is the force of gravity with which the earth attracts it.

Fig. 3.1 is a force–acceleration diagram for a falling object. It shows an object of mass m kg, with an acceleration of 9.8 m s^{-2}. Let the weight of the object be W newtons. Then, by Newton's second law,

$$W = m \times 9.8, \text{ or } 9.8m.$$

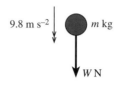

Fig. 3.1

> In SI units, the weight of an object of mass m kilograms is $9.8m$ newtons.

Example 3.2.1

Determine the weight of

(a) a table of mass 42 kg,   (b) a car of mass 1 tonne,   (c) a sack of mass 15 lb.

(a) Taking g as 9.8 m s^{-2}, the weight is 42×9.8 N ≈ 412 N.

(b) 1 tonne $= 1000$ kg. So the weight is 1000×9.8 N $= 9800$ N. You can, if you like, write this as 9.8 kilonewtons; a kilonewton (kN) is 1000 newtons.

(c) 1 kg is approximately 2.2 lb, so 15 lb is approximately $\dfrac{15}{2.2}$ kg $= 6.8...$ kg. The weight is therefore approximately $6.8... \times 9.8$ N $= 67$ N, correct to 2 significant figures.

Units such as the tonne and the kilonewton are called 'supplementary' SI units, to distinguish them from 'basic' SI units such as the kilogram and the newton.

Example 3.2.2

An injured seaman is being winched up to a rescue helicopter. The mass of the seaman is 55 kg. Find the tension in the cable when the seaman is being raised
(a) at a steady speed of 4 m s^{-1},
(b) with an acceleration of 0.8 m s^{-2}.

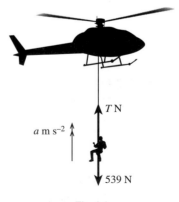

The two forces acting on the seaman, shown in Fig 3.2, are his weight and the tension T N in the cable. The weight is 55×9.8 N, which is 539 N.

(a) As the seaman is moving at a steady speed his acceleration is zero, so the forces are in equilibrium. That is, $T - 539 = 0$, or $T = 539$.

Fig. 3.2

The tension in the cable is 540 newtons, correct to 2 significant figures.

(b) The acceleration is now 0.8 m s^{-2}, so by Newton's second law,

$T - 539 = 55 \times 0.8$, which gives $T = 583$.

The tension in the cable is 580 newtons, correct to 2 significant figures.

If you are working algebraically, then you don't need to substitute a numerical value for g. Fig. 3.3 is a modified version of Fig. 3.1. It shows an object of mass m, falling with acceleration g. Let the weight of the object be W. (Notice that no units have been stated. You can use any units you like, provided that they are consistent.) Then, by Newton's second law,

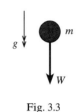

Fig. 3.3

$W = m \times g$, or just mg.

The weight of an object of mass m is mg.

Example 3.2.3
A pulley system is used to lift a heavy crate. There are six vertical sections of rope, each having tension T, and the crate has an upward acceleration a. Find the mass of the crate, expressing your answer in terms of T, a and g.

Denote the mass of the crate by m. The forces and the acceleration are shown in Fig. 3.4. The net force upwards on the container is $6T - W$, where $W = mg$. So, by Newton's second law,

$6T - mg = ma$.

In this example it is supposed that T, a and g are known, and the mass m is unknown. So write

$6T = mg + ma = m(g + a)$,

which gives $m = \dfrac{6T}{g + a}$.

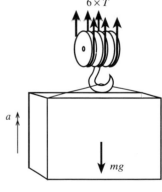

Fig. 3.4

Example 3.2.4
Machinery of total mass 280 kg is being lowered to the bottom of a mine by means of two ropes attached to a cage of mass 20 kg. For the first 3 seconds of the descent, the tension in each rope is 870 N. Then for a further 16 seconds, the tension in each rope is 1470 N. For the final 8 seconds, the tension in each rope is 1695 N. Find the depth of the mine.

The mass of the combined machinery and cage is 300 kg, so its weight is $300 \times 9.8 \text{ N}$, which is 2940 N. The forces are shown in Fig. 3.5.

The descent is in three stages and you can find the acceleration of the cage during each stage by using Newton's second law.

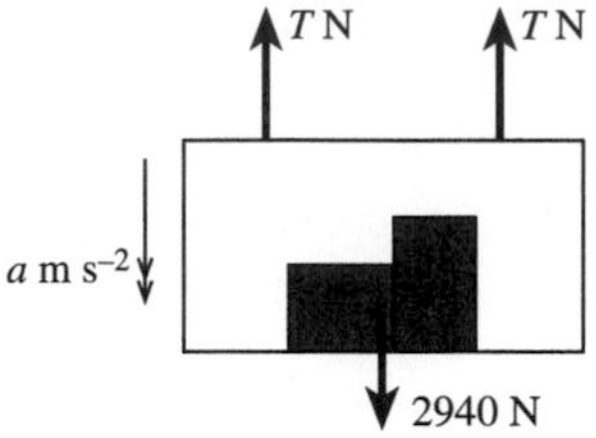

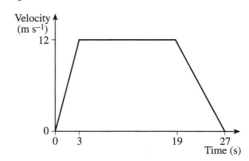

Fig. 3.5

Stage 1

With $T = 870$, $2940 - 2 \times 870 = 300a$, giving $a = 4$.

Stage 2

With $T = 1470$, $2940 - 2 \times 1470 = 300a$, giving $a = 0$.

Stage 3

With $T = 1695$, $2940 - 2 \times 1695 = 300a$, giving $a = -1.5$.

The descent is represented by the velocity–time graph shown in Fig. 3.6.

During Stage 1 the acceleration is 4 m s^{-2}, which means that the speed reached after 3 seconds is 12 m s^{-1}. You can now find the distance travelled by calculating the area of the region under the graph.

Fig. 3.6

This region is trapezium-shaped, with parallel sides of 27 and 16, and height 12. So the area is $\frac{1}{2}(27 + 16) \times 12 = 258$.

The depth of the mine is about 260 m.

Exercise 3A

1   Find the weight of

(a) a baby of mass 3 kg,   (b) a coin of mass 10 grams,   (c) a tree of mass 800 kg.

2   A piece of luggage weighs 170 N. Find its mass, to the nearest kilogram.

3   A crane is lifting a load of mass 350 kg. The tension in the cable as the load is lifted is 4200 N. Calculate the acceleration of the load.

4   A lift bringing miners to the surface of a mine shaft is moving with an acceleration of 1.2 m s^{-2}. The total mass of the cage and the miners is 1600 kg. Find the tension in the lift cable.

5   The total mass of a hot-air balloon, occupants and ballast is 1300 kg. What is the upthrust on the balloon when it is travelling vertically upwards with constant velocity? The occupants now release 50 kg of ballast. Assuming no air resistance, find the immediate acceleration of the balloon.

6   A steel ball of mass 1.8 kg is dropping vertically through water with an acceleration of 5.6 m s^{-2}. Find the magnitude of the force resisting the motion of the ball.

7   In a simulation of a spacecraft's lift-off an astronaut of mass 85 kg experiences a constant force of 7000 N from the seat. Calculate the acceleration of the astronaut in the simulation.

8   A boy of mass 45 kg is stranded on a beach as the tide comes in. A rescuer of mass 75 kg is lowered down, by rope, from the top of the cliff. They are both raised, initially with a constant acceleration of 0.6 m s^{-2}. Find the tension in the rope for this stage of the ascent.

    As they near the top of the cliff, the tension in the rope is 1150 N and they are moving with a constant deceleration. Calculate the magnitude of this deceleration.

9   The maximum load that a lift of mass 600 kg can hold is 480 kg. Find the tension in the cable when the lift is holding a maximum load and the lift is moving

    (a) upwards with an acceleration of 0.2 m s^{-2},

    (b) at a constant speed of 3 m s^{-1},

    (c) downwards with an acceleration of 0.2 m s^{-2},

    (d) downwards with a deceleration of 0.2 m s^{-2}.

10 The tension in the vertical cable of a crane is 1225 N when it is raising a girder with constant speed. Calculate the tension in the cable when it is raising the girder with an acceleration of 0.2 m s^{-2}, assuming no air resistance.

11 A balloon of total mass 840 kg is rising vertically with constant speed. As a result of releasing some ballast, the balloon immediately accelerates at 0.49 m s^{-2}. Calculate the mass of ballast released.

12 The resistance force, R N, experienced by a parachutist travelling with speed $v \text{ m s}^{-1}$ may be modelled as $R = 135v$. It may be assumed that the parachutist moves vertically downwards at all times. At the instant that he is moving with a speed of 8 m s^{-1} he has a deceleration of 2.2 m s^{-2}. Find his mass. The speed of the parachutist continues to drop until it reaches a constant value (the terminal speed); find this speed.

13 A stone of mass 0.1 kg drops vertically into a lake, with an entry speed of 15 m s^{-1}, and sinks a distance of 18 metres in 2 seconds. Find the resisting force, assumed constant, acting on the stone.

14 A pail of mass 4 kg is being lowered down a well at constant speed. Find the tension in the lowering rope. When filled with water, the pail is raised with a constant acceleration of 1.2 m s^{-2} for part of the ascent. The tension in the rope in this stage is 220 N. Calculate the mass of water in the pail.

15 A load of mass M is raised with constant acceleration, from rest, by a rope. The load reaches a speed of v in a distance of s. The tension in the rope is T. Find an expression for s in terms of M, T, v and g.

16 A container of total mass 200 kg is being loaded on to a cargo ship by using a pulley system, similar to that used in Example 3.2.3, but with only two vertical sections of rope. In this operation the container is lifted vertically off the ground to a height of h metres. For the first 3 s of the ascent the tension in each cable is 1200 N. For the next second it travels at constant speed. For the final 6 s, before it comes to rest, the tension in each rope is T N. Find the values of h and T.

17 A load of weight 7 kN is being raised from rest with constant acceleration by a cable. After the load has been raised 20 metres, the cable suddenly becomes slack. The load continues upwards for a distance of 4 metres before coming to instantaneous rest. Assuming no air resistance, find the tension in the cable before it became slack.

3.3 Normal contact force

A radio is placed on a table (Fig. 3.7). Why doesn't it fall through?

The obvious answer is 'because the table is there'. But mechanics requires an explanation in terms of forces. Since the radio doesn't move, the net force on it must be zero.

Fig. 3.7

You already know one force acting on the radio, its weight. So if the net force is zero, there must be a second force, with the same magnitude as the weight but acting upwards. This force comes from the contact between the radio and the table. It is called the 'normal contact force'. This is shown in Fig. 3.8.

The word 'normal' is used in the same sense as for a graph, where the normal is the line at right angles to the tangent. The direction of the contact force is at right angles to the region over which the table and the radio are in contact.

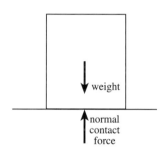

Fig. 3.8

When an object is in contact with a surface, there is a force on the object at right angles to the region of contact. This is called the **normal contact force**.

The normal contact force is sometimes called the **normal reaction**.

When an object of mass m rests on a horizontal surface, as in Fig. 3.9, the two forces on it are its weight mg and the normal contact force R, which acts vertically upwards. These forces are in equilibrium, so $R = mg$.

Fig. 3.9

It would be nicer to call the normal contact force N rather than R. But force is often measured in newtons, and it would be awkward to write N N. However, if you are doing an algebraic problem which doesn't involve units, there is no reason why you shouldn't use N for the force.

For a rounded object like a pebble or a ball there may
be only one point of contact with the surface, rather
than a region. The surface is then a tangent plane to
the object, and the contact force is at right angles to
this plane. This is illustrated in Fig. 3.10.

Fig. 3.10

Example 3.3.1

A book of mass 0.5 kg is placed flat on a horizontal shelf, as in Fig. 3.11. Find the
magnitude of the normal contact force.

The weight of the book is $0.5 \times 9.8 \, \text{N}$, which is
4.9 N. The only other force on the book is the
normal contact force, so this is also 4.9 N.

Fig. 3.11

Example 3.3.2

A container sits on the quayside waiting to be loaded on to a container ship. The mass of
the container is 6000 kg. A cable from a crane is attached to the container. At first, the
cable is slack; the tension is then gradually increased until the container rises off the
ground. Draw a graph to show the relationship between the normal contact force and the
tension in the cable.

There are three forces acting on the container: its
weight, the normal contact force from the ground
and the tension in the cable. (See Fig. 3.12.)

The weight of the container is 58 800 N. Denote
the normal contact force by R newtons, and the
tension by T newtons. Since the three forces are
in equilibrium the net force is zero, so

$$R + T - 58\,800 = 0.$$

This equation is represented by the graph in
Fig. 3.13. Note that it is drawn only for $T \geqslant 0$
and $R \geqslant 0$, because neither the tension nor the
contact force can be negative.

At first, while the cable is slack, $T = 0$ and
$R = 58\,800$. As the cable tightens, T increases
and R correspondingly decreases. Eventually,
when T reaches the value 58 800, $R = 0$ and
the container is on the point of being lifted from
the quayside.

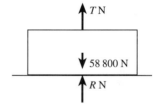

Fig. 3.12

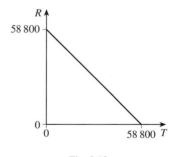

Fig. 3.13

3.4 Mass and weight

Some of the words used in science and mathematics are taken from everyday language,
but they are given a more precise meaning. One such word is 'weight'.

Here are some remarks which you might hear or read in a newspaper.

'This bag of potatoes has a weight of 3 kilograms.'
'The weight of an elephant is about 6 tonnes.'
'My rucksack weighs 35 pounds.'
'The boxer weighed in at 159 pounds.'

These are all statements for which, in mechanics, the correct usage would be to replace 'weight' by 'mass', and 'weighs' by 'has mass'.

In the case of the potatoes, you might be interested in both the mass and the weight. Mass is important from the point of view of feeding the family; but if you have to carry the bag home, it is the weight of about 30 newtons that will concern you, since this has to be supported by your arm muscles.

With the elephant, it is mass which matters if it charges your safari jeep; but if it walks across a bridge, it is the weight which might cause the bridge to collapse.

The mass of the rucksack remains constant, but its weight (about 160 newtons) decreases very slightly as you climb a mountain, because the value of g decreases with height.

For the boxer, the weight is irrelevant. It is his mass which determines how he can stand up to a punch, or how much he can damage his opponent.

A particular difficulty arises when you use measuring instruments, such as bathroom scales or a spring balance. People who use bathroom scales do so because they are worried about their mass. But mass is difficult to measure directly; it is much easier to measure force. So what the scales actually measure is the force with which they support your body, and this is equal to your weight. So if the scales indicate that your mass is 80 kg, what they are really measuring is a force of $80 \times 9.8 \text{ N} = 784 \text{ N}$.

You can demonstrate this by trying out an experiment like the next example.

Example 3.4.1

A mechanics student lives on the tenth floor of a tall building. She has just bought new bathroom scales, and decides to try them out by standing on them as she goes up in the lift. Initially the scales read 50 kg. After the doors have closed the reading briefly goes up to 60 kg, but then returns to 50 kg. As the lift nears the tenth floor, the reading drops to 35 kg. Explain.

Before the lift starts moving, the scales show 50 kg. This is the mass of the student. What the scales are really doing is measuring the normal contact force from the scales on her shoes. This is equal to her weight, which is 490 N.

As the lift starts to ascend, the scales show 60 kg. This does not mean that the student's mass has changed, but

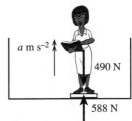

Fig. 3.14

that the normal contact force is now 588 N. It is the acceleration of the lift which has caused the change. The forces on the student are her weight and the normal contact force, as in Fig. 3.14.

Apply Newton's second law to the upward motion.

$$588 - 490 = 50a, \quad \text{which gives} \quad a = 1.96.$$

For a brief time at the start, the lift accelerates at just under 2 m s^{-2}.

Then the reading on the scales returns to 50 kg. So the normal contact force is 490 N, the same as her weight. The forces are in equilibrium. Since the lift is moving, it must be going at a constant speed.

Towards the end of the ascent, as the lift slows down, the scales show 35 kg. The normal contact force is now 343 N, as shown in Fig. 3.15. Newton's second law now gives

$$343 - 490 = 50a, \quad \text{so} \quad a = -2.94.$$

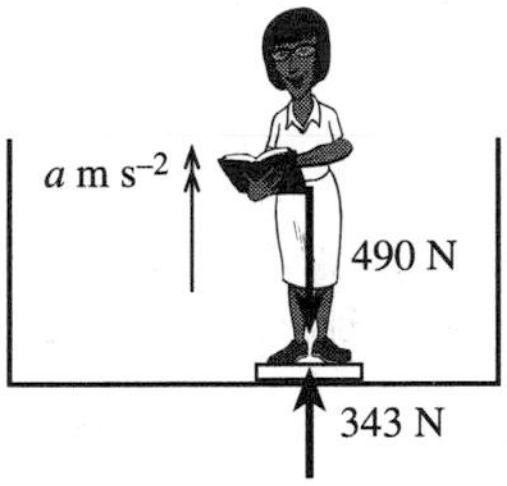

$a \text{ m s}^{-2}$

490 N

343 N

Fig. 3.15

For the final phase of the ascent, the lift is accelerating at about -3 m s^{-2}. That is, it is decelerating at about 3 m s^{-2}.

Example 3.4.2
A heavy mass m kg is suspended from the roof of a lift by a wire. The wire is cut, and a spring balance is inserted between the two free ends. When the lift is accelerating upwards at $a \text{ m s}^{-2}$, the reading on the balance is y kg. Find the equation connecting a and y.

The apparatus is shown in Fig. 3.16.

The usual function of a spring balance is to measure the mass of an object when the upper end is held stationary. This means that, when the balance reads y kg, the tension in the wire supporting the mass is yg N.

So, when the lift is accelerating, the forces on the mass are its weight, mg N, and the tension in the wire, yg N. By Newton's second law,

$$yg - mg = ma.$$

This can be rearranged as $a = \dfrac{g}{m} y - g$.

This apparatus can be used as an instrument for measuring acceleration. It is called an 'accelerometer'. You read the value of y from the spring balance, and then use the equation to calculate a.

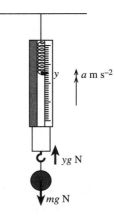

y $a \text{ m s}^{-2}$

yg N

mg N

Fig. 3.16

Exercise 3B

1 A book rests on a table. The magnitude of the normal contact force on the book from the table is 28 N. What is the mass of the book?

2 A truck of mass 4 tonnes is at rest on a platform. What is the magnitude of the normal contact force on the truck from the platform when the platform is

(a) stationary,   (b) descending with an acceleration of 0.5 m s^{-2}?

3 An oil drum of mass 250 kg rests on the ground. A vertical cable is attached to the drum and the tension is gradually increased. At one stage the tension in the cable has magnitude 1800 N. What is the magnitude of the normal contact force between the drum and the ground at this instant? What happens when the tension reaches 2450 N?

4 A girl of mass 38 kg is standing in a lift. Find the magnitude of the normal contact force on the girl's feet from the lift floor when the lift is

(a) stationary,   (b) moving upwards with an acceleration of 1.8 m s^{-2},

(c) moving upwards with a constant speed of 4 m s^{-1}.

5 A fork-lift truck is raising a container of car batteries with an acceleration of 1.2 m s^{-2}. The normal contact force on the container from the horizontal forks is 1485 N. Calculate the mass of the load.

6 A jet aircraft of mass 7 tonnes stands at rest on a part of the deck of an aircraft carrier that can be lowered to allow the jet to be housed in the hold of the carrier. Find the magnitude of the normal contact force on the wheels of the aircraft from the lowering part of the deck as it is lowered with an acceleration of 0.4 m s^{-2}.

7 The pilot of a hot-air balloon has mass 85 kg. As the balloon leaves the ground, the normal contact force on the pilot from the floor of the balloon immediately increases to 901 N and remains at this value for the first stage of the ascent. Calculate the acceleration of the balloon in this stage of its motion.

8 When a man stands on bathroom scales placed on the floor of a stationary lift the reading is 90 kg. While the lift is moving upwards he finds that the reading is 86 kg. Account for this change and describe the motion of the lift at this time.

9 A lift starting from rest moves downwards with constant acceleration. It covers a distance s in time t, where $s = \frac{1}{6}gt^2$. A box of mass m is on the floor of the lift. Find, in terms of m and g, an expression for the normal contact force on the box from the lift floor.

10 A spring balance is attached to the roof of a lift which is moving downwards. When an object of mass 7 kg is suspended from the balance the reading on the balance is 7.5 kg. Show that the lift is slowing down and find the magnitude of the deceleration.

11 A man of mass M kg and his son of mass m kg are standing in a lift. When the lift is accelerating upwards with magnitude 1.2 m s^{-2} the magnitude of the normal contact force exerted on the man by the lift floor is 880 N. When the lift is moving with constant speed the combined magnitude of the normal contact forces exerted on the man and the boy by the lift floor is 980 N. Find the values of M and m.

12 A spring balance hangs from the roof of a lift. A case of mass m kg is hung from the spring balance by a string. While the lift is accelerating upwards with magnitude a m s^{-2}, the reading on the balance is 12.5 kg; when the lift is moving downwards with an acceleration of a m s^{-2}, the reading is 9 kg. Find the values of m and a.

Miscellaneous exercise 3

1 A Red Cross food parcel of mass 80 kg is being lowered vertically to the ground, by means of a cable, from a helicopter. Assuming there is no air resistance, calculate the tension in the cable when the parcel is being lowered with acceleration 0.5 m s^{-2}.

2 A boy of mass 60 kg is standing in a lift that has an upward acceleration of magnitude 0.50 m s^{-2}. Describe the forces acting on the boy, and find their magnitudes. (OCR)

3 As a load moves downwards at a constant speed of 2 m s^{-1} the tension in the cable supporting it is 6000 N. Calculate the tension in the cable when the load is moving downwards with an acceleration of 1.96 m s^{-2}.

4 A balloon of total mass 420 kg is descending with a constant acceleration of 0.4 m s^{-2}. Find the upthrust acting on the balloon. When the balloon is moving at 1.5 m s^{-1}, enough ballast is released for the balloon to fall with a deceleration of 0.2 m s^{-2}. Calculate

   (a) how much ballast was released,

   (b) the time for which the balloon continues to fall before it begins to rise.

5 A cylindrical rock sample of mass 12 kg is being pulled by a cable up a deep vertical shaft with rough sides. The tension in the cable is kept constant, at 1520 N, for the first part of the operation, which takes 2 minutes and lifts the sample 1440 m. Calculate the resisting force, assumed constant, due to friction from the sides of the shaft.

6 A stone of mass m is released from rest on the surface of a tank of water of depth d. During the motion, the water exerts a constant resisting force of magnitude R. The stone takes t seconds to reach the bottom of the tank. Show that $R = m\left(g - \dfrac{2d}{t^2}\right)$.

7 A box of weight W rests on a platform. When the platform is moving upwards with acceleration a, the normal contact force from the platform on the box has magnitude kW. When the platform is moving downwards with acceleration $2a$, the box remains in contact with it. Find the normal contact force in terms of k and W, and deduce that $k < \frac{3}{2}$.

8 An acrobat of mass m slides down a vertical rope of height h. For the first three-quarters of her descent she grips the rope with her hands and legs so as to produce a frictional force equal to five-ninths of her weight. She then tightens her grip so that she comes to rest at the bottom of the rope. Sketch a (t, v) graph to illustrate her descent, and find the frictional force she must produce in the last quarter. If the rope is 30 metres high, calculate

   (a) her greatest speed,   (b) the time she takes to descend.

9   In a laboratory experiment the motion of a steel ball-bearing falling vertically in a tank containing liquid is observed.

    (a)   State why the acceleration of the ball-bearing is less than g.

    (b)   The ball-bearing of mass 0.15 kg is released from rest in the liquid, and after 0.60 seconds it has fallen a distance of 1.53 m. Assuming that the acceleration has a constant value of a m s^{-2}, find a and the magnitude of the force resisting the motion.

                                                        (OCR, adapted)

10   A lift travels vertically upwards from rest at floor A to rest at floor B, which is 20 m above A, in three stages as follows. At first the lift accelerates from rest at A at 2 m s^{-2} for 2 s. It then travels at a constant speed and finally it decelerates uniformly, coming to rest at B after a total time of $6\frac{1}{2}$ s. Sketch the (t, v) graph for this motion, and find the magnitude of the constant deceleration.

    The mass of the lift and its contents is 500 kg. Find the tension in the lift cable during the stage of the motion when the lift is accelerating upwards.   (OCR)

11   The diagram shows an approximate (t, v) graph for the motion of a parachutist falling vertically; v m s^{-1} is the parachutist's downwards velocity at time t seconds after he jumps out of the plane. Use the information in the diagram

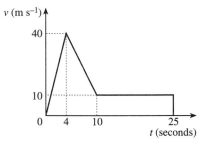

    (a)   to give a brief description of the parachutist's motion throughout the descent,

    (b)   to calculate the height from which the jump was made.

    The mass of the parachutist is 90 kg. Calculate the upwards force acting on the parachutist, due to the parachute, when $t = 7$.

    State two ways in which you would expect an accurate (t, v) graph for the parachutist's motion to differ from the approximate graph shown in the diagram.   (OCR)

4 Resolving forces

This chapter deals with the combined effect of all the forces on an object, including forces which are neither horizontal nor vertical. When you have completed it, you should

- understand the idea of resolving in a chosen direction
- know how to find the resolved part of a force in a given direction
- be able to solve problems by resolving in various directions.

4.1 Resolving horizontally and vertically

Suppose that a cyclist starts from rest and accelerates at 0.4 m s^{-2}. The combined mass of the cyclist and machine is 75 kg.

Since the cyclist and the bicycle have the same acceleration, they can be treated as a single object. What are the forces acting on it?

Clearly there is a force driving it forward, which is produced by the grip of the rear wheel on the road. Denote this by D newtons. There may also be some air resistance, R newtons, though at low speeds this will be small compared with the driving force; in a simplified model you might decide to neglect it.

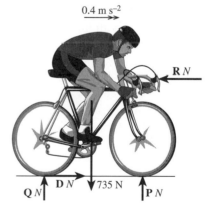

Also there is the combined weight of bicycle and rider, which is 735 newtons. This is opposed by the normal contact forces from the road on the front and rear wheels, P newtons and Q newtons respectively.

Fig. 4.1 shows all these forces, and the acceleration, in a single diagram.

Whenever you have to solve a problem about forces and acceleration, you should begin by drawing a diagram showing all the forces and the acceleration.

Fig. 4.1

Two equations for the forces can be written down. One uses Newton's second law of motion in a horizontal direction, the other states that the vertical forces are in equilibrium. These equations are $D - R = 75 \times 0.4$ and $P + Q - 735 = 0$.

Forming equations like this is called **resolving**. The first equation is 'resolving horizontally', and the second is 'resolving vertically'. A convenient shorthand for this is to write $\mathcal{R}(\rightarrow)$ and $\mathcal{R}(\uparrow)$. So you could set out the equations for the cyclist like this:

$$\mathcal{R}(\rightarrow) \quad D - R = 75 \times 0.4,$$

$$\mathcal{R}(\uparrow) \quad P + Q - 735 = 0.$$

When you write a resolving equation, you should always indicate, either in words or by using the $\mathcal{R}(\ )$ shorthand, which direction you are considering.

You can write the equilibrium equation $\mathcal{R}(\uparrow)$ either as $P+Q-735=0$ or as $P+Q=735$, whichever you prefer. The convention is that the arrow indicates the direction of the forces on the left side of the equation. But if you are using Newton's second law, it is best to put all the forces on the left and the 'ma' term by itself on the right.

4.2   Forces at an angle

So far all the forces considered have been either horizontal or vertical, but in many situations some forces act at an angle.

Suppose you are on a boating holiday with a friend. As you bring the boat into a lock, you turn off the engine and your friend jumps on to the side and steers the boat into the lock with a rope. Fig. 4.2 shows an aerial view of the situation. Suppose that the tension from the rope is T newtons, and that the rope is horizontal.

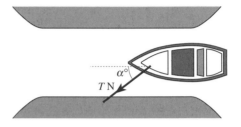

Fig. 4.2

For obvious reasons the rope can't be directed straight forward from the boat. Also, since the tension has to provide the forward movement of the boat, the rope can't be at right angles to the line of the boat. So the direction will make some acute angle, $\alpha°$, with the fore-and-aft line of the boat. The question then is, how much effect does the tension have in a forward direction?

The answer must be that it depends on both T and α. If α could be 0, then the forward effect would be the full T newtons. If α were 90, the forward effect would be zero. For values of α between 0 and 90, the forward effect must be rT newtons, where r is some number between 1 and 0 depending on α.

You can find the connection between r and α by doing experiments. (Some ideas for possible experiments are given later in this chapter and in Chapter 7.) It turns out that r is equal to $\cos\alpha°$.

You can see that this fits the requirements of the paragraph before last. When $\alpha=0$, the forward effect is $(\cos 0°)\times T$ newtons, which is $1\times T$ newtons, or just T newtons. When $\alpha=90$, the forward effect is $(\cos 90°)\times T$ newtons, which is zero. Between 0 and 90, the value of $\cos\alpha°$ is between 1 and 0.

You can make this into a general rule, illustrated in Fig. 4.3.

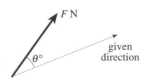

Fig. 4.3

If a force of F newtons makes an angle of $\theta°$ with a given direction, then the effect of the force in that direction is $F\times\cos\theta°$. This is called the **resolved part** of the force in the given direction.

It is now possible to write down equations for
the motion of the boat. Suppose that the boat is
brought in parallel to the side of the lock at a
steady speed. There is a resistance from the
water of R newtons to the forward motion of the
boat, and a force of S newtons preventing the
boat from moving sideways. Fig. 4.4 shows all
three horizontal forces on the boat. You can then
resolve parallel and perpendicular to the line of
the boat.

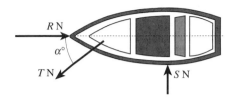

Fig. 4.4

$\mathcal{R}(\parallel$ to the line of the boat$)$ $\qquad T\cos\alpha° - R = 0$.

The rope makes an angle $(90 - \alpha)°$ with the sideways direction, so

$\mathcal{R}(\perp$ to the line of the boat$)$ $\qquad T\cos(90 - \alpha)° - S = 0$.

Notice that there are also vertical forces on the
boat: its weight and the buoyancy force from the
water. It is easier to show these in a separate
diagram (Fig. 4.5), to avoid having to draw a
three-dimensional picture.

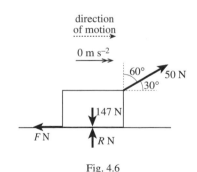

Fig. 4.5

Example 4.2.1
A box of mass 15 kg is dragged along the floor at a constant speed of 1.2 m s^{-1} by
means of a rope at $30°$ to the horizontal. The tension from the rope is 50 N. Calculate
the frictional force resisting the motion and the normal contact force from the floor.

Fig. 4.6 shows the four forces acting on the
box. The frictional force is F N, and the
normal contact force is R N. The weight
of the box is 147 N. The tension makes
angles of $30°$ with the horizontal and $60°$
with the vertical. You needn't show the
speed in the diagram, but because the box
is moving with constant speed it helps to
show the acceleration of 0 m s^{-2} in the
direction of motion.

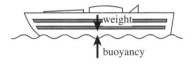

Fig. 4.6

$\mathcal{R}(\rightarrow)$ $\qquad 50\cos 30° - F = 15 \times 0$.

$\mathcal{R}(\uparrow)$ $\qquad R + 50\cos 60° - 147 = 0$.

These equations give $F = 50\cos 30° = 43.3...$ and $R = 147 - 50\cos 60° = 122$.

The frictional force is about 43 N, and the normal contact force is 122 N. Notice
that the normal contact force is less than the weight of the box, because the
tension in the rope is helping to support the weight.

Example 4.2.2

A child pushes a toy car of mass 2 kg across the floor with a force of 5 newtons at an angle of 35° to the horizontal. Find the acceleration of the car.

Fig. 4.7 shows the forces and the acceleration of a m s^{-2}.

$\mathcal{R}(\rightarrow)$ $5\cos 35° = 2a$.

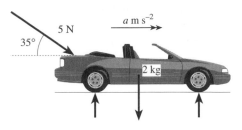

This gives $a = \dfrac{5\cos 35°}{2} = 2.04....$

The car accelerates at just over 2 m s^{-2}.

Fig. 4.7

Example 4.2.3

A small child is strapped into the seat of a swing which is supported by two ropes. To start her off, her father pulls the swing back with a horizontal force, so that the ropes make an angle of 20° with the vertical. The child and swing together have mass 18 kg. Calculate the tension in each rope, and the force exerted by her father before he lets go.

Denote the tension in each rope by T N, and the force from the father by F N. These forces, with the weight of 176.4 N, are shown in Fig. 4.8.

The forces are in equilibrium.

$\mathcal{R}(\rightarrow)$ $F = 2T\cos 70°$.

$\mathcal{R}(\uparrow)$ $2T\cos 20° = 176.4$.

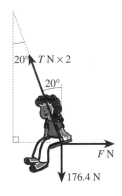

The second equation gives

$$T = \frac{176.4}{2\cos 20°} = 93.8....$$

Fig. 4.8

Substituting this in the first equation, $F = 64.2....$

Each rope acts on the swing with a tension of about 94 N. The father must pull the swing with a horizontal force of about 64 N.

Example 4.2.4

A game played on the deck of a ship uses wooden discs of mass 2 kg. These have a small depression in the top surface into which a broom handle can be inserted. Two parallel lines 6 metres apart are painted on the deck. Players begin with their discs on the back line and, by pushing on the broom handle, accelerate them towards the front line. When a disc crosses the front line the handle is pulled out and the disc slides across the deck until friction brings it to rest. When the broom handle is pushed with a force of 20 newtons at 60° to the horizontal, the frictional force is 4 newtons. After the handle is removed, the friction drops to 2 newtons. Find how far the disc travels beyond the front line.

The two stages of the motion are illustrated in
Fig. 4.9 and Fig. 4.10. Let the acceleration in the
first stage be a m s^{-2}, and the deceleration in the
second stage b m s^{-2}.

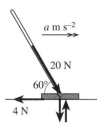

Fig. 4.9

Stage 1

$$\mathcal{R}(\rightarrow) \qquad 20\cos 60° - 4 = 2a,$$

so $\quad a = \dfrac{10-4}{2} = 3.$

Fig. 4.10

Stage 2

$$\mathcal{R}(\rightarrow) \qquad -2 = 2 \times (-b), \qquad \text{so } b = 1.$$

Fig. 4.11 is a velocity–time graph for the two
stages. The two line segments have gradients of 3
and -1, and the area of the triangle on the left is
6 because it represents the distance between the
two lines which the disc covers in Stage 1.

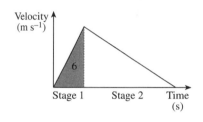

Fig. 4.11

You can deduce from the gradients that the bases
of the two triangles are in the ratio 1 to 3, and the
areas of the two triangles are in the same ratio. So
the area of the triangle on the right is $3 \times 6 = 18$.

This means that in Stage 2 the disc travels 18 metres.

Exercise 4A

1 For each of the diagrams shown below find the resolved parts of each of the forces $\mathbf{F}_1$ and
$\mathbf{F}_2$ in the directions Ox and Oy.

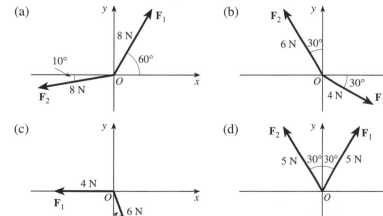

2 The diagram shows three coplanar forces acting on a particle P, which is in equilibrium. By resolving in the direction of the $5\,\text{N}$ force, calculate the value of θ; by resolving in the direction of the $X\,\text{N}$ force, calculate the value of X.

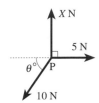

3 A toy of mass $1.8\,\text{kg}$ is pulled along a horizontal surface by a string inclined at $30°$ to the horizontal. Given that the tension in the string is $6\,\text{N}$ and that there are no forces resisting motion, calculate the acceleration of the particle.

4 A laundry basket of mass $5\,\text{kg}$ is being pulled, with constant speed, along a corridor by a rope inclined at $20°$ to the horizontal. Given that the frictional force has magnitude $33\,\text{N}$, find the tension in the rope.

5 A van of mass $750\,\text{kg}$ is being towed along a horizontal road with constant acceleration $0.8\,\text{m s}^{-2}$ by a breakdown vehicle. The connecting towbar is inclined at $40°$ to the horizontal. Given that the tension in the towbar has magnitude $1000\,\text{N}$, calculate the magnitude of the force resisting the motion of the car.

6 A car of mass $850\,\text{kg}$ is being pushed along a level road with a force of magnitude $T\,\text{N}$, directed upwards at $25°$ to the horizontal, and also pulled by a horizontal force of $283\,\text{N}$. There is a constant force of $600\,\text{N}$ opposing the motion. The car is moving at constant speed. Find the value of T, and the total normal contact force from the road.

7 A particle P of mass $4m\,\text{kg}$ is at rest on a horizontal table. A force of magnitude $50m\,\text{N}$, acting upwards at an acute angle $\theta°$ to the horizontal, is applied to the particle. Given that $\tan\theta° = \frac{3}{4}$ and that there is a resistance to motion of magnitude $20m\,\text{N}$, find the acceleration with which P moves. Find, in terms of m, the magnitude of the normal contact force of the table on P.

8 A shopper pushes a supermarket trolley in a straight line towards her car with a force of magnitude $20\,\text{N}$, directed downwards at an angle of $15°$ to the horizontal. Given that the acceleration of the trolley is $2.4\,\text{m s}^{-2}$, calculate its mass. Find also the magnitude of the normal contact force exerted on the trolley by the ground.

9 A lamp is supported in equilibrium by two chains fixed to two points A and B at the same level. The lengths of the chains are $0.3\,\text{m}$ and $0.4\,\text{m}$ and the distance between A and B is $0.5\,\text{m}$. Given that the tension in the longer chain is $36\,\text{N}$, show by resolving horizontally that the tension in the shorter chain is $48\,\text{N}$. By resolving vertically, find the mass of the lamp.

10 The three horizontal forces shown act on a mass of $4\,\text{kg}$. Given that the mass moves in the direction of the dotted line, show that $\theta = 30$ and find the magnitude of the acceleration.

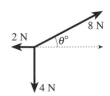

11 A paraglider of mass 90 kg is pulled by a rope attached to a speedboat. With the rope making an angle of 20° to the horizontal the paraglider is moving in a straight line parallel to the surface of the water with an acceleration of 1.2 m s^{-2}. The tension in the rope is 250 N. Calculate the magnitude of the vertical lift force acting on the glider, and the magnitude of the air resistance.

12 A child's toy of mass 5 kg is pulled along level ground by a string inclined at 30° to the horizontal. Denoting the tension in the string by T N, find, in terms of T, an expression for the normal contact force between the toy and the floor, and deduce that T cannot exceed 98.

13 A block of wood of mass 4.5 kg rests on a table. A force of magnitude 35 N, acting upwards at an angle of $\theta°$ to the horizontal, is applied to the block but does not move it. Given that the normal contact force between the block and the table has magnitude 30 N, calculate

(a) the value of θ,

(b) the frictional force acting on the block.

14 A container of mass 35 kg is pushed along a horizontal yard by a force of 130 N acting downwards at an angle of 30° to the horizontal, against a frictional force of 60 N. Calculate the acceleration of the container, and the magnitude of the normal contact force between the container and the floor.

15 A boy travelling in a railway carriage decides to try to calculate the acceleration of the train. He suspends a parcel of mass 2 kg from the roof of the carriage with a string and measures the angle that the string makes with the vertical. When the train is travelling with a constant acceleration of a m s^{-2} the angle is 8°. Find the value of a.

16 A concrete slab of mass m kg is being raised vertically, at a constant speed, by two cables. One of the cables is inclined at 10° to the vertical and has a tension of 2800 N; the other cable has a tension of 2400 N. Calculate the angle at which this cable is inclined to the vertical, and also find the value of m, assuming there is no air resistance.

17 A barge of mass 4 tonnes is pulled in a straight line by two tugs with an acceleration of 0.6 m s^{-2}. The tension in one tow-rope is 1800 N and the tension in the other is 1650 N. Given that the angles the ropes make with the direction of motion are 20° and $x°$ respectively, find the value of x and the resistance to motion of the barge.

18 A man is pulling a toboggan of mass 40 kg along a horizontal snow field with a force of 140 N inclined at 30° to the horizontal. His daughter is pushing with a force of 50 N directed downwards at 10° to the horizontal. The toboggan is moving with constant speed. Calculate the magnitude, F N, of the frictional force, and the magnitude, R N, of the normal contact force from the ground on the toboggan. Show that the ratio $F:R$ lies between 0.51 and 0.52.

4.3   Some useful trigonometry

If you write equations of resolving in two perpendicular
directions, and a force F makes an angle of $\theta°$ with one of
the directions, then it makes an angle of $(90-\theta)°$ with the
other (see Fig. 4.12). The force then has a resolved part of
$F\cos\theta°$ in one direction, and $F\cos(90-\theta)°$ in the other.

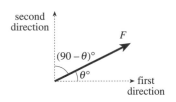

Fig. 4.12

You can write this second resolved part in another way. In
P1 Section 11.4 it was shown that $\cos(90-\theta)° = \sin\theta°$. So
the resolved parts of F in the two directions can be written
as $F\cos\theta°$ and $F\sin\theta°$.

Sometimes the second angle is $(90+\theta)°$, as in Fig. 4.13,
rather than $(90-\theta)°$. In that case you can use
$\cos(90+\theta)° = -\sin\theta°$, so that the second resolved part is
$-F\sin\theta°$.

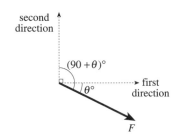

Another result that is sometimes useful is that
$\dfrac{\sin\theta°}{\cos\theta°} = \tan\theta°$. For example, in Example 4.2.3 the first

equation could have been written as $F = 2T\sin 20°$, and

you can notice from the second equation that $2T = \dfrac{176.4}{\cos 20°}$.

Substituting for $2T$ in the first equation gives

Fig. 4.13

$$F = \left(\frac{176.4}{\cos 20°}\right)\sin 20° = 176.4 \times \left(\frac{\sin 20°}{\cos 20°}\right) = 176.4\tan 20°.$$

From this you can find $F = 64.2\ldots$ directly, without first having to calculate T.

4.4   Resolving in other directions

You can write equations of resolving in any direction you like, not just horizontally and
vertically. One type of problem in which this is often useful is when an object is placed
on a track which is inclined at an angle to the horizontal.

Example 4.4.1

A crate of mass $30\,\text{kg}$ is at rest on a ramp which slopes at
an angle of $18°$ to the horizontal. It is prevented from
sliding down the ramp by friction. Find the frictional force
and the normal contact force.

Let the friction be $F\,\text{N}$ and the normal contact force
$R\,\text{N}$ (see Fig. 4.14). Notice that the normal contact
force is not vertical, but perpendicular to the plane of
the ramp. The weight is $294\,\text{N}$.

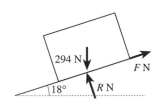

Fig. 4.14

The simplest directions to choose for resolving are
parallel to the ramp, and perpendicular to the
ramp. To do this, you are going to need to
calculate the angles marked $x°$ and $y°$ in
Fig. 4.15. It is easy to see that $x = 90 - 18 = 72$,
and $y = 90 - x = 90 - 72 = 18$.

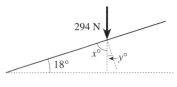

Fig. 4.15

$\mathcal{R}(\parallel \text{to ramp}) \qquad F - 294 \cos x° = 0.$

$\mathcal{R}(\perp \text{to ramp}) \qquad R - 294 \cos y° = 0.$

So $F = 294 \cos 72° = 90.8$ and $R = 294 \cos 18° = 279.6$, correct to 1 decimal place.

The frictional force is about 91 N and the normal contact force is about 280 N.

Example 4.4.2
Re-work Example 4.2.3 if the child's father pulls on the swing at right angles to the
ropes, rather than horizontally.

The diagram of forces now has the form of Fig. 4.16.
Notice that, although the situation being modelled is
quite different from that in the previous example, the
three forces are related in just the same way in
Fig. 4.14 and Fig. 4.16. This suggests resolving in the
directions corresponding to those in Example 4.4.1;
that is, perpendicular and parallel to the ropes.

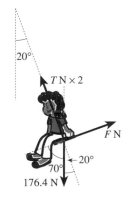

$\mathcal{R}(\perp \text{to ropes}) \qquad F = 176.4 \cos 70° = 60.3$, correct to 3
significant figures.

$\mathcal{R}(\parallel \text{to ropes}) \qquad 2T = 176.4 \cos 20°,$

Fig. 4.16

so $T = 88.2 \cos 20° = 82.9$, correct to 3 significant figures.

The father must pull on the swing with a force of about 60 N. Each rope acts on
the swing with a tension of about 83 N.

Example 4.4.3
A rail track is laid on the floor of a quarry,
sloping down at $11°$ to the horizontal from the
side of the cliff. A truck is filled with stone,
and when full may have mass up to 600 kg. It
is prevented from running downhill by a cable
from the truck to the top of the cliff, as shown
in Fig. 4.17. For safety reasons the tension of
the cable should not exceed 1600 N.

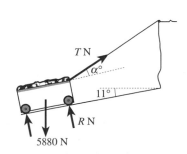

Fig. 4.17

Find
(a) the greatest angle that the cable should be allowed to make with the track,
(b) the smallest value of the total normal contact force on the truck.

(a) The maximum weight of a full truck is $5880\,\text{N}$. If the cable makes an angle $\alpha°$ with the track, and the tension from the cable is $T\,\text{N}$, then

$$\mathcal{R}(\parallel \text{to track}) \qquad T\cos\alpha° = 5880\cos79°.$$

So $\cos\alpha° = \dfrac{5880\cos79°}{T}$. The requirement $T \leqslant 1600$ means that

$$\cos\alpha° \geqslant \frac{5880\cos79°}{1600} = 0.7012\ldots, \text{ so } \alpha \leqslant 45.4\ldots.$$

The cable should make an angle no greater than $45°$ with the track.

(b) If the total normal contact force on all the wheels is $R\,\text{N}$,

$$\mathcal{R}(\perp \text{to track}) \qquad R + T\cos(90-\alpha)° = 5880\cos11°.$$

Since $\cos(90-\alpha)° = \sin\alpha°$,

$$R = 5880\cos11° - T\sin\alpha° = 5771.9\ldots - T\sin\alpha°.$$

The greatest acceptable value of T is 1600, and the greatest value of $\sin\alpha°$ is $\sin45.4\ldots° = 0.698\ldots$. So the least possible value of R is

$$5771.9\ldots - 1600\sin45.4\ldots° = 4631, \text{ correct to the nearest integer.}$$

The total normal contact force will never be less than $4630\,\text{N}$.

The final example takes the form of an experiment which you could carry out to test the theory that the resolved part of a force F at an angle $\theta°$ is $F\cos\theta°$. It could conveniently be performed in a gymnasium equipped with wall bars. You need a straight length of model railway track fixed on to a long plank. You also need a small wagon, which should be loaded to make it as heavy as possible; this reduces the relative effect of resistance forces. You need to fix brackets at one end of the plank which can be hooked over the wall bars, so that the height of that end of the plank can be varied.

Experiment 4.4.4 *[Safety!]*
A track of length d has one end on the floor and the other end at a height h above the floor. A wagon of mass m is placed at the upper end of the track, and runs freely down to the bottom. Show that the time T to reach the bottom of the track satisfies the equation

$$\frac{1}{T^2} = \left(\frac{g}{2d^2}\right)h.$$

Fig. 4.18 shows the wagon at some point of its run down the track, which is at an angle $\theta°$ to the horizontal. The weight of the wagon is mg, and its acceleration is a.

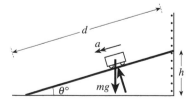

Fig. 4.18

$$\mathcal{R}(\text{down the track}) \qquad mg\cos(90-\theta)° = ma.$$

Since $\cos(90 - \theta)° = \sin \theta°$, this gives $a = g \sin \theta°$. Also $\sin \theta° = \dfrac{h}{d}$, so $a = \dfrac{gh}{d}$.

The time taken for the wagon to travel down the track can be found by using the constant acceleration equation $s = ut + \frac{1}{2}at^2$, with $u = 0$ and $a = \dfrac{gh}{d}$, so that $s = \left(\dfrac{gh}{2d}\right)t^2$. You know that $s = d$ when $t = T$, so $d = \left(\dfrac{gh}{2d}\right)T^2$.

This can be rearranged to give the required result,

$$\frac{1}{T^2} = \left(\frac{g}{2d^2}\right)h.$$

The reason for putting the equation into the form given is that it shows the connection between the two variables, h and T, in the experiment. By using different wall bars, h can be varied, and the value of T recorded for different values of h. The other quantities in the equation, g and d, remain constant.

You can then plot your results in a form like Fig. 4.19. If the theory is correct, the plotted points should lie approximately on a straight line through the origin.

As an additional spin off, you can measure from your graph the gradient of the straight line, which should equal $\dfrac{g}{2d^2}$. Since you know the length of the track, you can use the value of the gradient to estimate a value for g.

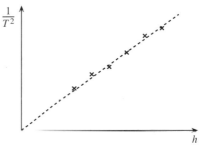

Fig. 4.19

Exercise 4B

1 For each of the forces defined below give their resolved parts in the Ox and Oy directions respectively, in terms of F and θ.

(a) 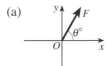 (b) 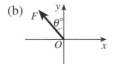 (c) 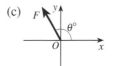 (d)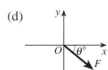

2 A block of wood of mass 4 kg is released from rest on a plane inclined at $30°$ to the horizontal. Assuming that the surface can be modelled as smooth (no friction), calculate the acceleration of the block, and its speed after it has moved 3 m.

3 A car of mass 850 kg is travelling, with acceleration 0.3 m s^{-2}, up a straight road inclined at $12°$ to the horizontal. There is a force resisting motion of 250 N. Calculate the magnitude of the driving force.

4　A cyclist of mass 60 kg free-wheels down a hill inclined at 6° to the horizontal. Assuming no resisting forces, calculate her acceleration down the hill, and show that her speed increases from 4 m s^{-1} to 16 m s^{-1} in about 117 m.

5　A sack of mass 8 kg is pulled up a ramp inclined at 20° to the horizontal by a force of magnitude 45 N acting parallel to a line of greatest slope of the ramp. The acceleration of the sack is 1.4 m s^{-2}. Find the frictional force.

6　A particle P is in equilibrium under the action of the three forces shown in the diagram. By resolving in the direction of the force of magnitude Y N, show that Y = 5. Calculate the value of X.

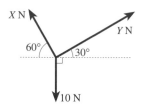

7　Calculate the magnitude of the horizontal force needed to maintain a crate of mass 6 kg in equilibrium, when it is resting on a frictionless plane inclined at 20°. Calculate also the magnitude of the normal contact force acting on the crate.

8　A skier of mass 78 kg is pulled at constant speed up a slope, of inclination 12°, by a force of magnitude 210 N acting upwards at an angle of 20° to the slope (see diagram). Find the magnitudes of the frictional force and the normal contact force acting on the skier.

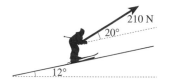

9　A particle of weight 10 N is placed on a smooth plane inclined at 35° to the horizontal. Find the magnitude of the force required to keep the particle in equilibrium if it acts

(a)　parallel to the plane,

(b)　horizontally,

(c)　upwards at an angle of 25° to a line of greatest slope of the plane,

Without making any calculations state, with a reason, which of the three cases has the greatest normal contact force.

10　A book of mass 1.8 kg is resting on the flat top of a desk. The desk lid is raised so that it makes an angle of 15° with the horizontal, as shown in the diagram.

(a)　Find the frictional force, given that the book does not move.

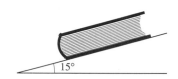

As the desk lid is raised further, the book begins to move when the lid is inclined at $\theta°$ to the horizontal.

(b)　Given that the maximum magnitude that the frictional force can attain is 8.45 N, find the maximum value of θ for which equilibrium remains unbroken.

The book is held at rest and the lid is raised until it is inclined at 40° to the horizontal. The book is then released.

(c)　Find the acceleration of the book down the desk lid, assuming the maximum frictional force still acts.

11 A metal sphere of weight 500 N is suspended from a fixed point O by a chain. The sphere is pulled to one side by a horizontal force of magnitude 250 N and the sphere is held in equilibrium with the chain inclined at an angle $\theta°$ to the vertical. Find, in either order, the tension in the string and the value of θ.

12 A picture of mass 12 kg is supported in equilibrium by two strings, inclined at 20° and 70° to the horizontal. Calculate the tension in each string.

13 A box of mass 12 kg is dragged, with a constant acceleration of 1.75 m s^{-2}, up a path inclined at 30° to the horizontal. The force pulling the box has magnitude $2X$ N and acts at 10° to the path, as shown in the diagram. The frictional force has magnitude X N. Calculate the value of X and the magnitude of the normal contact force of the path on the box.

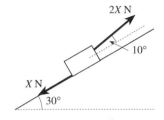

14 A toboggan of mass 20 kg is pulled, with a rope, up a snow-covered hill inclined at 15° to the horizontal. The rope is inclined at 30° to the horizontal, as shown in the diagram.

(a) Explain why the tension in the rope must certainly be greater than 52.5 N.

Given that the tension in the rope is 65 N, and that the toboggan is moving at constant speed, calculate

(b) the magnitude of the normal contact force exerted on the toboggan by the hill,

(c) the magnitude of the frictional force.

15 A boat on a trailer is held in equilibrium on a slipway, which is inclined at 20° to the horizontal, by a cable which is inclined at $\theta°$ to a line of greatest slope of the slipway, as shown on the diagram. The combined mass of the boat and trailer is 1250 kg. The cable may break if the tension exceeds 7000 N. Find the maximum value of θ.

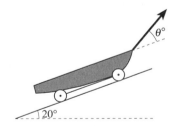

16 A glider of weight 2500 N is being towed with constant speed by a four-wheel drive vehicle. The tow-rope is inclined at 25° to the horizontal and the glider is inclined at 30° to the horizontal as shown in the diagram. The air resistance has magnitude R N and the lift has magnitude L N; the directions in which they act are shown in the diagram. Calculate the values of R and L, given that the tension in the rope is 3000 N.

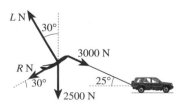

Miscellaneous exercise 4

1   A particle is in equilibrium under the
action of the three coplanar forces shown
in the diagram. Find P and Q.   (OCR)

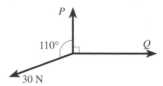

2   Susie uses a strap to pull her suitcase, at a constant speed in a straight line, along the
horizontal floor of an airport departure lounge. The strap is inclined at $50°$ to the
horizontal and the frictional force exerted on the case by the floor has magnitude 20 N.
Modelling the suitcase as a particle, find the tension in the strap.   (OCR)

3   The diagram shows a particle of mass 2.6 kg
maintained in equilibrium in a vertical plane by
forces of $5P$ N and $12P$ N which are
perpendicular. Find

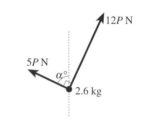

(a) $\alpha°$, the angle at which the force of
$5P$ N is inclined to the vertical,

(b)   the value of P.   (OCR)

4   A particle is in equilibrium under the
action of the three coplanar forces whose
magnitudes and directions are shown in the
diagram. Find the values of P and Q.

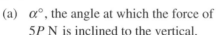

The force of magnitude 4 N is now
removed from the system. State the
direction in which the particle begins to
move.   (OCR)

5   A ramp, of length 5 m, is inclined at $30°$ to the horizontal. A parcel of mass 1 kg,
which may be modelled as a particle, is placed at rest at the top of the ramp and allowed
to slide down. The speed of the parcel at the bottom of the ramp is 7 m s^{-1}. Is this data
consistent with the ramp being smooth and there being no air resistance? Justify your
answer.   (OCR)

6   The diagram shows a small metal ball, of mass
2 kg, resting in the horizontal groove between two
smooth planes inclined at $20°$ and $40°$ to the
horizontal. Find the magnitudes of the contact
forces **P** and **Q**.   (OCR)

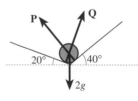

7   A child is sitting on a swing. The child's mother is
holding the seat of the swing so that it is in
equilibrium. The forces acting on the seat of the swing
are as shown in the diagram. The horizontal force has
magnitude R, and the force inclined at $40°$ to the
vertical has magnitude T. Find R and T.   (OCR)

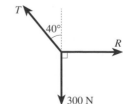

8 A cyclist starts from rest and moves along a straight, horizontal track. The forward driving force is a constant 72 N and the resistances to forward motion are a constant 20 N. The combined mass of the bicycle and cyclist is 80 kg.

(a) Calculate the acceleration of the cyclist.

(b) How long does it take the cyclist to reach a speed of 8 m s^{-1}? How far does the cyclist travel in this time?

The cyclist starts to climb a hill when her speed reaches 8 m s^{-1}. The hill is at a constant angle of $10°$ to the horizontal. The driving force and resistances to motion are unchanged.

(c) Show that the cyclist is now decelerating at about 1.05 m s^{-2}. (MEI, adapted)

9 A particle P rests in equilibrium on a smooth horizontal surface under the action of the four horizontal forces shown in the diagram. The angles between the forces of magnitudes 1.2 N and 2 N, and between the forces of magnitudes X N and Y N, are each $90°$. The angle between the forces of magnitudes 2 N and Y N is $130°$. Find the values of X and Y.

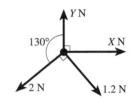

The force of magnitude 1.2 N is now removed. Given that the mass of P is 0.4 kg, find the magnitude of the acceleration with which P starts to move, and show clearly on a diagram the direction of this acceleration. (OCR)

10 The diagram shows a particle P attached to points A and B by two light inextensible strings, AP of length 30 cm and BP of length 16 cm. The points A and B are at the same horizontal level and P hangs freely with angle APB equal to $90°$. Given that the tension in the string BP is 15 N, find

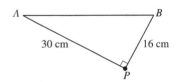

(a) the tension in the string AP,

(b) the mass of P.

Particle P is now replaced by a heavier particle Q. Given that the tension in either string must not exceed not exceed 120 N, find the greatest possible mass of Q. (OCR)

11 A hanging flower basket H, of weight 50 N, is held in equilibrium by two light inextensible strings. One string is attached to a fixed point A and this string makes an angle of $60°$ with the vertical; the other string is attached to a fixed point B and this string makes an angle of $\theta°$ with the vertical, as shown in the diagram. Given that the tension in the string attached to A is T and the tension in the string attached to B is $2T$, find the values of θ and T.

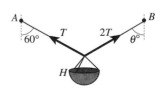

(MEI)

12 A box of mass 80 kg is to be pulled along a
    horizontal floor by means of a light rope. The
    rope is pulled with a force of 100 N and the rope
    is inclined at 20° to the horizontal, as shown in
    the figure.

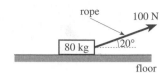

(a) Explain briefly why the box cannot be in
    equilibrium if the floor is smooth.

In fact the floor is not smooth and the box is in equilibrium.

(b) Draw a diagram showing all the external forces acting on the box.

(c) Calculate the frictional force between the box and the floor, and also the normal
    reaction of the floor on the box, giving your answers correct to three significant
    figures.

The maximum value of the frictional force between the box and the floor is 120 N and the
box is now pulled along the floor with the rope always inclined at 20° to the horizontal.

(d) Calculate the force with which the rope must be pulled for the box to move at a
    constant speed. Give your answer correct to three significant figures.

(e) Calculate the acceleration of the box if the rope is pulled with a force of 140 N. (MEI)

13 A block of mass 20 kg is held in equilibrium on
    a plane by means of a string which is at an angle
    of 25° to the greatest slope of the plane. The
    plane is at 40° to the horizontal, as shown in the
    figure.

    The situation is first modelled by assuming that
    the plane is smooth.

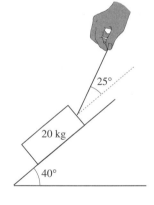

(a) Draw a diagram showing all the forces
    acting on the block.

(b) Show that the tension in the string is about
    139 N and find the normal reaction of the
    plane on the block.

An experiment shows that when the tension in the string is increased to 172 N, the block is
still in equilibrium. The model is now refined to take account of friction.

(c) Draw a diagram showing the forces acting on the block and calculate the frictional
    force.

(d) Without further calculations, state with a reason whether the normal reaction of the
    plane on the block is the same in parts (b) and (c).   (MEI)

14 A toboggan of mass 15 kg carries a child of mass 25 kg. It starts from rest on a snow slope
    of inclination 10°. Given that the acceleration is 1.2 m s^{-2} and that air resistance may be
    ignored, find the frictional force.

    Having reached the bottom of the slope, the toboggan and child are pulled back up the
    slope, at a constant speed, by a light rope which is parallel to a line of greatest slope. Find
    the tension in the rope, assuming that the same frictional force is acting.   (OCR)

15

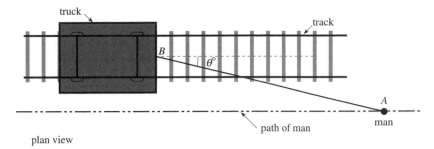

plan view

Railway trucks in coal mines were sometimes pulled by men. One such truck is standing on a straight, horizontal section of track. The man pulls on a light inextensible rope AB. The rope is horizontal and at an angle $\theta°$ to the direction of the track. The man walks parallel to the track.

Initially the magnitude of the tension in the rope is 100 N and $\theta = 10$. This tension in the rope is not enough to move the truck from rest.

(a) Calculate the resolved parts of the tension in the rope parallel and perpendicular to the track.

(b) What force prevents the truck from moving perpendicular to the track?

(c) What is the magnitude of the resistance to the forward motion of the truck?

The man now pulls harder to move the truck. The truck moves from rest against a resistance to its forward motion of $(100 + 44 \sin \theta°)$ N at all times. There is a constant tension in the rope and θ has the constant value of 10. It takes the man 15 seconds to reach his normal walking speed of 1.5 m s^{-1}.

(d) Explain briefly why the acceleration of the truck is constant. With what force must the man pull on the rope to maintain the speed of 1.5 m s^{-1}? How far does the man walk before he reaches his normal walking speed?

(e) In order to avoid an obstacle, the man follows a path in which θ is increased. Assuming that the force in the rope does not change, what effect does this have on the motion of the truck? (MEI)

5 Friction

In this chapter frictional force is analysed in detail. When you have completed it, you should

- be familiar with the mathematical model of friction and the properties of frictional forces
- understand the idea of limiting equilibrium
- know what is meant by the coefficient of friction and be able to use it
- be able to solve problems on motion and equilibrium in which friction is one of the forces acting on an object.

5.1 Basic properties of frictional forces

Imagine that you are trying to drag a heavy box along a horizontal platform (Fig. 5.1). One of two things may happen. If you pull hard enough, the box will start to move in the direction you are pulling in. If you don't pull so hard, the box will stay where it is. But in either case your pull will be opposed by a frictional force.

Fig. 5.1

This frictional force acts horizontally, in the plane where the base of the box is in contact with the platform. Its direction is opposite to the direction in which it is moving, or in which it would move if it could. Fig. 5.2 shows the four forces acting on the box, whether or not it is moving.

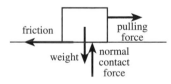

Fig. 5.2

If the box doesn't start to move, then the forces are in equilibrium. This means that the friction exactly balances the pull. If you pull a bit harder, the friction will increase; if you don't pull so hard, the friction will decrease. If you stop pulling, the friction will vanish.

If you pull hard enough for the box to move, the friction is smaller than the pull. There is a limit to the amount of friction that the base of the box and the platform can produce. If you pull with a force greater than this limit, the box will start to move.

When part of the surface of an object is in contact with a fixed surface, and forces are tending to move the object across the surface, these forces will be opposed by a frictional force. Its direction is opposite to the direction of motion or possible motion.

The frictional force cannot exceed a certain magnitude, called the **limiting friction**. If the object is at rest and equilibrium is possible with a frictional force less than this limiting friction, the object will remain in equilibrium.

If the object is at rest and the forces are in equilibrium with the limiting friction, the object is said to be in **limiting equilibrium**, and to be 'on the point of moving'.

Example 5.1.1

A dustbin of mass 20 kg is placed on a path which is at an angle of $10°$ to the horizontal. The limiting friction between the bin and the path is 50 N.
(a) Will the bin slide down the path?
(b) A force parallel to the slope is applied to the bin so that it is on the point of moving up the path. How large is this force?

(a) There are three forces on the bin: its weight, the normal contact force, and friction acting up the path (Fig. 5.3). Only the weight and the friction have any effect parallel to the path.

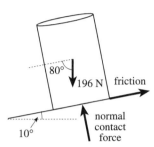

Fig. 5.3

The weight is 196 N, and its resolved part down the path is $196\cos 80°$, which is about 34 N. This is less than the limiting friction, so there can be equilibrium with a frictional force of 34 N up the path.

The bin will not slide down the path.

(b) Since the bin is on the point of sliding up the path, the friction has its limiting value of 50 N and acts in the opposite direction, down the path. Let the applied force be P N up the path. Then the forces on the bin are as in Fig. 5.4.

$\mathcal{R}$(up the path) $P - 50 - 196\cos 80° = 0$.

This gives $P = 50 + 34 = 84$.

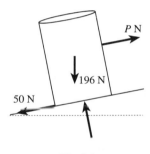

Fig. 5.4

If a force of 84 N is applied, the bin is on the point of sliding up the path.

How large is the friction when the object starts to move? In theory it might stay at its limiting value, it might be smaller, or it might get larger but not so large as the force moving it. Experiments suggest that in practice the friction when there is motion is slightly smaller than limiting friction, but to a first approximation it is often taken to equal the limiting friction. This is the model you should use, unless you are told otherwise.

> When an object slides over a fixed surface, the frictional force has its limiting value and acts in a direction opposite to the direction of motion.

Example 5.1.2

If, with the data in Example 5.1.1, a force of 90 N is applied to the dustbin up the path, calculate the acceleration with which the bin will move.

The forces in Fig. 5.5 are the same as in Fig. 5.4, except that P is now 90. As the bin is moving, friction has its limiting value of 50 N. Let the acceleration be a m s^{-2}.

$$\mathcal{R}(\text{up the path}) \qquad 90 - 50 - 196\cos 80° = 20a.$$

This gives $20a = 90 - 50 - 34 = 6$, so $a = \frac{6}{20} = 0.3$.

The bin will accelerate up the path at 0.3 m s^{-2}.

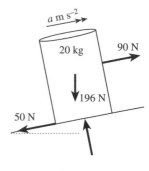

Fig. 5.5

The properties of friction described in this section apply only when the surfaces in contact are dry and fairly rigid. If there is a layer of oil or water separating the surfaces, then you need to use a different model of friction.

5.2 Limiting friction

The next question to ask is, how large is the limiting friction?

This might depend on a number of factors, such as
- the materials that the surfaces in contact consist of,
- the shape and area of the region of contact between the surfaces,
- the other forces acting on the object.

The first of these is obviously important. Other things being equal, wood sliding across gravel produces much more friction than polished steel sliding across ice. Any model of friction has to take account of the difference in roughness of various materials.

Experiments suggest that shape and area do not have much effect on the size of the limiting friction. However, there are exceptions to this. For example, a new car tyre with a well-designed tread can produce more friction than a worn tyre, even though both are made of the same material.

The effect of the other forces certainly needs to be taken into account. You can show this by carrying out a simple experiment. *[Safety!]*

Take two books, one heavier than the other, and stand each upright on a table. Now clench your fists, and try to lift each book off the table, as in Fig. 5.6. To do this, you will need to push with your knuckles against the covers of the book. If the book has weight W, and the friction on each cover is F, then $2F = W$, so that $F = \frac{1}{2}W$. This means that the frictional force has to be larger for the heavier book.

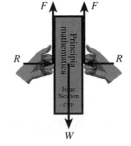

Fig. 5.6

Now reduce the forces R from your knuckles until the book is on the point of slipping. Friction is then limiting. You will find that you need to push harder on the covers to support the heavier book. This is because the limiting friction depends on the normal contact force. Since the limiting friction has to be larger for the heavier book, the normal contact force also has to be larger.

Notice that it is the same for the box pulled across the platform in Fig. 5.1. If the box is made heavier, then you need to pull harder before it starts to move. The limiting friction depends on the normal contact force, and in this case the normal contact force has the same magnitude as the weight.

If you carry out more precise experiments, you find that there is a direct proportional relationship connecting the limiting friction and the normal contact force. For example, if you double the normal force, the limiting friction is doubled. The rule for calculating limiting friction can then be summarised as follows.

> The limiting frictional force between two surfaces is proportional to the normal contact force. If the limiting friction is $F_{\lim}$ and the normal contact force is R, then $F_{\lim} = \mu R$, where μ is a constant.
>
> The constant μ is called the **coefficient of friction**. Its value depends mainly on the materials of which the surfaces consist.

The symbol μ is the Greek letter 'm', pronounced 'mu'. It is always used to denote the coefficient of friction. For most surfaces, the value of μ lies between 0.3 and 0.9, but smaller or larger values (even greater than 1) can occur.

If μ is very small, you may get useful approximate results by taking μ to be 0, so that friction is ignored. In that case, the surfaces are said to be **smooth**. If μ is greater than 0, the surfaces are said to be **rough**, and you will need to consider friction. The term 'very rough' is sometimes used to describe surfaces for which μ is so large that there is no practical likelihood that one will slide over the other.

Example 5.2.1

A person tries to pull a small cupboard across the floor. The mass of the cupboard is 80 kg and the coefficient of friction is 0.5. Describe what happens if the cupboard is pulled with a horizontal force of (a) 200 N, (b) 400 N.

The forces on the cupboard are shown in Fig. 5.7. The normal contact force, R N, is equal to the weight of the cupboard, which is 784 N

Fig. 5.7

The limiting friction is $0.5R$ N, that is 392 N.

(a) The pull of 200 N is less than the limiting friction. The pull is therefore opposed by a frictional force of 200 N, and the cupboard doesn't move.

(b) The pull of 400 N is greater than 392 N, so that friction is limiting and the cupboard will start to move. Denote its acceleration by a m s^{-2}.

$\mathcal{R}(\rightarrow)$ $400 - 392 = 80a$,   which gives $a = 0.1$.

The cupboard starts to move with acceleration 0.1 m s^{-2}.

Example 5.2.2

A boy kicks a stone of mass 100 grams across the playground. The coefficient of friction between the stone and the playground is 0.25. If the stone comes to rest 31 m away, find the speed with which the boy kicked it.

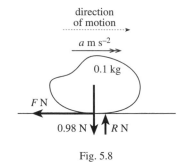

Fig. 5.8

You have to assume that the playground is flat, so that the stone stays in contact with it. The mass of the stone is 100 grams, which is 0.1 kg, so its weight is 0.98 N. The other forces on the stone are the normal contact force, R N, and friction, F N (see Fig. 5.8).

Resolving vertically gives $R = 0.98$. So long as the stone is moving, friction has its limiting value, which is 0.25×0.98 N $= 0.245$ N.

You can use Newton's second law to find the acceleration, a m s^{-2}.

$$\mathcal{R}(\rightarrow) \quad -0.245 = 0.1a, \quad \text{so } a = -2.45.$$

To finish the problem, you need a connection between velocity and distance. The acceleration is constant, so you can use the equation $v^2 = u^2 + 2as$. You have found that $a = -2.45$, so while the stone is moving $v^2 = u^2 - 4.9s$. You now want to find the value of u.

You are told that the stone goes 31 m, which means that $v = 0$ when $s = 31$. So $0 = u^2 - 4.9 \times 31$, which gives $u = \sqrt{151.9} = 12.3$, correct to 3 significant figures.

The boy kicked the stone with a speed of approximately 12.3 m s^{-1}.

5.3 Some experiments

The model of friction described in the last two sections is based on a mixture of reasoning and experiment. Here are two experiments which you could try for yourself.

Experiment 5.3.1 *[Safety!]*

You need a suitcase and a spring balance. Begin by using the spring balance to weigh the case. Then place the case flat on a table and attach the spring balance to the handle. Pull the case across the table at a steady speed with the spring balance, as shown in Fig. 5.9, and read the force on the spring balance. Repeat the experiment with various objects inside the case, and investigate the relationship between the force and the weight.

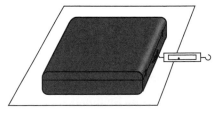

Fig. 5.9

The forces on the case are the same as those in Fig. 5.2. Since the case is moving at a steady speed, the forces are in equilibrium. That is, the friction is equal to the pull and the normal contact force is equal to the weight. So you can find the normal contact force and the friction by measuring the weight and the pull.

Also, since the case is moving, friction is limiting.

One complication is that most spring balances are calibrated as if they measure mass rather than weight. (This was discussed in Section 3.4.) So when you weigh the case, if the spring balance shows x kg, the weight is $9.8x$ newtons.

Similarly, when you measure the pull, if the spring balance reads y kg, this means that the pull is $9.8y$ newtons.

The theory predicts that the limiting friction is proportional to the normal contact force, so that the pull is proportional to the weight. This is expressed by the equation $9.8y = \mu(9.8x)$, which gives $y = \mu x$.

So if, as you carry out the experiment with different objects in the case, you plot y against x, the points should lie on a straight line through the origin. If they do, then the gradient of the line will give the value of the coefficient of friction.

Experiment 5.3.2 *[Safety!]*

You need several books of different masses, with covers all made of similar materials. Take one book and place it flat on the table. Then tilt the table, gradually increasing the angle by placing sheets of card under two adjacent legs. Continue until the book is on the point of sliding down the table. Measure the height of the legs above the floor, and hence calculate the angle of tilt. Repeat the experiment with each book in turn.

If the book has mass m, then the forces on the book are its weight mg, the normal contact force R and the friction F, which is limiting when the book is on the point of sliding (Fig. 5.10). Theory predicts that F is equal to μR. Denote the angle of tilt by $\alpha°$.

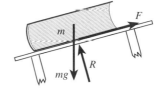

Fig. 5.10

$R(\perp$ to table top) $mg\cos\alpha° = R$.

$R(\parallel$ to table top) $mg\cos(90-\alpha)° = \mu R$.

Since $\cos(90-\alpha)° = \sin\alpha°$, this last equation can be written as

$\quad mg\sin\alpha° = \mu R$.

Combining this with the first equation,

$\quad mg\sin\alpha° = \mu mg\cos\alpha°$,   so $\sin\alpha° = \mu\cos\alpha°$.

This can be simplified by using $\dfrac{\sin\alpha°}{\cos\alpha°} = \tan\alpha°$, to give $\tan\alpha° = \mu$.

If the theory is correct, the angles at which sliding begins should be the same for all the books, whatever their masses. If so, then the coefficient of friction is the tangent of the angle $\alpha°$.

You can extend this experiment by turning the books round on the table top, or by using books with covers of different sizes, to see if this makes any difference to the angle of tilt.

5.4   Friction and motion

You may have gained the impression that friction always acts so as to prevent motion. People often try to reduce the magnitude of the frictional force, for example by applying oil to moving parts, or by polishing surfaces which move over each other.

However, for many types of motion friction is essential. Imagine trying to run on a slippery pavement, trying to ride a bicycle on an ice-rink or driving a car in mud. In all these cases, the problem is that the magnitude of the frictional force is not large enough. It is friction which makes it possible to run, ride bicycles or drive cars.

The athlete would slip without the friction between her shoe and the ground. Pedalling causes the bicycle's back (driving) wheel to rotate, and the bicycle moves forward because of the friction between the tyre and the ground. The car's engine causes the driving wheels to rotate, and friction is needed for the car to be able to move. These situations are illustrated in Figs. 5.11, 5.12 and 5.13.

Fig. 5.11

Fig. 5.12

Fig. 5.13

Exercise 5A

1 The diagram shows horizontal forces of magnitudes P N and Q N acting in opposite directions on a block of mass 5 kg, which is at rest on a horizontal surface. State, in terms of P and Q, the magnitude and direction of the frictional force acting on the block when

(a) $P > Q$,   (b) $Q > P$.

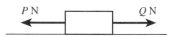

· 2 The diagram shows horizontal forces of magnitudes P N and 100 N acting in opposite directions on a block of weight 50 N, which is at rest on a horizontal surface. Given that the coefficient of friction between the block and the surface is 0.4, find the range of possible values of P.

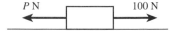

· 3 The diagram shows a force of magnitude 8 N acting downwards at 30° to the horizontal on a block of mass 3 kg, which is at rest on a horizontal surface. Calculate the frictional force on the block.

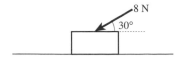

4 An airline passenger pushes a 15 kg suitcase along the floor with his foot. A force of 60 N is needed to move the suitcase. Find the coefficient of friction. What force would be needed to give the suitcase an acceleration of 0.2 m s^{-2}?

5 A block of mass 6 kg is accelerating at 1.25 m s^{-2}, on a horizontal surface, under the action of a horizontal force of magnitude 22.5 N. Calculate the coefficient of friction between the block and the surface.

6 A horizontal cable from a winch is attached to a dinghy of mass 800 kg which rests on horizontal ground. The coefficient of friction is $\frac{3}{4}$. The tension in the cable is increased in steps of 1000 N. What is the frictional force when the tension is

(a) 4000 N,   (b) 5000 N,   (c) 6000 N?

Describe what happens in each of these cases.

7 The diagram shows a block of weight 50 N at rest on a plane inclined at an angle $\alpha°$ to the horizontal, under the action of a force of magnitude P N acting up the plane. Find, in terms of P, the magnitude and direction of the frictional force acting on the block when

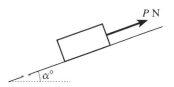

(a) $P > 50 \sin\alpha°$,   (b) $P < 50 \sin\alpha°$.

8 The diagram shows a block of mass 4 kg at rest on a plane inclined at 35° to the horizontal, under the action of a force of magnitude P N acting up the plane. The coefficient of friction between the block and the plane is 0.45. Find the range of possible values of P.

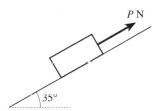

9 A bowl of mass 500 grams is placed on a table, which is tilted at various angles to the horizontal. The coefficient of friction is 0.74. Calculate the net force on the bowl down a line of greatest slope of the table when the angle of tilt is

(a) 36°,   (b) $36\frac{1}{2}°$,   (c) 37°.

Describe what happens in each of these cases.

10 In the game of shove-ha'penny a coin of mass 5 grams is struck and slides across a horizontal wooden board. If the coefficient of friction is 0.4, and the coin is struck with a speed of 1.5 m s^{-1}, how far will it slide until it comes to rest?

11 A solid cylinder of mass 6 kg is lightly held, with its axis vertical, in the jaws of a vice, and is on the point of slipping downwards. The magnitude of the force exerted by each of the jaws is 70 N. Calculate the coefficient of friction between the vice and the cylinder.

12 A builder holds up a vertical piece of plate glass of weight 40 N by pressing the two sides with forces of P N from the palms of his hands. If the coefficient of friction is $\frac{1}{4}$, what is the least value of P needed if the glass is not to slip?

13 A shopper picks up a 2 kg packet of pasta with the thumb and index finger of one hand. The coefficient of friction between his fingers and the wrapping is 0.3. What horizontal force must he exert to prevent the packet from slipping?

14 A cyclist and her bicycle have mass 75 kg. She is riding on a horizontal road, and positions herself so that 60% of the normal contact force acts on the back wheel and 40% on the front wheel. The coefficient of friction between the tyres and the road is 0.8. What is the greatest acceleration she can hope to achieve?

Whilst riding at 6 m s^{-1} she applies both brakes to stop the wheels rotating. In what distance will she come to a stop?

15 A crate of bottles, with total mass 6 kg, is placed on the floor of a milk float. The coefficient of friction is 0.4. What is the greatest acceleration possible if the crate is not to slip on the floor?

16 A table of mass 15 kg stands on the floor of a restaurant. The coefficient of friction is 0.5 when there is no motion, but it drops to 0.4 when the table starts to move. A waiter pushes the table across the floor with a gradually increasing horizontal force until the table starts to move. Find the acceleration with which the table starts to move.

5.5 Problems involving friction

When you have a problem to solve which involves friction, you use the method of resolving which was described in Chapter 4, together with equations expressing the properties of friction. These can be summarised as follows, using F and R to denote friction and normal contact force.

- If motion is taking place (whether at constant speed or with acceleration), friction is limiting and in a direction opposite to the direction of motion.
- If the object is on the point of moving, friction is limiting and in a direction opposite to that in which the object is about to move.
- If friction is limiting, then $F = \mu R$.
- Whether friction is limiting or not, $F \leqslant \mu R$.

Example 5.5.1

A block of weight 20 N is at rest on a horizontal surface. When a force of magnitude 12 N is applied to the block at an angle of $30°$ above the horizontal, it is on the point of moving. Find the coefficient of friction between the block and the surface.

The forces acting on the block are shown in Fig. 5.14. Since the block is about to move towards the right, friction is acting towards the left. This is a case of limiting equilibrium, so $F = \mu R$.

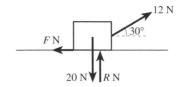

Fig. 5.14

$$\mathcal{R}(\leftarrow) \qquad F = 12\cos 30° = 10.39\ldots$$

$$\mathcal{R}(\uparrow) \qquad R + 12\cos 60° = 20, \quad \text{giving} \quad R = 14.$$

Therefore $\mu = \dfrac{F}{R} = \dfrac{10.39\ldots}{14} = 0.74$, correct to 2 significant figures.

The coefficient of friction is approximately 0.74.

A common mistake in situations like this is to think that $R = 20$. When resolving vertically, you must include every force with a vertical resolved part.

Example 5.5.2

A snow-covered hill is at an angle of $13°$ to the horizontal. A toboggan of weight 75 N is placed on the hill. Given that the coefficient of friction between the toboggan and the hill is 0.15, find whether the toboggan will slide down the hill by itself.

The three forces acting on the toboggan are shown in Fig. 5.15.

$\mathcal{R}(\perp$ to the hill$)$ $R = 75\cos 13° = 73.07\ldots$

The maximum value of the friction is μR N, where

$$\mu R = 0.15 \times 73.07\ldots = 10.96\ldots.$$

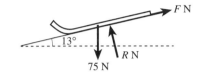

Fig. 5.15

The resolved part of the weight which acts down the hill is
$$75\cos 77°\ \text{N} = 16.87\ldots\ \text{N}.$$

As this force acting down the slope is greater than the maximum possible frictional force acting up the slope, the toboggan will slide down the hill by itself.

Example 5.5.3

Part of an assault course consists of a taut cable 25 metres long fixed at $35°$ to the horizontal. A light rope ring is placed round the cable at its upper end. A soldier of mass 80 kg grabs hold of the ring and slides down the cable. If the coefficient of friction between the ring and the cable is 0.4, find how fast the soldier is moving when he reaches the bottom.

Fig. 5.16 shows the forces on the soldier with the ring at some point of his descent. The normal contact force is R N, the friction is F N, and the acceleration is a m s^{-2}. The weight of the soldier is 784 N, and the weight of the ring can be neglected.

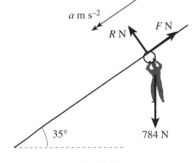

Fig. 5.16

$\mathcal{R}(\parallel$ to the cable$)$ $784\cos 55° - F = 80a$.

$\mathcal{R}(\perp$ to the cable$)$ $784\cos 35° = R$.

Since there is motion, friction is limiting, so that $F = 0.4R$. So

$$784\cos 55° - 0.4 \times 784\cos 35° = 80a,$$

$$a = 9.8\cos 55° - 3.92\cos 35° = 2.409\ldots.$$

The acceleration is constant, and you want to find the velocity when the soldier has travelled 25 m down the cable. So use the equation $v^2 = u^2 + 2as$ with $u = 0$, $a = 2.409\ldots$ and $s = 25$. This gives

$$v^2 = 0^2 + 2 \times 2.409\ldots \times 25 = 120.4\ldots, \text{ giving } v = \sqrt{120.4\ldots} = 10.97\ldots.$$

The soldier reaches the bottom of the cable at a speed of just under 11 m s^{-1}.

Example 5.5.4

A block of weight 200 N is placed on a slope at $\beta°$ to the horizontal, where $\sin \beta° = 0.6$ and $\cos \beta° = 0.8$. It is kept from moving by a horizontal force of P newtons. For different values of the coefficient of friction μ, find the range of possible values of P.

If P is too small, the block might slide down the slope; if P is too large, the block might be pushed up the slope. So the frictional force, F N, might act either up the slope (Fig. 5.17) or down the slope (Fig. 5.18). The normal contact force is R N.

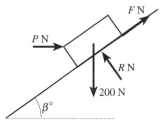

Fig. 5.17

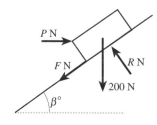

Fig. 5.18

For Fig. 5.17:

$\mathcal{R}(\perp \text{ to the slope}) \quad P \times 0.6 + 200 \times 0.8 = R$.

$\mathcal{R}(\parallel \text{ to the slope}) \quad P \times 0.8 + F = 200 \times 0.6$.

Equilibrium is not necessarily limiting, so $F \leqslant \mu R$. This gives

$$120 - 0.8P \leqslant \mu(0.6P + 160), \text{ which can be rearranged as}$$

$$40(3 - 4\mu) \leqslant (0.8 + 0.6\mu)P, \quad \text{giving} \quad (4 + 3\mu)P \geqslant 200(3 - 4\mu).$$

Notice that, if μ is greater than $\frac{3}{4}$, the expression on the right is negative, but the expression on the left is positive, so the inequality is always satisfied. This links with the result of Experiment 5.3.2, where you found that the book would not slide until the table is tilted so that $\tan \alpha° = \mu$. In this example $\tan \beta° = \frac{0.6}{0.8} = \frac{3}{4}$; so if $\mu > \frac{3}{4}$, the block will not slide down the slope even if the force P is removed.

However, if μ is less than $\frac{3}{4}$, P must be at least $\dfrac{200(3 - 4\mu)}{4 + 3\mu}$ to prevent the block from sliding down the slope.

For Fig. 5.17, the equation for resolving at right angles to the slope is the same as before, but the equation $\mathcal{R}(\parallel \text{ to the slope})$ changes to

$$0.8P = F + 120.$$

The condition $F \leqslant \mu R$ then leads to the inequality

$$0.8P - 120 \leqslant \mu(0.6P + 160), \quad \text{giving} \quad (4 - 3\mu)P \leqslant 200(3 + 4\mu).$$

Again, there are two cases. If μ is less than $\frac{4}{3}$, P cannot be greater than $\dfrac{200(3 + 4\mu)}{4 - 3\mu}$; otherwise the block would start to slide up the slope.

But if μ is greater than $\frac{4}{3}$, the expression on the left is negative and the expression on the right is positive, so the inequality is always satisfied. This means that, however hard you push, the block can never slide up the slope.

What is happening is that, as you increase P, the normal contact force from the slope increases. If μ is large, this produces a large increase in the limiting friction. So although the resolved part of P up the slope also increases, it is not enough to overcome the available friction.

The results of this example can be illustrated with graphs. In Fig. 5.19 values of P are plotted against μ. The lower graph has equation $P = \dfrac{200(3 - 4\mu)}{4 + 3\mu}$ from $\mu = 0$ to $\mu = \frac{3}{4}$, after which $P = 0$. The upper graph has equation $P = \dfrac{200(3 + 4\mu)}{4 - 3\mu}$ from $\mu = 0$ to $\mu = \frac{4}{3}$. If, for a particular value of μ, the value of P lies between the two graphs, the block will be in equilibrium. If the value of P lies below the lower graph, the block will slide down the slope. If the value of P lies above the upper graph, the block will slide up the slope.

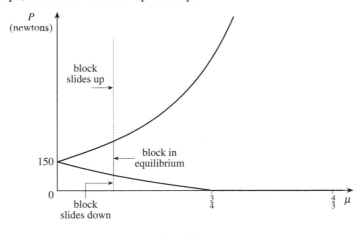

Fig. 5.19

Exercise 5B

1 A crate stands on the floor of a moving train. The crate has a tendency to slide backwards relative to the train. State the direction of the frictional force, and whether the train is accelerating or decelerating.

The acceleration or deceleration has magnitude 4 m s^{-2} and the crate is on the point of sliding. Find the coefficient of friction between the crate and the floor.

2   A cyclist and his bicycle have a total mass of 90 kg. He is travelling along a straight horizontal road, at 7 m s^{-1}, when he applies the brakes, locking both wheels. He comes to rest in a distance of 5 m. Find the coefficient of friction between the tyres and the road surface.

3   The coefficient of friction between a waste skip of mass 500 kg and the horizontal ground on which it stands is 0.6. What is the maximum mass of waste material that the skip can contain if it is to be moved by a horizontal force of magnitude 7350 N?

4   A car is travelling on a horizontal straight road at 14 m s^{-1} when its brakes are applied, locking all four wheels. The coefficient of friction between the road and the wheels is 0.8. Find the distance travelled by the car from the instant that the brakes are applied until it comes to rest.

5   The diagram shows a horizontal force of magnitude 30 N acting on a block of mass 2 kg, which is at rest on a plane inclined at $50°$ to the horizontal. Find the magnitude and direction of the frictional force on the block.

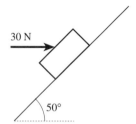

6   An ice-hockey puck is struck from one end of a rink of length 40 m towards the other end. The initial speed is 7 m s^{-1}, and the puck rebounds from the boundary fence at the other end with a speed which is 0.75 times the speed with which it struck the fence, before just returning to its starting point. Calculate the coefficient of friction between the puck and the ice.

7   A railway engine is travelling at 49 m s^{-1}, without carriages or trucks, when the power is shut off and the brakes applied, locking the wheels of the engine. The engine comes to rest in 25 seconds. Calculate the coefficient of friction between the wheels and the track.

8   A block of mass 5 kg accelerates at 0.8 m s^{-2}, down a plane inclined at $15°$ to the horizontal, under the action of a force of magnitude 30 N acting down the plane. Calculate the coefficient of friction between the block and the plane.

9   A sledge of mass 350 kg is released from rest at the top of a straight ice track of length 80 m, which is inclined at an angle of $20°$ to the horizontal. The coefficient of friction between the sledge and the track is 0.05. Calculate the frictional force on the sledge, and the speed of the sledge at the bottom of the track, given that the sledge

    (a) is empty,   (b) contains passengers of total mass 150 kg.

10 A child starts from rest at the top of a playground slide and reaches a speed of 5.5 m s^{-1} at the bottom of the sloping part, which makes an angle of $35°$ with the horizontal. The coefficient of friction between the child and the slide is 0.25. Find the length of the sloping part of the slide, and the length of time for which the child is on the sloping part.

11 A car travels down a hill which is inclined at $6°$ to the horizontal, with its engine switched off. When the car's speed reaches 10 m s^{-1} the brakes are applied, locking all four wheels. The car comes to rest in a distance of 8 m. Find the coefficient of friction between the tyres and the road.

12 A fridge magnet of mass 0.05 kg is held against the door of a refrigerator and then released from rest. The magnetic effect is only partially effective and so the magnet moves vertically downwards, remaining in contact with the door. The magnet travels 1.4 m in 2 seconds. Assuming the acceleration of the magnet is constant, find the frictional force on the magnet.

Given that the coefficient of friction between the door and the magnet is 0.3, calculate the normal contact force exerted by the door on the magnet.

13 A cyclist free-wheels down a slope inclined at 7° to the horizontal. When her speed gets to 4 m s^{-1} she applies the brakes, locking both wheels. The cyclist comes to rest 1 s after applying the brakes. Find the coefficient of friction between the tyres and the slope.

14 The diagram shows a force of magnitude 20 N acting downwards at 25° to the horizontal on a block of mass 4 kg, which is at rest in limiting equilibrium on a horizontal surface. Calculate the coefficient of friction between the block and the surface.

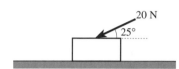

The direction of the force of magnitude 20 N is now reversed. Calculate the acceleration with which the block starts to move.

15 The diagram shows a horizontal force of magnitude 10 N acting on a block of mass 6 kg, which is at rest in limiting equilibrium on a plane inclined at 20° to the horizontal. Calculate the coefficient of friction between the block and the plane.

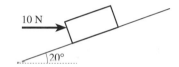

The direction of the horizontal force is now reversed. Find the acceleration with which the block starts to move.

Miscellaneous exercise 5

1 A book, which may be modelled as a particle of weight 8 N, rests in equilibrium on a desk top inclined at 28° to the horizontal. Find the frictional force acting on the book.

The coefficient of friction between the book and the desk top is 0.6. Determine whether the equilibrium is limiting. (OCR)

2 A coin is projected with speed 6 m s^{-1} along the horizontal surface of a bench. The coefficient of friction between the coin and the surface is 0.7. Modelling the coin as a particle and assuming no air resistance, find the speed of the coin after 0.3 s. (OCR)

3 A heavy ring of mass 5 kg is threaded on a fixed rough horizontal rod. The coefficient of friction between the rod and the ring is $\frac{1}{2}$. A light string is attached to the ring and pulled downwards with a force acting at a constant angle of 30° to the horizontal (see diagram). The magnitude of the force is T newtons, and is gradually increased from zero. Find the value of T that is just sufficient to make the equilibrium limiting. (OCR)

4 A straight path is inclined at an angle of 15° to the
horizontal. A loaded skip of total mass 1500 kg is at
rest on the path and is attached to a wall at the top of the
path by a rope. The rope is taut and parallel to a line of
greatest slope of the path, as shown in the diagram.
Calculate the normal and frictional components of the
contact force exerted on the skip by the path when the tension in the rope is 2000 N.

After the rope is cut the skip is on the point of slipping down the path. Calculate the
coefficient of friction between the skip and the path.   (OCR)

5 A parcel, of mass 5 kg, rests on a rough plane inclined at
45° to the horizontal. The parcel is held in equilibrium by
a force of magnitude 20 N inclined at 30° to a line of
greatest slope of the plane, as shown in the diagram.
Draw a diagram showing all the forces acting on the
parcel, and show that the normal contact force between
the parcel and the plane has magnitude 24.6 N, correct to
3 significant figures.

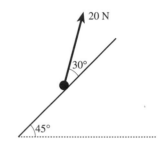

Given that the equilibrium is limiting, with the parcel on the point of moving down the
plane, find the coefficient of friction between the parcel and the plane.   (OCR)

6 A straight footpath makes an angle of $\alpha°$ with the
horizontal. An object P of weight 1250 N rests on
the footpath. The coefficient of friction between the
object and the footpath is 0.1. The least magnitude of
a force, acting up the footpath, which will hold the
object at rest on the footpath is 50 N (see diagram). By treating the object as a particle,
show that the value of α satisfies $10\sin\alpha° - \cos\alpha° = 0.4$.   (OCR)

7 A book of mass 0.8 kg is placed on a rough plane inclined at an angle of 60° to the
horizontal. The book is just prevented from sliding down the plane by a force of magnitude
5 N acting parallel to a line of greatest slope of the plane. Find the coefficient of friction
between the book and the plane.

8

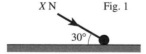

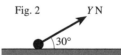

A loaded crate of mass 80 kg is to be moved along rough horizontal ground. A student was
asked to compare the least 'pushing' force needed with the least 'pulling' force needed.
The student modelled the crate as a particle, and looked at this problem by considering only
'pushing' forces and 'pulling' forces inclined at 30° to the horizontal. In Fig. 1 the least
'pushing' force has magnitude X newtons. Given that the coefficient of friction between
the crate and the ground is 0.6, find X.

In Fig. 2 the least 'pulling' force has magnitude Y newtons. Determine which of the
statements (a), (b) or (c) given below is true, and justify your conclusion.

(a) $X > Y$,   (b) $X = Y$,   (c) $X < Y$.   (OCR)

9

A small toy has mass 1.2 kg. When a child tries to move the toy along a horizontal floor by pushing with a force of magnitude 5 N, acting downwards at an angle of 30° to the horizontal as shown in Fig. 1, she is unsuccessful. When the child tries to move the toy by pulling with a force of magnitude 5 N, acting upwards at an angle of 30° to the horizontal as shown in Fig. 2, she is successful. Show that the coefficient of friction between the toy and the floor lies between 0.30 and 0.47 correct to two significant figures. (OCR)

10 A log, of mass 80 kg, rests on horizontal ground. When a force of magnitude 240 N is applied to the log in an upward direction that makes an angle of 20° with the horizontal, the log is on the point of moving. Modelling the log as a particle, calculate the coefficient of friction between the log and the ground. (OCR)

11 A laundry basket of mass 3 kg is being pulled along a rough horizontal floor by a light rope inclined upward at an angle of 30° to the floor. The tension in the rope is 8 N. Considering the laundry basket as a particle, calculate the magnitude of the normal contact force exerted on the laundry basket by the floor.

Given that the acceleration of the laundry basket is 0.2 m s^{-2}, find the coefficient of friction between the laundry basket and the floor. (OCR)

12 A parcel of mass 3 kg is released from rest at the top of a straight chute which is fixed at 40° to the horizontal. Given that the coefficient of friction between the parcel and the chute is 0.2, and neglecting any other resistances, calculate the acceleration of the parcel as it slides down the chute. (OCR)

13 A coin of mass 8 grams is placed flat on a rough board, which is inclined at an angle of 25° to the horizontal. The coin moves downwards with acceleration 1.5 m s^{-2}. Find the coefficient of friction between the coin and the board. (OCR)

14 Initially a small block of wood is at a point O on a rough plane inclined at 15° to the horizontal. The block is projected directly up the plane with initial speed 4 m s^{-1}. The coefficient of friction between the block and the plane is $\frac{1}{10}$. The block comes instantaneously to rest at A. Find the distance OA.

Find the speed of the block as it passes through O when moving back down the plane. (OCR)

15 A wooden box is pulled along a rough horizontal floor by means of a constant force of magnitude 150 N acting at an angle of 40° above the horizontal. The box may be modelled as a particle of mass 45 kg, and air resistance may be neglected. Draw a diagram showing all the forces acting on the box, and show that the normal contact force of the floor on the box is approximately 345 N.

The coefficient of friction between the box and the floor is 0.3. Calculate the time taken for the box to move 40 m from rest. (OCR, adapted)

16 A girl sitting on a wooden board slides down a line of greatest slope, which is inclined at
    $10°$ to the horizontal, on a snow-covered mountain. The combined mass of the girl and the
    board is 65 kg, and the magnitude of the frictional force between the board and the slope is
    125 N. Air resistance may be ignored. Show that the coefficient of friction between the
    board and the slope is 0.20 correct to 2 significant figures, and verify that the girl and the
    board are slowing down.

    The girl passes a point A travelling at 5 m s^{-1}. Calculate her speed at the point B, where
    B is 40 m down the slope from A.

    Later in the day the girl, still sitting on the board, is pulled up the same slope, with constant
    speed, by a rope inclined at $30°$ above the horizontal. The surface of the slope may now be
    assumed to be smooth. Calculate the magnitude of the force exerted on the board by the
    slope.   (OCR)

17 A schoolboy slides a box, of mass 6 kg, down a straight path inclined at $20°$ to the
    horizontal. The initial speed of the box is 5 m s^{-1}, and the coefficient of friction between
    the box and the path is 0.8. Assuming constant acceleration, find the distance travelled
    before the box comes to rest.   (OCR)

6 Motion due to gravity

This chapter applies the constant acceleration formulae to the special case of motion due to the force of gravity, either vertical or along a slope. When you have completed it, you should

- understand that motion upwards and downwards can be covered by a single set of equations, with velocity and displacement either positive or negative
- appreciate the effect of friction for motion on a slope, and of air resistance for vertical motion.

6.1 Objects falling from a height

You know from Chapter 3 that an object falling freely under the force of gravity has a constant acceleration of about 9.8 m s^{-2}, often denoted by g. This acceleration is the same whatever the mass of the object, but the model is based on the assumption that the effect of air resistance is so small that it can be ignored in calculations.

Since the acceleration is constant, you can use the formulae in Section 1.5 to answer questions about the time it takes to fall a certain height, the speed after falling a certain distance, and so on.

Example 6.1.1
At a swimming pool a girl steps from a diving board 4 m above the surface of the water. How fast is she moving when her feet hit the water?

The girl's initial velocity is 0 and her acceleration in metre–second units is 9.8. You want a connection between the velocity v and the displacement s, so use the formula $v^2 = u^2 + 2as$ to get $v^2 = 0 + 2 \times 9.8 \times s$, giving $v^2 = 19.6s$. When $s = 4$, $v^2 = 78.4$, so $v = \sqrt{78.4}$, or $8.85\ldots$.

The girl is moving at just under 9 m s^{-1} when her feet hit the water.

Example 6.1.2
A brick is dislodged from the top of a tall block of flats. A resident on a 7th-floor balcony sees it passing, and a second later hears it hit the ground. Each storey has a height of 3.5 m. How tall is the block of flats, and how fast is the brick moving when it hits the ground?

As in the previous example, $u = 0$ and $a = 9.8$. You are interested in the distance the brick moves in a certain time, so use the formula $s = ut + \frac{1}{2}at^2$ to get the displacement–time equation $s = 4.9t^2$.

Suppose that the height of the block of flats is h metres and that the brick takes T seconds to fall to the ground. The height of the balcony above ground level is 7×3.5 metres, which is 24.5 metres. So $s = h$ when $t = T$, and $s = h - 24.5$ when $t = T - 1$. Substituting these pairs of values in $s = 4.9t^2$ gives

$$h = 4.9T^2 \quad \text{and} \quad h - 24.5 = 4.9(T-1)^2.$$

Subtract the second equation from the first. This gives

$$h - (h - 24.5) = 4.9T^2 - 4.9(T-1)^2,$$

which simplifies to

$$24.5 = 4.9(2T - 1), \quad \text{so} \quad T = 3.$$

From this you can calculate $h = 4.9 \times 3^2 = 44.1$, so the block of flats is about 44 m high.

To find how fast the brick is moving when it hits the ground, use the formula $v = u + at$, which with the known values of u and a becomes $v = 9.8t$. So when $t = 3$, $v = 29.4$. The brick hits the ground with a speed of just under 30 m s^{-1}.

Exercise 6A

Air resistance may be ignored, and you may assume that the moving objects do not encounter any obstacles (such as the ground) unless specifically mentioned in the question.

1 A stone is dropped from rest. Find the velocity of the stone and the distance it has fallen after 3 seconds.

2 A ball is dropped from rest at a height 10 metres above the ground. Find the velocity of the ball just before it hits the ground.

3 A girl standing on a bridge over a river drops a stone from rest. The stone hits the water after 1.5 seconds. How high is the bridge?

4 A ball is thrown downwards with an initial velocity of 3.5 m s^{-1}, and hits the ground when its velocity is 17.5 m s^{-1}. From what height was the ball thrown?

5 A stone is thrown downwards from a height of 14.7 metres and hits the ground after 1.4 seconds. Find the velocity of the stone just before it hits the ground.

6.2 Objects projected upwards

When a cricketer makes a catch he often celebrates by throwing the ball vertically up into the air. To do this he has to give the ball an initial velocity, and the force producing this comes from his hands. But once the ball is in the air, the only force on it is the force of gravity.

While the ball is rising, its displacement and velocity are upwards, but the force is downwards. Gravity therefore produces a deceleration of 9.8 m s^{-2}, so that in the constant acceleration formulae you must write $a = -9.8$.

Example 6.2.1
A ball is thrown vertically upwards and rises a height of 10 metres. Find the speed with which it was thrown, and its velocity when it has risen $7\frac{1}{2}$ metres.

In this example you are not interested in the time, so use the formula which leaves out t, which is $v^2 = u^2 + 2as$. The initial velocity u is unknown, but $a = -9.8$. The equation connecting velocity and displacement is therefore $v^2 = u^2 - 19.6s$.

Since the ball rises a height of 10 m, its velocity is 0 when $s = 10$. Therefore $0 = u^2 - 19.6 \times 10$, so $u^2 = 196$, giving $u = 14$. That is, the ball was thrown with an initial velocity of 14 m s^{-1}.

You can now substitute 14 for u in the velocity–displacement equation to get $v^2 = 196 - 19.6s$. So when $s = 7\frac{1}{2}$, $v^2 = 196 - 19.6 \times 7.5 = 49$, giving $v = \sqrt{49} = 7$. That is, when it has risen $7\frac{1}{2}$ metres the ball is moving upwards at a speed of 7 m s^{-1}.

The questions asked in this example refer only to the upward motion of the ball. But what goes up must come down, and you could go on to ask questions about the complete throw from the moment when the ball leaves the fielder's hands until the moment when he catches it again. For example, how long is it in the air for, and how fast is it moving when it is caught?

You could answer these questions by splitting the throw into two parts: the upward motion, and then the downward motion, in which the ball falls from a height of 10 metres. But this is not necessary. You can use just one set of equations, which hold for both the upward and the downward motion.

Consider the velocity–time equation $v = u + at$, which in this example takes the form $v = 14 - 9.8t$. The upward part of the throw lasts until $v = 0$, when $t = \frac{14}{9.8} = \frac{10}{7}$; so the ball reaches its greatest height of 10 metres after $\frac{10}{7}$ seconds. After that the equation gives a negative value for v.

Notice that in setting up the model for this example, and in stating that $u = 14$ and $a = -9.8$, it is implied that quantities measured in the upward direction are to count as positive. So if v turns out to be negative, this means that the ball is moving downwards.

This illustrates the difference between the terms 'speed' and 'velocity'. For example, if you take $t = 2$, you get $v = 14 - 9.8 \times 2 = -5.6$. You would say that the ball has a velocity of -5.6 m s^{-1} in the upward direction, but that it is moving with a speed of 5.6 m s^{-1}.

Now consider the displacement–time equation $s = ut + \frac{1}{2}at^2$, which for this example takes the form $s = 14t - 4.9t^2$. You can check from this that, when $t = \frac{10}{7}$, $s = 20 - 10 = 10$, which confirms that the ball reaches its greatest height, 10 metres, after $\frac{10}{7}$ seconds. After that the displacement starts to decrease. For example, when $t = 2$, you get $s = 14 \times 2 - 4.9 \times 4 = 8.4$. So after 2 seconds the ball is at a height of 8.4 metres.

By writing the equation for s as $s = 0.7t(20 - 7t)$, you can see that $s = 0$ when $t = \frac{20}{7}$. This means that after $t = \frac{20}{7}$ seconds the displacement s, that is the height of the ball, is zero. So the complete throw lasts for $\frac{20}{7}$ seconds.

Finally, substituting $t = \frac{20}{7}$ in the equation $v = 14 - 9.8t$ gives $v = 14 - 28 = -14$. This means that, when the ball is caught, its velocity is -14 m s^{-1}; that is, it is descending with a speed of 14 m s^{-1}.

It is interesting to notice that the ball takes just the same time to go up as to come down, and that it is caught with the same speed as it is thrown. This is always true for an object moving under the force of gravity alone which is thrown up and caught at the same level. You are asked to prove this in Exercise 6B, Question 13.

Figs. 6.1 and 6.2 show the velocity–time and displacement–time graphs for the throw. Fig. 6.1 shows that v is positive up to $t = \frac{10}{7}$ and negative for t between $\frac{10}{7}$ and $\frac{20}{7}$, but that the whole throw can be thought of as part of one continuous motion. Fig. 6.2 shows s increasing to a maximum value of 10 when $t = \frac{10}{7}$ and then decreasing to 0 when $t = \frac{20}{7}$.

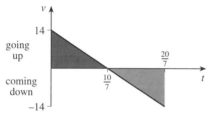

Fig. 6.1

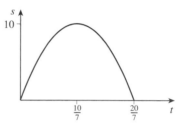

Fig. 6.2

It is important to notice how the displacement is found from the velocity–time graph. The region between the graph and the time-axis consists of two triangles, shaded dark and light grey in the figure. Both these triangles have area $\frac{1}{2} \times \frac{10}{7} \times 14 = 10$. The dark triangle shows that the displacement increases by 10 metres between $t = 0$ and $t = \frac{10}{7}$. But the light triangle, which lies below the axis, shows that the displacement *decreases* by 10 metres between $t = \frac{10}{7}$ and $\frac{20}{7}$, so that by the time $t = \frac{20}{7}$ the displacement is $10 + (-10)$, which is zero.

This illustrates the difference between the terms 'distance' and 'displacement'. During the throw the ball moves a distance of $10 + 10 = 20$ metres, but since it ends up where it started the displacement at the end of the throw is zero.

Example 6.2.2
Juliet's balcony is 3.9 metres above the ground. Romeo throws a bunch of forget-me-nots up to her with a speed of 11.2 m s^{-1}. Juliet responds by throwing him an orange, which she throws upwards with a speed of 1 m s^{-1}. Find the time for which each gift is in the air, and the speed at which it is moving when it is caught.

For Romeo's flowers you have $u = 11.2$ and $a = -9.8$, so that the displacement–time and velocity–time equations are $s = 11.2t - 4.9t^2$ and $v = 11.2 - 9.8t$. Juliet catches them when $s = 3.9$, which is when $11.2t - 4.9t^2 = 3.9$, or $49t^2 - 112t + 39 = 0$. This factorises as $(7t - 3)(7t - 13) = 0$. There are therefore two possibilities, $t = \frac{3}{7}$ or $t = \frac{13}{7}$.

You can see the reason for this by calculating the corresponding values of v, which are $11.2 - 9.8 \times \frac{3}{7} = 7$ and $11.2 - 9.8 \times \frac{13}{7} = -7$. Juliet has two chances of catching the flowers: either as they go past the balcony on the way up, after $\frac{3}{7}$ seconds with a speed of 7 m s^{-1}, or on the way down again, after $\frac{13}{7}$ seconds and with the same speed.

For Juliet's orange $u = 1$ and $a = -9.8$, so that $s = t - 4.9t^2$ and $v = 1 - 9.8t$. In this case s stands for the displacement above Juliet's hands when she throws the orange, so to find when Romeo catches it you must take s to be -3.9. A negative displacement means that the object is in the negative direction from the point where it started.

This leads to the equation $t - 4.9t^2 = -3.9$, or $49t^2 - 10t - 39 = 0$, which factorises as $(t - 1)(49t + 39) = 0$. Since t cannot be negative in this model, $49t + 39$ cannot be zero, so the only possibility is $t - 1 = 0$, or $t = 1$. This gives the value $v = 1 - 9.8 \times 1 = -8.8$. So Romeo catches the orange after 1 second, when it is coming down with a speed of 8.8 m s^{-1}.

A detail that you should notice in this example is that 3.9 m is given as the height of the balcony above the ground, but the gifts in fact move from the hands of one of the lovers to the hands of the other. So in taking the displacement to be $\pm 3.9 \text{ m}$ it has been assumed that each throws the gift at the same height above the floor as the other catches it.

One final point should be made. There is nothing special about taking the positive direction to be upwards. You could equally well take it to be downwards, in which case the signs of u, a, v and s (but not t) would be reversed. But it seems more natural to take the positive direction upwards, since that is the direction in which the object is moving at first. If you look back at Section 6.1, where the motion was only downwards, the obvious choice was to take the positive direction downwards.

Exercise 6B

Air resistance may be ignored, and you may assume that the moving objects do not encounter any obstacles (such as the ground) unless specifically mentioned in the question.

1 A machine projects a tennis ball vertically upwards with an initial velocity of 25 m s^{-1}. Find the velocity and the height of the ball after 2 seconds.

2 A juggler throws a ball vertically upwards with an initial velocity of 5.6 m s^{-1}. Find the greatest height of the ball.

3 A ball is thrown vertically upwards and reaches a maximum height of 22.5 metres. Find the initial velocity of the ball.

4 A stone is thrown upwards and reaches a maximum height of 35 metres. Find the time taken to reach the maximum height.

5 A cricket ball is hit vertically upwards and reaches its maximum height after 2.2 seconds. Find the maximum height of the ball.

6 A boy throws a ball upwards with an initial velocity of 8 m s^{-1} from a point 2.5 metres below the ceiling. Find the time between throwing the ball and the ball hitting the ceiling.

7 A stone is thrown upwards with an initial velocity of 20 m s^{-1}. Find the velocity and the height of the stone after 3 seconds.

8 A ball is thrown upwards and is caught (at the same height) 3.2 seconds later. Find the initial velocity of the ball.

9 A stone is thrown upwards with an initial velocity of 18 m s^{-1}. Find the time when the stone returns to the point of projection, and the velocity of the stone at this instant.

10 A ball is thrown upwards with an initial velocity of 15.4 m s^{-1}. For how long is the ball higher than 10.5 metres?

11 A ball is thrown upwards with an initial velocity of 12 m s^{-1} from a point 2.5 metres above the ground. Find the time when the ball reaches the ground, and the velocity of the ball at this instant.

12 A stone is thrown upwards with an initial speed of 15 m s^{-1} from the top of a cliff. It lands at the bottom of the cliff after 5.4 seconds. Find the height of the cliff.

13 An object is thrown vertically upwards with initial speed u. Show that it reaches its maximum height after time $\dfrac{u}{g}$ and show that the maximum height is $\dfrac{u^2}{2g}$.

Show that the object returns to the point of projection after total time $\dfrac{2u}{g}$ and find its velocity at this instant.

Deduce that the time moving upwards is the same as the time moving downwards, and that the speed of the object when it returns to the point of projection is equal to its initial speed.

14 A trampolinist bounces upwards and lands (at the same level) 1.8 seconds later. Find the initial velocity of the trampolinist, and her greatest height.

15 A stone is thrown upwards with an initial velocity of 24.5 m s^{-1} from a point 29.4 metres above the ground.

   (a) Find the maximum height of the stone (above the ground).
   (b) Find the time when the stone hits the ground.
   (c) Display the (t, v) graph for the motion of the stone (up to the time when it hits the ground).
   (d) Display a graph showing the height of the stone as a function of time.

6.3 Motion on a sloping plane

You can use a similar method to investigate the motion of an object sliding up and down a slope under the action of the force of gravity, but the acceleration in this case is not so large. This is illustrated by the next two examples. In the first the slope has a smooth surface, and in the second friction is introduced.

Example 6.3.1

A path runs up a hillside, at an angle of $\alpha°$ to the horizontal, such that $\sin\alpha° = \frac{5}{7}$ and $\cos\alpha° = \frac{2}{7}\sqrt{6}$. A block is placed on the path, and is prevented from sliding down by a low kerbstone. The block is struck and starts to move up the path at a speed of 21 m s^{-1}. The path is icy, so the effect of friction can be neglected. Find how far up the path the block moves, the speed with which it hits the kerbstone on its return, and the time it is in motion.

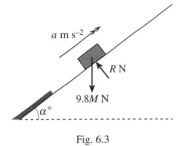

The only two forces on the block as it slides on the path are its weight and the normal contact force, shown in Fig. 6.3. The mass of the block is not given, so take it to be M kg. Then the weight of the block is $9.8M$ newtons, and the resolved part of this weight down the plane is $9.8M\cos(90-\alpha)°$ newtons, which is $9.8M\sin\alpha° = 7M$ newtons. So if the acceleration of the block up the plane is $a\text{ m s}^{-2}$,

Fig. 6.3

$\mathcal{R}(\|$ to the plane) $-7M = Ma$,   which gives $a = -7$.

The first two questions can be answered from the velocity–displacement equation $v^2 = u^2 + 2as$, which with $u = 21$ and $a = -7$ takes the form $v^2 = 441 - 14s$.

At the furthest point up the path $v = 0$, so $s = \frac{441}{14} = 31.5$. Later, when the block hits the kerbstone again, the displacement is 0, so $v^2 = 441$. Since by this time it is sliding down the path, the velocity must be negative, so $v = -21$.

There are several ways of finding the time for which the motion lasts. One is to use the velocity–time equation $v = u + at$ in the form $v = 21 - 7t$. You know that when it hits the kerbstone $v = -21$, so $-21 = 21 - 7t$, which gives $t = \frac{42}{7} = 6$.

So the block travels 31.5 metres up the plane, and after 6 seconds it hits the kerbstone with a speed of 21 m s^{-1}.

Example 6.3.2

For the situation in Example 6.3.1, when the ice melts the coefficient of friction between the block and the path is $\frac{1}{\sqrt{6}}$.

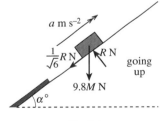

Fig. 6.4 shows the forces on the block while it is sliding up the path. To find the frictional force you first need to know the normal contact force, R newtons.

Fig. 6.4

$\mathcal{R}(\perp$ to the path) $R = 9.8M\cos\alpha°$,   so $R = 2.8\sqrt{6}M$.

Since the block is in motion, friction is limiting and equal to

$$\frac{1}{\sqrt{6}} \times 2.8\sqrt{6}M \text{ newtons, or } 2.8M \text{ newtons.}$$

$\mathcal{R}(\|$ to the path) $-7M - 2.8M = Ma$,   which gives $a = -9.8$.

Using the equations $v = u + at$ and $v^2 = u^2 + 2as$ for the motion up the path,

$v = 21 - 9.8t$ and $v^2 = 441 - 19.6s$. So at the highest point, when $v = 0$, $t = \frac{21}{9.8} = 2.14\ldots$ and $s = \frac{441}{19.6} = 22.5$.

For the return part of the motion the direction of the frictional force is reversed, and the forces are as shown in Fig. 6.5. It is now simpler to take the positive direction to be down the path, since the displacement and the velocity are both in that direction. Calling the acceleration a',

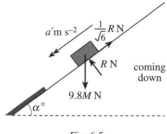

Fig. 6.5

$\mathcal{R}(\parallel$ to the path$)$ $7M - 2.8M = Ma'$,   so $a' = 4.2$.

For this part of the motion $u = 0$ and $a' = 4.2$, so the equations $v^2 = u^2 + 2as$ and $s = ut + \frac{1}{2}at^2$ take the forms $v^2 = 8.4s$ and $s = 2.1t^2$. The block hits the kerbstone when $s = 22.5$, so $v = \sqrt{8.4 \times 22.5} = 13.74\ldots$ and $t = \sqrt{\dfrac{22.5}{2.1}} = 3.27\ldots$.

So the block now travels 22.5 metres up the path, is in motion for a total time of about $2.14\ldots + 3.27\ldots$, or 5.4 seconds correct to 1 decimal place, and hits the kerbstone with a speed of about 13.7 m s^{-1}.

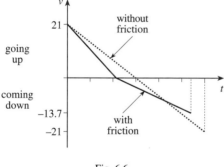

Fig. 6.6

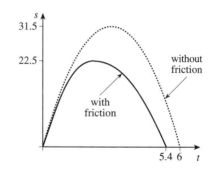

Fig. 6.7

Fig. 6.6 and Fig. 6.7 show the velocity–time and displacement–time graphs for Example 6.3.1 (the broken line) and Example 6.3.2 (the solid line), with the direction up the path taken as positive. The graphs for the motion without friction take the form of a single straight line and parabola, but those for the motion with friction consist of two straight lines and two half-parabolas joined together. In Fig. 6.6, for both velocity–time graphs, the areas of the triangles above and below the time-axis are equal.

6.4 Vertical motion with air resistance

When an object is moving vertically there is no frictional force between solid surfaces, but there will usually be resistance from the air. An important difference between these forces is that, in the standard model, the size of the frictional force does not depend on the speed, but air resistance increases with the speed of the object.

The size of the air resistance force depends also on the shape of the object, the surface area, the material of which the surface is made, and the density of the air. These factors are combined to give a constant of proportion k in the equation defining the model. A useful approximation is that at low speeds the air resistance is proportional to the speed, and that at higher speeds it is proportional to the square of the speed.

For a falling object, there is a speed at which the air resistance is so large that it exactly balances the weight. When this occurs, no further acceleration is possible. This speed is called the **terminal speed**.

Example 6.4.1

Three people step out of an aircraft, and fall vertically before opening their parachutes. The first, who has a mass of 80 kg, remains upright as he falls, and has a terminal speed of 50 m s^{-1}. The second is a soldier wearing heavy clothing and carrying equipment; his mass is 120 kg, and he also remains upright. The third is a skilled skydiver, of mass 70 kg, who takes up a horizontal position with arms and legs stretched out; this enables her to multiply the air resistance constant by a factor of 12. Find the terminal speed of the soldier and the skydiver.

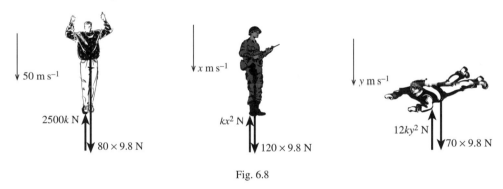

Fig. 6.8

Fig. 6.8 shows the forces on the three people. Suppose that the air resistance on the first is given by the formula kv^2 newtons, where v is his speed in m s^{-1}. The resistance on the soldier will not be very different, since he adopts the same upright position. For the skydiver the resistance is given to be $12kv^2$ newtons.

Let the terminal speeds of the soldier and the skydiver be x m s^{-1} and y m s^{-1} respectively. Then, equating the weight to the air resistance in each case,

$$80 \times 9.8 = k \times 50^2, \quad 120 \times 9.8 = kx^2 \quad \text{and} \quad 70 \times 9.8 = 12ky^2.$$

The first equation gives $k = \dfrac{80 \times 9.8}{50^2} = 0.3136$. Substituting this in the second and

third equations gives $x = \sqrt{\dfrac{120 \times 9.8}{0.3136}} = 61.2\ldots$ and $y = \sqrt{\dfrac{70 \times 9.8}{12 \times 0.3136}} = 13.5\ldots$.

So the soldier will have a terminal speed of just over 60 m s^{-1}, but the skydiver can reduce hers to less than one-quarter of that value.

Notice that although the gravitational acceleration is the same for all three people, regardless of their mass, the soldier's greater weight causes him to fall with a faster terminal speed than the first person. On the other hand, by presenting a larger surface area to the air stream, the skydiver can reduce her terminal speed to allow much more time to enjoy the fall and to carry out spatial manoeuvres before she needs to open her parachute.

A detailed analysis of motion against air resistance involves quite advanced mathematics, which must wait until the module Mechanics 3. However, it is possible at this stage to give an approximate description of how air resistance affects vertical motion.

Example 6.4.2*

A cannonball is projected vertically upwards from a mortar with an initial velocity of 49 m s^{-1}. The mortar is situated at the edge of a cliff 180 metres above the sea. On the way down, the cannonball just misses the cliff. In vertical fall the cannonball would have a terminal speed of 70 m s^{-1}. Calculate the acceleration of the cannonball just after it leaves the mortar barrel, and at the highest point of its path. Draw graphs to compare the actual motion with the motion predicted if there were no air resistance.

For the motion without air resistance $u = 49$ and $a = -9.8$, so the constant acceleration formulae give $v = 49 - 9.8t$ and $s = 49t - 4.9t^2$. The cannonball would reach its highest point when $v = 0$, which is when $t = 5$, at which time $s = 122.5$. It would enter the sea when $s = -180$, and you can easily check that this is when $t = \frac{90}{7}$, that is, about 13 seconds after it is fired. The velocity–time graph is the dotted line in Fig. 6.10.

To find the acceleration for the actual motion you need to know the formula for the air resistance. Suppose that this has the form kv^2 newtons, and that the mass of the cannonball is M kg. Then since the terminal speed in vertical fall is 70 m s^{-1}, the weight $9.8M$ must balance the resistance kv^2 when $v = 70$. This is expressed by the equation

$$9.8M = 4900k, \quad \text{so} \quad k = 0.002M.$$

Fig. 6.9 shows the forces on the cannonball as it leaves the mortar barrel. Since the speed is 49 m s^{-1}, the resistance is $2401k$, or $4.802M$ newtons.

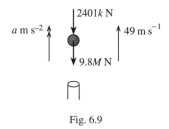

Fig. 6.9

$\mathcal{R}(\uparrow) \quad -9.8M - 4.802M = Ma,$

so $\quad a = -14.602.$

The cannonball therefore has a deceleration of about 14.6 m s^{-2} as it leaves the barrel.

At its highest point $v = 0$, so the air resistance is zero. Here, therefore, the cannonball simply has the acceleration due to gravity, 9.8 m s^{-2}.

These calculations show that the velocity–time graph has the shape of Fig. 6.10. When $t = 0$ the gradient is -14.6, steeper than the gradient of -9.8 for the dotted line representing the motion without resistance. But when $v = 0$, as it crosses the time-axis, the gradient is -9.8, so it is parallel to the dotted line. Since the terminal speed is 70 m s^{-1}, the graph can never go below $v = -70$.

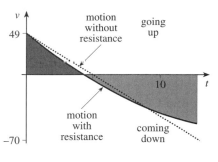

Fig. 6.10

The greatest height of the cannonball is shown by the area of the region shaded dark grey. It looks as if this is roughly four-fifths of the corresponding area for the dotted line, which is 122.5, so the cannonball rises to a height of about 100 m. The time when the cannonball enters the sea is shown by the value of t for which the area of the light grey region exceeds that of the dark grey region by 180. This is not so easy to estimate, but it is probably not very different from the value for the motion without resistance.

Exercise 6C

1   A particle of mass $\frac{1}{2}$ kg is placed at a point O on a track inclined at an angle $\sin^{-1}\frac{25}{49}$ to the horizontal. It is projected up the track with a speed of 12 m s^{-1}. There is a frictional force of magnitude 2 N, which acts in a direction opposite to the direction of motion.

(a) Find the deceleration of the particle when it is moving up the track, and the acceleration when it is moving down.

(b) Find how far the particle goes up the track, and how long it takes to do so.

(c) Find how long it takes for the particle to return to O, and its speed when it reaches O.

(d) Draw the (t, v) graph for the motion of the particle up to the time when it gets back to O, and sketch the (t, s) graph.

What would be the answers to (b) and (c) if there were no friction? Compare the corresponding (t, v) and (t, s) graphs with those you have already drawn.

2   A smooth track is inclined to the horizontal at an angle of $\sin^{-1}\frac{3}{5}$. A particle of mass m is placed on the track at a point O, and projected directly up the track with speed 28 m s^{-1}. Find how far the particle goes up the track, the speed at which it returns to O, and the time that it takes from the instant of projection until it gets back to O.

What would the corresponding answers be if the plane were rough with coefficient of friction $\frac{9}{20}$?

3   A rock of mass 20 kg falls from a height. As it falls, it experiences air resistance of magnitude $0.0784v^2$ newtons, where v is its speed in m s^{-1}. Find the terminal speed of the rock. With what acceleration will it be falling when its speed is 25 m s^{-1}?

4   A cat falls from a branch of a tall tree and lands on the ground 3 seconds later. Neglecting air resistance, estimate the height of the branch and the speed at which the cat is falling just before it lands.

If air resistance is taken into account, will the height and the speed be larger or smaller than the values you have calculated?

The air resistance is modelled by an expression of the form kv newtons, where v is the cat's speed in m s^{-1}. If the cat has mass $2\frac{1}{2}$ kg, and its terminal speed is 49 m s^{-1}, find the value of the constant k. Calculate the cat's acceleration when it is falling at 10 m s^{-1}.

5   A child is on the balcony of a flat, 10 metres above the ground. He drops his teddy-bear over the railing, and it falls to the ground below. Neglecting air resistance, calculate how long it takes to fall, and how fast it is moving when it hits the ground.

The mass of the teddy-bear is 1 kg, and when falling at v m s^{-1} the air resistance has magnitude $0.98v$ newtons. What is the terminal speed of the teddy-bear? Find a formula for its acceleration when it is falling with speed v m s^{-1}.

Draw a sketch to compare the (t, v) graphs for the fall, using the models without and with air resistance. What can you say about the values given by the two models for

(a)   the speed when the teddy-bear hits the ground,

(b)   the time that it takes to fall?

6   A skydiver of mass m kg steps out of an aircraft and starts to fall. The air resistance when his speed is v m s^{-1} is given by kv^2 newtons. If his terminal speed is 56 m s^{-1}, find an expression for k in terms of m.

When his speed reaches 21 m s^{-1} he adopts a position for which the air resistance is $4kv^2$ newtons. Find his new terminal speed. Find also the acceleration with which he is falling

(a)   just before he adopts the new position,

(b)   just after he adopts the new position.

7   A child throws a ball of mass 0.1 kg vertically upwards with a speed of 7 m s^{-1} from a height of 0.5 m above the ground, and catches it at the same level. Ignoring air resistance, calculate the greatest height of the ball above the ground, and the time it is in the air.

Suppose that the air resistance is modelled by the expression $0.02v$ newtons, where v is the speed of the ball in m s^{-1}. Calculate the acceleration of the ball

(a)   just after it is thrown,   (b) at the highest point.

With this model, what can you say about

(i)   the greatest height of the ball above the ground,

(ii)   the speed at which it is falling just before it is caught,

(iii) the acceleration of the ball just before it is caught?

On another occasion the child drops the ball from the top of a high tower. What can you say about the speed at which it hits the ground?

Miscellaneous exercise 6

1   Humpty Dumpty sat on a wall 3.6 m high. When he fell off, how long did he take to reach the ground, and how fast was he moving when he hit it?

2   A coin is thrown vertically upwards, with speed 5 m s^{-1}, from the top of a wishing-well. There is no water in the well and the coin hits the bottom of the well 3 s after being thrown. Modelling the coin as a particle, and ignoring air resistance, calculate the depth of the well to the nearest metre.   (OCR)

3   A ball is projected vertically upwards, from a point O, with speed 32 m s^{-1}. Ignoring air resistance, find the time it takes the ball to return to O.

Sketch the (t, v) graph for this motion.   (OCR)

4   Bill is standing on the flat roof of a house 6 m high, and Ben is on the ground vertically below. Ben throws a ball up to Bill with a speed of 16.7 m s^{-1}, and Bill catches it on the way down. How long is the ball in the air, and how fast is it moving as Bill catches it?

5   A ball is projected vertically upwards from the point A with speed $u \text{ m s}^{-1}$. The ball returns to A after 8 s. Ignoring air resistance, find the value of u.

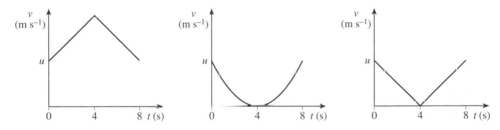

Students were asked to draw a graph of velocity against time to model the motion of the ball. Three of the (t, v) graphs presented are shown above.

(a)   Explain why the middle graph is incorrect.

(b)   If you think either of the others is correct, state which one. If you think neither is correct, sketch the correct graph.   (OCR)

6   In a laboratory experiment the motion of a steel ball-bearing falling vertically in a tank containing a liquid is observed.

(a)   State why the acceleration of the ball-bearing is less than g.

(b)   The ball-bearing is released from rest in the liquid, and after 0.60 s it has fallen a distance of 1.53 m. Assuming that the acceleration of the ball-bearing has a constant value $a \text{ m s}^{-2}$, find a and find also the speed of the ball-bearing after 0.60 s.

(c)   At a time of 0.30 s after release the ball-bearing had fallen a distance of 0.41 m. Show how this observation contradicts the assumption of constant acceleration made in (b).   (OCR)

7   A very deep shaft is drilled vertically through the earth. When a brick is dropped into the shaft, the sound of the brick hitting the bottom is heard 11.4 seconds later. Taking the speed of sound to be 350 m s^{-1}, find the depth of the shaft.

8 A helicopter is hovering 490 m above the ground. A package is dropped from the helicopter, and 2 seconds later a second package is dropped from the same position. Find expressions for the difference in height of the two packages, distinguishing the cases $0 \leqslant t \leqslant 2$, $2 < t \leqslant 10$, $10 < t \leqslant 12$ and $t > 12$. Sketch a graph to show this difference in height, and find its greatest value.

9 A parachutist with her equipment has mass 75 kg. The speed with which she lands is equal to the speed with which she would hit the ground if she jumped off a wall $2\frac{1}{2}$ m high. Taking this to be her terminal speed with the parachute open, and supposing the air resistance when she is falling at v m s^{-1} to be given by the expression kv newtons, find the value of k.

When she jumps from an aircraft, she falls a distance of 40 m before opening her parachute. Neglecting air resistance, calculate how fast she is then falling.

What is her deceleration when she first opens her parachute? Draw a rough sketch of the (t, v) graph for the complete drop.

10 When an object falls through a liquid, three forces act on it: its weight, the buoyancy and the resistance of the liquid. Two spheres, of mass $\frac{1}{2}$ kg and $1\frac{1}{2}$ kg respectively, have the same radius, so that they have the same buoyancy of 3.2 newtons, and the same resistance formula, $5v$ newtons when falling at speed v m s^{-1}. Both spheres enter the liquid falling vertically at 1 m s^{-1}. Calculate the terminal speeds of the two spheres, and the acceleration or deceleration when they enter the liquid. Using the same axes, sketch (t, v) graphs for the two spheres.

If the depth of the liquid is 10 m, show that the heavier sphere reaches the bottom after a time between 4 and 10 seconds. Find bounds for the time that the lighter sphere takes to reach the bottom.

11 An object of mass m kg falling from rest has terminal speed 14 m s^{-1}. Two models are suggested for the air resistance force: $k_1 v$ newtons or $k_2 v^2$ newtons, where k_1, k_2 are constant and v is the speed in m s^{-1}. Find expressions for k_1 and k_2 in terms of m, and hence find expressions for the acceleration of the object at speed v m s^{-1} according to the two models. Using the same axes, draw graphs of these two expressions and show that, at all speeds up to 14 m s^{-1}, the acceleration predicted by model 2 is greater than that predicted by model 1.

Sketch (t, v) graphs for the falling objects according to the two models. Which model predicts the shorter time to fall a given distance from rest?

Revision exercise 1

1 An iceberg breaks off from the Antarctic continent and floats due north at constant velocity. Its latitude south decreases by $1°$ in 8 days. Taking the circumference of the earth to be 40 000 km, calculate the speed of the iceberg in m s^{-1}.

2 A train increases speed from 40 m s^{-1} to 60 m s^{-1} in a distance of 2 km. If the acceleration is constant, find

(a) the acceleration,   (b) the time it takes.

3 A motorcyclist leaves a town travelling at 15 m s^{-1}, and accelerates at 2.5 m s^{-2}. Write expressions for the distance travelled in the next t seconds, and the speed after that time. How long will he take to go 200 m, and how fast will he then be going?

4 A shopper pushes a loaded supermarket trolley of total mass 60 kg with a horizontal force of 40 N. There is a resistance to motion of 25 N. Find how long she takes to reach a walking speed of 1.5 m s^{-1} from rest, and how far the trolley goes in that time.

5 An airliner of mass 60 tonnes lands at a speed of 70 m s^{-1}. The reverse thrust of the engines reduces this speed to 20 m s^{-1} in 10 s. Neglecting air resistance, calculate the magnitude of the reverse thrust.

Would you get a larger or smaller value than this if air resistance is taken into account?

6 A rowing crew with its boat has a total mass of 800 kg. Starting from rest, the boat reaches a speed of 5 m s^{-1} in 25 s. If the resistance of the water is 320 N, find the average contribution to the forward force on the boat made by each of the eight rowers.

7 A crane lowers a container of mass 5 tonnes gently on to a quay. At a height of 10 m above the quay the container is descending at 4 m s^{-1}. This is reduced to zero with constant deceleration. Calculate the tension in the cable.

8 A car accelerates using three gears to reach a speed of 30 m s^{-1} from rest. The speed ranges and the corresponding accelerations are given in the table for each gear. Each gear-change takes 1 second, during which time the speed of the car is constant.

Gear	first	second	third
Speed range (m s^{-1})	0 to 5	5 to 20	20 to 30
Acceleration (m s^{-2})	2.5	1.5	1

Draw a (t, v) graph to show the motion of the car. Calculate the time the car takes to reach 30 m s^{-1}, and the distance travelled while it does so.

9 A loaded airport luggage trolley has a total weight of 900 N. It is being wheeled down a ramp at an angle of $8°$ to the horizontal. What force parallel to the ramp must be exerted to hold it steady?

A similar trolley is being pushed up the ramp by a force applied at an angle of $15°$ to the ramp. What force must be exerted to keep it moving at a constant speed?

10 A car of mass 1500 kg making an emergency stop leaves skid marks 7 m long on the road. If the coefficient of friction between the tyres and the road is 1.5, calculate how fast the car was travelling when the brakes were applied.

11 A train braking with constant deceleration covers 1 km in 20 s, and a second kilometre in 30 s. Find the deceleration. What further distance will it cover before coming to a stop, and how long will this take?

12 A yachtsman fires a distress flare vertically upwards with a speed of 40 m s^{-1}. How high above the sea does it rise? For how long will it be more than 50 m above the sea?

13 A quarry 20 m deep is surrounded by a high fence. A boy standing on the rim behind the fence throws a brick upwards with a speed of 5 m s^{-1}, so that it goes over the fence and drops into the quarry. How long does the brick take to land on the floor of the quarry?

14 A magnetic hook of weight 0.8 N is placed on the side of a fridge. The force of magnetic attraction is 13 N, and the coefficient of friction between the base of the hook and the fridge is 0.6. What is the largest weight that the hook can support?

15 A sack of weight 600 N is being loaded on to a truck up a ramp inclined at 18° to the horizontal. A rope attached to the sack is held at an angle of 25° to the ramp. The coefficient of friction between the sack and the ramp is 0.3. What tension in the rope is needed

(a) to prevent the sack from sliding down the ramp,

(b) to pull the sack up the ramp at a steady speed?

16 A marker buoy of mass 5 kg is dropped into the sea from a helicopter at a height of 40 m. After the buoy enters the water it experiences a buoyancy force of 329 N. If there is no loss of speed as the buoy enters the water, find how far it sinks below the surface. Find also how long after it is dropped the buoy returns to the surface.

Discuss how these answers would be affected if the resistance of the air and of the water were included in the calculation.

17 A naval gun has a barrel 4 m long. When fired horizontally, a shell of mass 2 kg emerges from the muzzle at a speed of 500 m s^{-1}. The force from the expanding gases inside the barrel may be taken to have a constant value of 80 kN. Calculate the resistance to the motion of the shell from the sides of the barrel.

Would the answer be substantially different if the barrel was angled at 40° to the horizontal?

18 A balloon of mass 490 kg is descending at a speed of 5 m s^{-1} with an acceleration of 0.2 m s^{-2}. What mass of ballast must be thrown out to reduce the acceleration to zero?

If twice this amount of ballast is thrown out, how much further will the balloon descend before it starts to climb?

19 The speed limit on a motorway is 120 km per hour, but because of road works there is a stretch of 2.4 km for which the speed limit is reduced to 80 km per hour. There is a warning notice 0.5 km before the restriction starts. A law-abiding driver begins to slow down as she passes the notice, with constant deceleration, so that her speed has dropped to the required level as she reaches the road works. After the end of the restriction she accelerates back to the regular speed limit in 9 seconds. Illustrate her journey with a (t, v) graph, and find how much time she loses as a result of the road works.

20 A box of mass m has to be moved across a horizontal stage. If it is pulled with a force of $\frac{1}{2}mg\sqrt{2}$ at $45°$ to the upwards vertical, it will move. If it is pushed with a force of $\frac{1}{2}mg\sqrt{2}$ at $45°$ to the downward vertical, it won't move. What can you deduce about the coefficient of friction?

21 A sideboard has to be pushed across a room. If one person pushes, the sideboard will move with acceleration a_1. If two or three people push, it will move with acceleration a_2 or a_3 respectively. Assuming that each person pushes with force of the same magnitude, and that the resistance to motion is the same in each case, show that $a_3 = 2a_2 - a_1$.

22 A toboggan accelerates down a hill with a gradient of 28% (that is, at an angle of $\sin^{-1} 0.28$ to the horizontal). At the foot of the hill the ground flattens out horizontally, and the toboggan comes to rest in 40 m after 10 s. Find the speed at the bottom of the hill, and the value of the coefficient of friction.

Assuming that the coefficient of friction is the same throughout the ride, find the acceleration down the hill, and how far up the hill the toboggan was to begin with.

23 A cyclist of total mass 100 kg is free-wheeling at a constant speed of 14 m s^{-1} down a hill with a gradient of 10%. He wants to slow down to a safer speed, so he applies the brake lightly to produce a constant braking force of 80 N. The air resistance is proportional to the square of the speed.

(a) Calculate the deceleration when he first applies the brake.

(b) Calculate the deceleration when his speed has dropped to 10 m s^{-1}.

(c) At what speed will his deceleration be reduced to zero?

Draw a sketch of the (t, v) graph for the motion.

24 Explain why a runner's acceleration cannot exceed 9.8μ m s^{-2}, where μ is the coefficient of friction between her shoes and the track.

The highest speed that a runner can keep up in an 800-metre race is 7 m s^{-1}. Show that the fastest time she can hope to achieve from a standing start is $\left(\frac{800}{7} + \frac{5}{14\mu}\right)$ seconds. By how much could she better her time by changing running shoes, increasing μ from 0.6 to 1.2?

25 A valley is formed between two hills, which are at angles of $\alpha°$ and $\beta°$ to the horizontal. A skier starts from rest on the slope of the first hill, at a height h above the valley floor. Find her acceleration down the first hill and her deceleration up the opposite hill, supposing that there is no friction. Show that, if she exerts no force with her ski sticks, she ends up at the same height h as she started.

Suppose now that $\alpha = 15$, $\beta = 10$ and that the coefficient of friction is 0.1. Show that she ends up at a height of about $0.4h$ above the valley floor.

7 Newton's third law

Previous chapters have been about the equilibrium or motion of a single object. This chapter is concerned with situations in which there are two objects which interact with each other. When you have completed it, you should

- understand that forces occur in equal and opposite pairs, and be able to identify the objects on which each of the pair of forces acts
- be able to apply Newton's third law in situations involving two interacting objects
- understand what is meant by the tension in a string
- be able to solve problems on pairs of objects connected by a string, which may pass over a smooth peg or a light pulley.

7.1 Forces in pairs

Imagine two cars travelling along a motorway, one in front of the other. The front car slows down just as the car behind it accelerates. The cars collide, and both suffer damage.

The front car is damaged because it experiences a large force from behind. The rear car experiences a large force in the opposite direction, from the front. These forces are shown in Fig. 7.1. The third of Newton's laws of motion states that the two forces are equal in magnitude.

Fig. 7.1

> **Newton's third law**
>
> If an object A exerts a force on an object B, then B exerts a force on A of the same magnitude in the opposite direction.

This is neatly summarised by Newton's own statement, which (translated) was that 'action and reaction are always equal and opposite'. But in the case of the cars it is not clear which force is the 'action' and which the 'reaction'. Both drivers contributed to the accident, and each would probably say that it was the action of the other that caused it.

The important point about Newton's third law is that it applies to every kind of force. Here are some more examples.

Normal contact forces   Think of a person riding a horse. Fig. 7.2 shows the forces on the rider: her weight W and the normal contact force of magnitude R from the horse supporting her.

Forces on rider

Fig. 7.2

Forces on horse

Fig. 7.3

What about the horse? The forces on the horse (Fig. 7.3) similarly include its weight and normal contact forces from the ground. But the horse is also aware of the rider, because there is a normal contact force acting downwards on its back. Newton's third law states that this force also has magnitude R.

It is important to understand that this last force is *not* the weight of the rider. The definition of weight is that it is the force with which the earth attracts the rider. It is a force on the rider, not on the horse.

If the rider is simply moving horizontally, then R would equal W, so that the force on the horse's back would have the same magnitude as the rider's weight. But if the rider is moving up and down in the saddle, then she will have some vertical acceleration, and in that case R will not equal W.

Notice that to show the forces two diagrams were needed, one for the rider and one for the horse. You shouldn't try to economise by putting all these forces on a single diagram, because it wouldn't then be clear which forces act on the rider and which on the horse.

Frictional forces   Here is an experiment for you to try. You need a trolley with a roughish top and a large, full teapot. Place the teapot on the trolley, and get a friend to hold the trolley still. Now place your hand on the side of the teapot facing the end of the trolley, and gradually increase the force until the teapot moves along the top of the trolley.   *[Safety!]*

Now ask your friend to let go, and repeat the experiment with the trolley free to move. This time you will probably find that as you push the teapot it is the trolley which moves, and the teapot stays in the same position on the trolley.

What is the force which makes the trolley move? It can't be your push, because that is a force on the teapot, not on the trolley.

Fig. 7.4 and Fig. 7.5 analyse the forces on the teapot and on the trolley respectively. In the first part of the experiment, when your friend is holding the trolley, you have to increase your push until it exceeds the limiting friction between the teapot and the top of the trolley. Since the teapot is full, and the normal contact force equals the weight of the teapot, this limiting friction will be quite a large force.

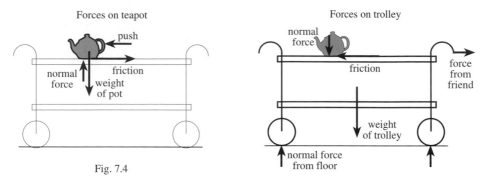

Fig. 7.4

Fig. 7.5

There are two forces from the trolley on the teapot: the normal contact force and the friction. So by Newton's third law there are equal and opposite forces from the teapot on the trolley. The frictional force on the trolley is balanced by the force exerted by your friend. As your push increases, the friction increases, so your friend's force must also increase. But once the teapot starts to move, friction has reached its limiting value, and your friend won't have to increase his force any more.

When the trolley is free to move, your push on the teapot is still opposed by friction, and there is an equal and opposite frictional force on the trolley, but there is no other horizontal force acting against it. So the trolley will start to accelerate. And because the frictional force is much less than its limiting value, the teapot will not slide on the trolley top but will also accelerate with the trolley.

Gravity forces   The force which causes the moon to go round the earth is the force of the earth's gravity. If there weren't any gravity, then you know from Newton's first law that the moon would move in a straight line rather than (approximately) in a circle.

The force on the moon has a magnitude of about 2×10^{20} newtons. By Newton's third law, the moon exerts a gravitational force of the same magnitude on the earth. The most obvious evidence of this force is in the oceans; tides are caused mainly by the gravitational attraction of the moon.

You might ask why the moon's gravity doesn't make the earth rotate round the moon. The answer is that, to a small extent, it does. In fact, both the earth and the moon rotate about a common point; but because the earth is so much heavier, that point is below the earth's surface, and you would need very accurate instruments to detect the effect.

If you drop a brick, its weight is the force of attraction from the earth. By Newton's third law, the brick also attracts the earth with an equal force in the opposite direction. But since the earth has mass about 10^{25} times that of the brick, the effect of this force is insignificant.

7.2 Calculations using Newton's third law

Example 7.2.1

A pick-up truck of mass 1200 kg tows a trailer of mass 400 kg. There is air resistance of 140 N on the truck , but the resistance to the motion of the trailer is negligible. Find the force from the coupling, and the driving force on the truck , when the truck and trailer accelerate at 0.5 m s^{-2}.

Fig. 7.6 shows the horizontal forces on the trailer and on the truck. (To avoid complicating the diagrams, the vertical forces, weights and normal contact forces from the ground, are left out.) The only horizontal force on the trailer is the force from the coupling, denoted by C N. By Newton's third law, there is an equal force in the opposite direction on the truck . The driving force on the truck is denoted by D N.

Fig. 7.6

For the trailer,

$\mathcal{R}(\rightarrow) \quad C = 400 \times 0.5$, so $C = 200$.

For the truck,

$\mathcal{R}(\rightarrow) \quad D - C - 140 = 1200 \times 0.5$.

Since $C = 200$, this gives $D = 200 + 140 + 600 = 940$.

The force from the coupling is 200 N, and the driving force is 940 N.

Example 7.2.2

A man of weight 750 N tries to push a bookcase of weight 1200 N across the floor. The coefficient of friction between the bookcase and the floor is 0.4. How rough must the contact between his shoes and the floor be for this to be possible?

The forces on the bookcase and on the man are shown in Fig. 7.7.

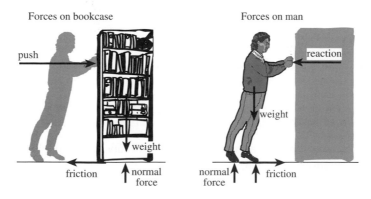

Fig. 7.7

The normal contact force on the bookcase is equal to its weight of 1200 N, so the maximum frictional force is 0.4×1200 N, which is 480 N. To move the bookcase, he must push with a force larger than this.

There is a force equal to this in the opposite direction acting horizontally on the man, and this is balanced by the friction from the soles of his shoes. So this frictional force must be larger than 480 N.

The normal contact force on the man's shoes is equal to his weight, which is 750 N. The coefficient of friction between his shoes and floor must therefore be greater than $\frac{480}{750}$, which is 0.64.

Example 7.2.3
A bar magnet of mass 0.2 kg hangs from a string. A metal sphere, of mass 0.5 kg, is held underneath the magnet by a magnetic force of 20 N. The string is then pulled upwards with a force of T N. Find the largest possible value of T if the sphere is not to separate from the magnet.

So long as the sphere remains attached to the magnet, there are two forces between them: the magnetic force and a normal contact force of R N. By Newton's third law, these act in opposite directions on the magnet and the sphere. Suppose that they accelerate upwards at a m s^{-2}.

Fig. 7.8 shows the forces on the sphere and on the magnet, whose weights are 4.9 N and 1.96 N respectively.

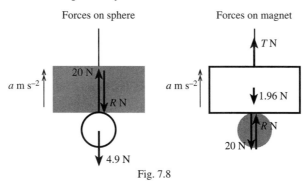

Fig. 7.8

For the sphere, $\mathcal{R}(\uparrow)$ $20 - R - 4.9 = 0.5a$.

For the magnet, $\mathcal{R}(\uparrow)$ $T - 1.96 - 20 + R = 0.2a$.

You can eliminate a from these two equations and deduce that

$$2(20 - R - 4.9) - 5(T - 1.96 - 20 + R) = 2(0.5a) - 5(0.2a) = 0,$$

so $40 - 2R - 9.8 - 5T + 9.8 + 100 - 5R = 0$, which simplifies to $5T + 7R = 140$.

Since contact is maintained, the normal contact force cannot be negative. It follows that $5T \leqslant 140$, so $T \leqslant 28$.

If the sphere is not to separate from the magnet, the force from the string cannot exceed 28 newtons.

Example 7.2.4

A student has two books lying flat on the table, one on top of the other. She wants to consult the lower book. To extract it, she pushes it to the left with a force of Q N. To prevent the upper book moving as well, she exerts a force of P N on it to the right. The lower book then slides out, and the upper book remains stationary. The weights of the upper and the lower book are 8 N and 7 N respectively. Between the two books the coefficient of friction is 0.25, and between the lower book and the table it is 0.4. Calculate P and Q.

The forces on each book are shown in Fig. 7.9. The motion of the lower book is opposed by two frictional forces, F N from the upper book and G N from the table, both acting to the right. By Newton's third law, there is a frictional force of F N on the upper book acting to the left.

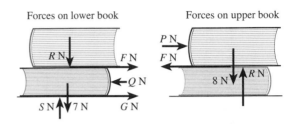

Fig. 7.9

There are normal contact forces of R N between the books, and S N on the lower book from the table. Since there is motion, the frictional forces will have their limiting values, $F = 0.25R$ and $G = 0.4S$.

If the lower book moves at a steady speed, the forces on both books will be in equilibrium.

For the upper book, $\mathcal{R}(\rightarrow)$ $P - F = 0$, $\mathcal{R}(\uparrow)$ $R - 8 = 0$.

For the lower book, $\mathcal{R}(\rightarrow)$ $F + G - Q = 0$, $\mathcal{R}(\uparrow)$ $S - 7 - R = 0$.

From these equations you can calculate $R = 8$, $S = 15$, $F = 2$, $G = 6$, $P = 2$, $Q = 8$.

She pushes the lower book to the left with a force of 8 newtons, and prevents the upper book from moving with a force of 2 newtons to the right.

Exercise 7A

1   A crate of weight 80 N is stacked on top of a crate of weight 100 N, on horizontal ground as shown. Make separate sketches showing the forces acting on the upper and lower crates. Indicate the magnitudes of the forces in your sketches.

2   A birdbath consists of a concrete pillar of weight 1000 N surmounted by a concrete bowl of mass 200 N, as shown in the diagram. State the magnitude and direction of the force exerted by

(a) the pillar on the bowl,   (b) the bowl on the pillar,

(c) the ground on the pillar.

3 A sack is in contact with both the base and the
vertical back of an excavator scoop, as shown in
the diagram. The excavator is moving forwards
at constant speed in a straight line. Make
separate sketches showing the forces acting on

(a) the sack,   (b) the scoop.

4 A man of mass 75 kg travels upwards in a lift which is decelerating at 0.4 m s^{-2}. Make a
sketch showing the forces acting on the man.

Find the magnitude of the force exerted by the man on the floor of the lift.

5 A reckless truck-driver loads two identical
untethered crates stacked one upon the other
as shown in the diagram. No sliding takes
place. Make separate sketches to show the
forces acting on each crate when the truck
travels on a horizontal straight road

(a) with constant speed,   (b) while accelerating,   (c) while decelerating.

Each crate has mass 250 kg. Calculate the magnitude of the frictional force exerted on

(i) the upper crate by the lower,   (ii) the lower crate by the deck of the truck,

when the acceleration of the truck is 1.5 m s^{-2}.

6 In an archaeological reconstruction a group of students try to drag a trireme along a beach.
This requires a horizontal force of $50\,000$ N. The average weight of a student is 6000 N,
and the coefficient of friction between the student's feet and the sand is 0.2. How many
students are needed?

7 A steel block of weight W rests on a horizontal surface in an inaccessible part of a
machine. The coefficient of friction between the block and the surface is μ. To extract the
block, a magnetic rod is inserted into the machine and this rod is used to pull the block at a
constant speed along the surface with a force F. The magnetic force of attraction between
the rod and the block is M. Explain why

(a) $M > \mu W$,   (b) $F = \mu W$.

8 A car of mass 1200 kg, towing a caravan of mass 800 kg, is travelling along a motorway
at a constant speed of 20 m s^{-1}. There are air resistance forces on the car and the caravan,
of magnitude 100 N and 400 N respectively. Calculate the magnitude of the force on the
caravan from the towbar, and the driving force on the car.

The car brakes suddenly, and begins to decelerate at a rate of 1.5 m s^{-2}. Calculate the force
on the car from the towbar. What effect will the driver notice?

9 From the instant that a pile-driver of mass 2000 kg comes into contact with a pile of mass
600 kg, they move vertically downwards together, with common deceleration 0.8 m s^{-2},
until they come to rest. Make separate sketches showing the forces acting on the pile-driver
and on the pile.

Find the magnitudes of all the forces exerted on the pile

(a) when it is moving,   (b) after it has come to rest.

10 A drop-forge hammer, of mass 1500 kg, falls under gravity on to a piece of hot metal which rests in a fixed die. From the instant that the hammer strikes the piece of metal until it comes to rest, the hammer is decelerating at 1.5 m s^{-2}. Make sketches showing the forces on the hammer and on the metal while they are in contact.

Find the magnitude of the force exerted by the hammer on the piece of metal

(a) while the hammer is decelerating,

(b) after the hammer has come to rest.

11 Three identical boxes, each of weight W, are to be stacked one on top of another against a vertical wall. The lowermost box is in contact with the wall, and the other two boxes are positioned as shown in the diagram. The middle box is pushed into position by the application of a horizontal force of magnitude P. Make separate sketches showing the forces acting on

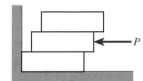

(a) the uppermost box,   (b) the middle box.

Show that $P > 2\mu W$, where μ is the coefficient of friction between any two boxes.

Show also that, if $P > 4\mu W$, sliding takes place between the upper and middle boxes, and that if $P \leqslant 4\mu W$, sliding between these boxes does not take place.

12 With the situation in Question 11, suppose that the force is first applied to the top box, until it touches the wall. How large a force will be required? Will the middle box move as well?

Once the top box is touching the wall, a force is applied to the middle box. How large a force will be needed to move it?

13 Two cylinders of equal radii each have weight W. They are at rest on a smooth slope of inclination $\alpha°$ to the horizontal, the lower of the two cylinders being in contact with a smooth vertical wall as shown in the diagram. Find, giving your answer in terms of W and $\alpha°$, the magnitude of the force exerted by

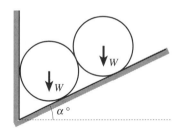

(a) the slope on the upper cylinder,

(b) the lower cylinder on the upper cylinder,

(c) the upper cylinder on the lower cylinder,

(d) the wall on the lower cylinder,

(e) the slope on the lower cylinder.

7.3   Strings, ropes, chains and cables

In Fig. 7.10 one end of a string is tied to a hook in a wall. You hold the other end so that the string is horizontal, and pull on it with a force of magnitude P (in any units) to the left.

Fig. 7.10

Usually the weight of the string is very small compared with the size of P. It can be left out of the calculations without much loss of accuracy. The string in the model is then described as 'light', which means that its weight, and its mass, are taken to be zero.

Now consider the equilibrium of the string. There must be a force on it to counteract your pull, and that comes from the hook. So the hook also exerts a force on the string of magnitude P to the right (see Fig. 7.11).

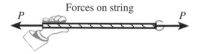

Fig. 7.11

However you are not pulling on the hook, but on the string. You pull on the string with a force P to the left, so by Newton's third law the string exerts on you a force of magnitude P to the right.

Newton's third law applies similarly at the other end. The hook exerts on the string a force P to the right, so the string exerts on the hook a force P to the left.

For this reason, when you draw a string in a diagram, you show it with a line and arrows pointing inwards, as in Fig. 7.12. These arrows indicate the force which the string exerts on the objects attached to its two ends.

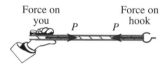

Fig. 7.12

> A light string exerts forces of equal magnitude on the objects attached to its two ends. These forces act along the line of the string, and are directed inwards at each end. The magnitude of the force at either end is called the **tension** in the string.

The same ideas apply to other objects such as ropes, chains, cables and rods, provided that their weight can be neglected by comparison with the forces which act on them.

The difference between a rod and a string, rope or cable is that it can also exert forces which are directed outwards at each end. The magnitude of such a force is called the **thrust** in the rod.

The objects at the end of the string may be stationary, as in the example just discussed, or they may move. For example, the same ideas could be applied to the cable joining two trucks in Fig. 7.13.

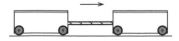

Fig. 7.13

In this case, another important property of the cable is that it remains the same length as the trucks move. The cable is then said to be 'inextensible'. It follows from this that the two trucks have the same speed, and the same acceleration.

Example 7.3.1

Suppose that in Fig. 7.13 the truck on the left has mass 30 kg, and the truck on the right has mass 50 kg. The truck on the right is pulled along with a force of 120 N. Calculate the tension in the cable.

Let the common acceleration of the two trucks be a m s^{-2}, and denote the tension in the cable by T N. In Fig. 7.14 the middle part of the cable is shown as a light grey line. This is a reminder of what the problem is about, but separates out the forces on the two trucks. Only the horizontal forces are shown in the diagram.

For the left truck,

$\mathcal{R}(\to) \quad T = 30a$.

For the right truck,

$\mathcal{R}(\to) \quad 120 - T = 50a$.

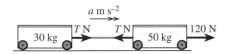

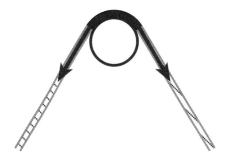

Fig. 7.14

It is probably simplest to begin by finding a, by substituting $30a$ for T in the second equation, which gives $120 - 30a = 50a$, so $a = \frac{120}{80} = 1.5$. Then

$$T = 30 \times 1.5 = 45.$$

The tension in the cable is 45 newtons.

7.4 Pegs and pulleys

Another property of a string is that it is flexible, so that it can be passed round a fixed peg. The string then has two straight sections and a curved section where it is in contact with the peg, as in Fig. 7.15. The argument used above to explain the force on the hook can be applied to each of the straight sections of the string. This means that the tension in each of the straight sections acts on the curved section round the peg.

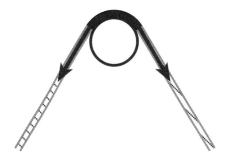

Fig. 7.15

If the contact between the string and the peg is rough, there could be some friction acting on the string round the circumference of the peg, and in that case the tensions in the two straight sections would be different. But if the contact is smooth, the tensions in the two straight sections are the same.

Another possibility is for the string to pass round a pulley, which can rotate on a fixed axis. Now, if the surface is rough, the pulley will go round with the string. (The same applies when a chain passes round a cog wheel.) To make the pulley go round, the tensions in the two straight sections have to be different. But if the mass of the pulley is small, and if it runs on smooth bearings, the difference in the tensions is very small, so it can be neglected in a first approximation.

Smooth pegs and light pulleys are further examples of mathematical models often used in mechanics. You will never find them in practice, but you can often use the models in calculations with only a small loss of accuracy.

> When a string passes round a smooth peg, or a light pulley with smooth bearings, the tension in the string is the same on either side.

Example 7.4.1

Repairs are being carried out in a tall block of flats. A wheel is attached at the top of the scaffolding with its axis horizontal. A rope runs over the rim of the wheel and has buckets of mass 2 kg tied to it at both ends. One bucket is filled with 3 kg of rubble and then released, so that it descends to ground level. With what acceleration does it move?

As always, modelling approximations have to be made. In this example, assume that the mass of the rope and the wheel can be neglected, that the wheel rotates on smooth bearings, and that the rope doesn't stretch. Then the tension in the string will be the same at both ends, and the upward acceleration of the empty bucket will have the same magnitude as the downward acceleration of the filled bucket. Denote the tension by T N, and the acceleration by a m s^{-2}.

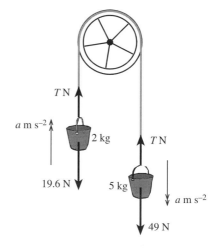

Fig. 7.16 shows the forces on each bucket during the motion. The weights of the buckets are 19.6 N and 49 N.

For the empty bucket,

$$\mathcal{R}(\uparrow) \qquad T - 19.6 = 2a.$$

For the filled bucket,

$$\mathcal{R}(\downarrow) \qquad 49 - T = 5a.$$

Adding,

$$(T - 19.6) + (49 - T) = 2a + 5a,$$

which gives $7a = 29.4$, so $a = 4.2$.

Fig. 7.16

The filled bucket descends to ground level with acceleration of 4.2 m s^{-2}.

Example 7.4.2

A box of mass 2 kg is placed on a table. A string attached to the box passes over a smooth peg at the edge of the table, and a ball of mass 1 kg is tied to the other end. The two straight sections of the string are horizontal and vertical. If the coefficient of friction between the box and the table is 0.2, find the acceleration of the box and the ball.

Fig. 7.17 shows the forces on the box and the
ball. Because the peg is smooth, the tension in
the string has the same magnitude, T N, at each
end. The normal contact force on the box is
R N, the friction is F N, and the acceleration is
a m s^{-2}. The weights are 19.6 N and 9.8 N
respectively.

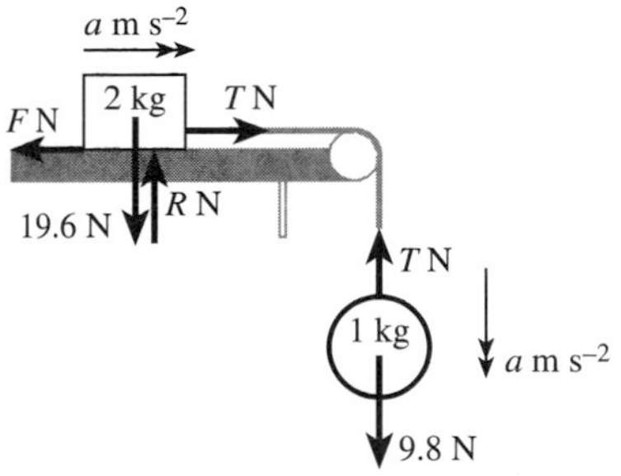

Resolving vertically for the box gives $R = 19.6$.
Since the system is in motion, friction will be the
largest possible, so $F = 0.2 \times 19.6 = 3.92$.

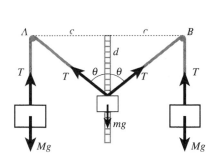

Fig. 7.17

For the box, $\mathcal{R}(\rightarrow)$ $T - F = 2a$.

For the ball, $\mathcal{R}(\downarrow)$ $9.8 - T = a$.

Adding the two equations and substituting $F = 3.92$ gives $9.8 - 3.92 = 3a$, so $a = 1.96$.

The box and the ball have an acceleration of just under 2 m s^{-2}.

The next example can be used as the basis of an experiment to verify the rule for finding
the resolved part of a force, given in Section 4.2.

Example 7.4.3

In the apparatus illustrated in Fig. 7.18 a mass
m is attached to two strings of equal length,
each of which carries a mass M at its other
end. The strings are placed symmetrically over
smooth nails A and B, which are at the same
level. The whole system is in equilibrium. The
distance between the nails is $2c$, and the mass
m is at a depth d below the mid-point of AB.
Find an equation connecting M, m, c and d.

Fig. 7.18

Let the tension in each of the strings be T N, and suppose that the sloping
sections of each string make an angle θ with the vertical.

For each mass M, $\mathcal{R}(\uparrow)$ $T - Mg = 0$.

For the mass m, $\mathcal{R}(\uparrow)$ $2T\cos\theta - mg = 0$.

Substituting Mg for T in the second equation and dividing by g gives $m = 2M\cos\theta$.

The sloping sections of the strings have length $\sqrt{c^2 + d^2}$, so that $\cos\theta = \dfrac{d}{\sqrt{c^2 + d^2}}$.

This gives $m = \dfrac{2Md}{\sqrt{c^2 + d^2}}$.

To use this as an experiment, keep the masses M constant but vary the mass m.
[*Safety!*] Set a scale down the line of symmetry to measure the depth d, and
calculate $\cos\theta = \dfrac{d}{\sqrt{c^2 + d^2}}$. If you plot $\cos\theta$ against m, you should get points
which lie on a line through the origin with gradient $\dfrac{1}{2M}$.

Example 7.4.4

On a construction site a truck of mass 400 kg is pulled up a $10°$ slope by a chain. The
chain runs parallel to the slope up to the top, where it passes over a cog wheel of negligible
mass. It then runs horizontally and is
attached to the rear of a locomotive of
mass 2000 kg. Neglecting any
resistances, calculate the driving force
needed to accelerate the truck up the
slope at 0.1 m s^{-2}.

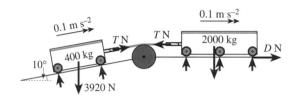

Fig. 7.19 shows the forces on the
truck and the locomotive. Denote
the tension in the chain by T N.
The weight of the truck is 3920 N.

Fig. 7.19

For the truck,　　$\mathcal{R}(\parallel$ to the slope)　　$T - 3920\cos 80° = 400 \times 0.1$,

which gives $T = 720.7\ldots$.

The locomotive also has acceleration 0.1 m s^{-2}.

For the locomotive,　　$\mathcal{R}(\rightarrow)$　$D - T = 2000 \times 0.1$,

so $D = 720.7\ldots + 200 = 920.7\ldots$.

The driving force required is about 920 N.

7.5* A way of simplifying calculations

When you have a problem to solve about two or more objects, you sometimes find that the
equations have several terms which depend on the value of g. Some people find it simpler
not to substitute the numerical value 9.8 at first, but to replace it by a letter. You can then
make a single substitution of the numerical value at the end, when you calculate the answer.

Normally the letter g is used in place of the numerical value 9.8. For example, in
Example 7.4.2, the weights of the box and the ball could be written as $2g$ newtons and
g newtons respectively. The friction would then be $0.2 \times 2g$ newtons, which is $0.4g$
newtons. The two equations for the box and the ball would then be

$$\mathcal{R}(\rightarrow)\ \ T - 0.4g = 2a \qquad \text{and} \qquad \mathcal{R}(\uparrow)\ \ g - T = a,$$

which can be added to give $g - 0.4g = 3a$, so $a = 0.2g$. A single substitution of 9.8 for
g then produces the answer $a = 1.96$.

In fact, using the letter g for the number 9.8 can be rather confusing, because in algebraic applications you have used g to stand for the quantity 9.8 m s^{-2}, which could be written in other units such as 0.0098 km s^{-2} or 980 cm s^{-2}. So in working a particular problem you need to be clear whether you are using the letter g as an abbreviation for the number 9.8, or whether it stands for the quantity which is the acceleration due to gravity. In the first case you need to include units in your answers, for example a force of $0.4g$ N or an acceleration of $0.2g \text{ m s}^{-2}$; in the second case the units are included in the symbol for the quantity, and it would be wrong to add a unit to the symbol.

All the same, this is a useful way of avoiding over-complicated arithmetic, and you would find it useful in several of the questions in Exercise 7B. A further advantage is that in some problems the value of g cancels out, which can save you a lot of unnecessary arithmetic.

Exercise 7B

1   In the cases illustrated in the following diagrams the strings pass over small light pulleys. The contacts between the blocks and the surfaces are rough, except where they are indicated as smooth in parts (d), (e) and (f). The blocks are at rest and the strings taut. In each case find the tension in the string and the frictional force exerted by each surface on the block with which it is in contact.

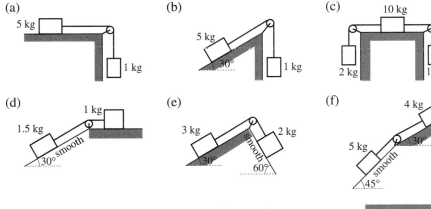

2   A tape is wound round two smooth cylinders as shown. The higher cylinder is fixed, but the lower cylinder sits in a loop formed by the tape. If the 5 kg mass descends at constant speed, calculate the mass of the lower cylinder.

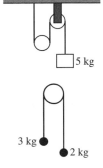

3   In the system illustrated the string passes over a smooth fixed peg. The particles are held in the positions shown, with the string taut; they are then released from rest. Find the tension in the string and the acceleration of the particles.

4   Suppose that in each of the cases illustrated in Question 1 the pulleys can rotate freely and that all the contacts between the blocks and surfaces are smooth. The blocks are held in the positions shown, with the string taut. The blocks are then released from rest. Find the acceleration of the blocks in each case.

5   A particle of mass 3 kg is attached to one end of
    each of two strings s_1, and s_2. A particle of
    mass 2.5 kg is attached to the other end of s_1,
    and a particle of mass 1 kg is attached to the
    other end of s_2. The particles are held in the
    positions shown, with the strings taut and s_1
    passing over a smooth fixed peg. The system is
    released from rest. Find the acceleration of the
    particles, and the tensions in s_1, and s_2.

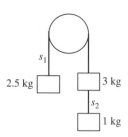

6   In the system illustrated in Question 2 suppose that the mass of the lower cylinder is 12 kg.
    The system is held at rest in the position shown, with the tape taut, and then released. Find
    the acceleration of

    (a) the lower cylinder,   (b) the 5 kg mass.

7   Two particles are connected by a light inextensible string which passes over a smooth fixed
    peg. The heavier particle is held so that the string is taut, and the parts of the string not in
    contact with the pulley are vertical. When the system is released from rest the particles
    have an acceleration of $\frac{1}{2}g$. Find the ratio of the masses of the particles.

8   A particle of mass m is placed on a rough track which goes up at an angle $\alpha°$ to the
    horizontal, where $\sin\alpha° = 0.6$ and $\cos\alpha° = 0.8$. The coefficient of friction is 0.5. A string
    is attached to the particle, and a particle of mass M is attached to the other end of the
    string. The string runs up the track, passes over a smooth bar at the top of the track, and
    then hangs vertically. Find the interval of values of M for which the system can rest in
    equilibrium.

    Find expressions for the acceleration with which the system will move if the value of M
    lies outside this interval.

7.6 Internal and external forces

Suppose that a vehicle of mass 1600 kg accelerates at 0.5 m s^{-2}, and that the motion is
opposed by a resistance of 140 newtons. What is the driving force, D newtons?

You can answer this question using the methods of Chapter 2. By Newton's second law,
$D - 140 = 1600 \times 0.5$, so that $D = 940$.

Now compare this with Example 7.2.1, in which a pick-up truck of mass 1200 kg tows a
trailer of mass 400 kg against a resistance of 140 newtons with acceleration 0.5 m s^{-2}.
You found there that the driving force required is also 940 newtons.

This is hardly surprising. If the 'vehicle' in the first paragraph consists of a truck and a
trailer, then it makes no difference whether you treat this as a single object or as two
connected objects moving with the same velocity and acceleration.

But what you can't find by applying Newton's
law to the truck-and-trailer vehicle is the force
from the coupling. If you draw a diagram for
the horizontal forces on the vehicle, it will look
like Fig. 7.20. The only forces affecting the
motion are the driving force and the resistance.

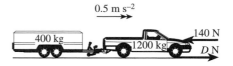

Fig. 7.20

These are called the 'external' forces on the combined vehicle. The force from the
coupling on the truck and on the trailer, which had to be included in Fig. 7.6, become
'internal' forces when you are thinking of the truck-and-trailer as a single vehicle.

> When an object is made up of two parts, each of which has the
> same velocity and acceleration, you can apply Newton's second
> law either to the object as a whole or to the parts separately.
>
> For the object as a whole, forces of interaction between the two
> parts are **internal forces**, and are not included in the equation.
>
> For the separate parts, the forces of interaction of each on the other
> are **external forces**, and are included in the equations.

This principle also applies in Example 7.3.1. Since both trucks are moving on the same
track and connected by an inextensible cable, they have the same velocity and acceleration.
You can therefore treat the two trucks together as a single object of mass 80 kg, and the
only horizontal external force is the pull of 120 newtons; the tension in the cable is an
internal force. The acceleration of the trucks is $\frac{120}{80}$ m s^{-2}, which is 1.5 m s^{-2}.

But to calculate the tension in the cable you must use one or other of the Newton's law
equations for the separate trucks. When you have to carry out calculations for the
motion of an object which splits into two parts, you will often find it simplest to write
equations for the object as a whole and for just one of the parts.

Example 7.6.1
A dynamo of mass 1500 kg is placed in a cage of mass 500 kg, which is raised
vertically by a cable from a crane. The tension in the cable is 20 000 N. Find the
acceleration of the cage, and the contact force between the cage and the dynamo.

The cage and the dynamo have the same
acceleration, a m s^{-2}, so they can be treated
as one object (Fig. 7.21). The only external
forces are the tension in the cable and the
combined weight of 2000×9.8 N, which is
19 600 N.

For the cage-and-dynamo,

$$\mathcal{R}(\uparrow) \quad 20\,000 - 19\,600 = 2000a,$$

so $a = 0.2$.

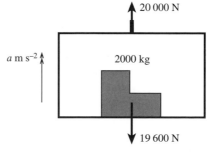

Fig. 7.21

To find the contact force, R N, you must consider either the cage or the dynamo separately. It is simpler to take the dynamo, because there are fewer forces acting on it (see Fig. 7.22). You now know that $a = 0.2$.

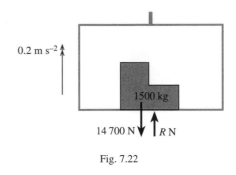

Fig. 7.22

For the dynamo alone,

$\mathcal{R}(\uparrow) \quad R - 14\,700 = 1500 \times 0.2$,

so $R = 15\,000$.

The acceleration of the cage is 0.2 m s^{-2}; the contact force is $15\,000$ N.

Example 7.6.2

Three barges travel down a river in line. Only the rear barge has an engine, which produces a forward force of 400 kN. The masses of the front, middle and rear barges are 1600 tonnes, 1400 tonnes and 2000 tonnes, and the water exerts on them resistances of 100 kN, 20 kN and 30 kN respectively. Find the forces in the couplings joining the barges.

The three aerial views in Fig. 7.23 show the horizontal forces on all three barges, on the front two barges and on the front barge. The acceleration is a m s^{-2}, and the forces in the couplings are R kN and S kN.

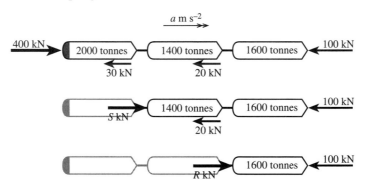

Fig. 7.23

Notice that, although tonnes (1000 kg) and kilonewtons (1000 N) are not basic SI units, they do form part of a system which is consistent with metres and seconds, so that the equation $F = ma$ can be used without any need for conversion.

There are three unknowns, but the forces in both couplings are internal forces if you take all three barges together.

For all three barges,

$\mathcal{R}(\text{forwards}) \quad 400 - 100 - 20 - 30 = (1600 + 1400 + 2000)a$.

This gives $a = \frac{250}{5000} = 0.05$.

For the front two barges,

$\mathcal{R}$(forwards) $S - 100 - 20 = (1600 + 1400) \times 0.05$.

For the front barge,

$\mathcal{R}$(forwards) $R - 100 = 1600 \times 0.05$.

These equations give $S = 270$ and $R = 180$.

The forces in the front and rear couplings are 180 kN and 270 kN respectively.

Notice that if you use this method each equation involves just one of the unknown quantities, so you have no simultaneous equations to solve.

You can if you wish check your answers by considering the forces on one of the other barges by itself. For example, Fig. 7.24 shows the forces on the middle barge. The forces in both couplings are external forces on this barge, and the forward force is $(S - R - 20)$ kN. With the values of R and S found, this is 70 kN. Since $70 = 1400 \times 0.05$, you have a check that the equation $F = ma$ is satisfied for the middle barge.

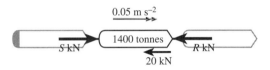

Fig. 7.24

Exercise 7C

1   A car of mass 1000 kg is towing a camping trailer of mass 250 kg along a straight road. There are constant resistances to the motion of the car and the trailer of magnitude 150 N and 50 N respectively. The driving force on the car has magnitude 800 N. Calculate the acceleration of the car and the trailer, and the tension in the towbar, when

(a)   the road is horizontal,

(b)   the road is inclined at $\sin^{-1}\frac{2}{49}$ to the horizontal and the car is travelling uphill.

2   When a car of mass 1350 kg tows a trailer of mass 250 kg along a horizontal straight road, the resistive forces on the car and trailer have magnitude 200 N and 50 N respectively. Find the magnitude of the driving force on the car when the car and trailer are travelling at constant speed, and state the tension in the towbar in this case.

Find the acceleration or deceleration of the car and the trailer, and the tension in the towbar, when the driving force exerted by the car has magnitude

(a) 330 N,   (b) 170 N,   (c)   zero.

Find also the deceleration of the car and the trailer, and the magnitude of the force in the towbar, stating whether this force is a tension or thrust, when the driver applies the brakes and the braking force exceeds the driving force by

(d) 30 N   (e) 70 N,   (f) 150 N.

3 A car of mass M pulls a trailer of mass m down a straight hill which is inclined at angle $\alpha°$ to the horizontal. Resistive forces of magnitudes P and Q act on the car and the trailer respectively, and the driving force on the car is F. Find an expression for the acceleration of the car and trailer, in terms of F, P, Q, M, m and α.

Show that the tension in the towbar is independent of α.

In the case when $F = P + Q$, show that the acceleration is $g \sin \alpha°$ and that the tension in the towbar is Q.

4 Five spheres, each of mass m, are joined together by four inextensible strings. The spheres hang in a vertical line as shown in the diagram, and are held at rest by a force applied to the uppermost sphere, of magnitude $5mg$, acting vertically upwards. Find the tension in each of the strings.

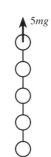

The force on the uppermost sphere is now removed. If the total air resistance acting vertically upwards on the spheres is $\frac{1}{2}mg$, find the acceleration of the system in the subsequent motion.

Find also the tension in each of the four strings if

(a) the air resistance on each individual sphere is $\frac{1}{10}mg$,

(b) the air resistance on the uppermost sphere is $\frac{3}{5}mg$ and the air resistance on each of the other four spheres is $\frac{1}{20}mg$.

Miscellaneous exercise 7

1 A girl of mass 55 kg is standing in a lift which is moving with an upwards acceleration of 0.15 m s^{-2}. The force exerted on the floor of the lift by the girl has magnitude R newtons. Draw a diagram showing the forces acting on the girl, who may be modelled as a particle, and find the value of R.   (OCR)

2 A child of mass 30 kg is standing in a lift which is descending. The force exerted on the floor of the lift by the child has magnitude 270 N. Find the magnitude of the acceleration of the lift and state whether the lift is speeding up or slowing down.   (OCR)

3 Two bodies, of masses 3 kg and 5 kg, are attached to the ends of a light inextensible string. The string passes over a smooth fixed pulley and the particles are moving vertically with both vertical parts of the string taut. Find the tension in the string.   (OCR)

4 Two children P and Q, of masses 40 kg and 50 kg respectively, are holding on to the ends of a rope which passes over a thick horizontal branch of a tree. The parts of the rope on either side of the branch are vertical and child Q is moving downwards. A model is to be used in which the children may be considered as particles, and in which the rope is light and inextensible and is moving freely in a smooth groove on the branch. Show that the acceleration of each child has magnitude 1.09 m s^{-2}, and find the tension in the rope.

When child Q is moving at 2 m s^{-1} she lets go of the rope. Child P continues to rise for a further distance h metres before falling back to the ground. Calculate the value of h.

Choose one of the assumptions stated in the model and comment briefly on how realistic you think it is.   (OCR)

5 Two small bodies P and Q, of masses 6 kg and 2 kg respectively, are attached to the ends of a light inextensible string. The string passes over a pulley fixed at a height of 4 m above the ground. Initially Q is held on the ground and P hangs in equilibrium at a height of 2 m above the ground (see diagram). Both hanging parts of the string are vertical. Q is released. The modelling assumptions are that there is no air resistance and that the pulley is smooth. Find the speed of Q when P hits the ground, and find also the greatest height, above the ground, reached by Q in the subsequent motion.

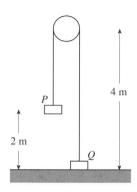

When Q reaches its highest point the string is cut. Find the speed of Q just before it hits the ground.

Without further calculation, sketch the (t, v) graph of the motion of Q from the start until it hits the ground. Show clearly, by shading, a region on your sketch whose area is equal to the greatest height, above the ground, reached by Q.   (OCR)

6 Two particles P and Q, of masses 2 kg and m kg respectively, are connected by a light inextensible string. Particle P is held on a smooth horizontal table. The string passes over a smooth pulley R fixed at the edge of the table, and Q is at rest vertically below R (see diagram). When P is released the acceleration of each particle has magnitude 0.81 m s^{-2}. Assuming that air resistance may be ignored, find the tension in the string and the value of m.   (OCR)

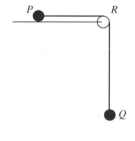

7 The diagram shows a light inextensible string passing over a fixed smooth pulley. Particles A and B, of masses 0.03 kg and 0.05 kg respectively, are attached to the ends of the string. The system is held at rest with A and B at the same horizontal level and the string taut. The two parts of the string not in contact with the pulley are vertical. The system is released at time $t = 0$, where t is measured in seconds. The particle B moves downwards for 2 s before being brought to rest as it hits the floor. The string then becomes slack and B remains at rest. Neglecting air resistance, show that the string becomes taut again when $t = 3$.

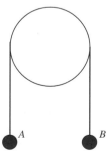

Draw, on separate diagrams, the (t, v) graphs for A and B, for $0 \leqslant t \leqslant 3$, clearly indicating the velocity of A when $t = 2$ and when $t = 3$.   (OCR)

8   Particles A and B, of masses 0.5 kg and 0.8 kg respectively, are joined by a light
    inextensible string. A is held at rest on a smooth horizontal platform. The string passes
    over a small smooth pulley at the edge of the platform, and B hangs vertically below the
    pulley. A is 1.3 m from the pulley. A is released, with the string taut, and the particles
    start to move. Find the tension in the string, and the speed of A immediately before it
    reaches the pulley, stating any assumption you make.

    Immediately before A reaches the pulley it becomes detached from the string. Given that
    B reaches the floor 1.21 s after the release of A, calculate the initial height of B above the
    floor.   (OCR)

9   Particles A and B, of masses 0.2 kg and
    0.1 kg respectively, are joined by a light
    inextensible string. Particle A is placed on a
    fixed smooth plane inclined at 10° to the
    horizontal, and is held at rest by a force of
    magnitude X newtons which acts in a
    direction parallel to a line of greatest slope
    of the plane. The string passes over a
    smooth pulley P fixed at the bottom of the
    plane, and the part PB of the string hangs
    vertically, as shown in the diagram. Find X.

    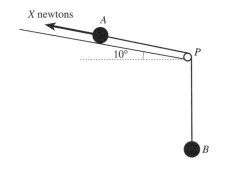

    The force of magnitude X newtons is now removed. Ignoring air resistance, find the
    tension in the string in the subsequent motion.   (OCR, adapted)

10 Machinery of mass 300 kg is placed on the floor of a lift of mass 450 kg. The magnitudes
    of the tension in the cable holding the lift, and the normal contact force between the
    machinery and the lift floor, are T newtons and R newtons respectively. By considering
    the forces acting on the machinery, find the value of R when the lift is moving upwards
    with a deceleration of 2.2 m s^{-2}. By considering the motion of the machinery and the lift
    as one body, find the value of T for the same deceleration.

11 Two particles P and Q, of masses 4 kg
    and 6 kg respectively, are connected by a
    light inextensible string which passes over
    a light smooth pulley A. Particle P is held
    at rest on a rough horizontal table and
    particle Q rests on a smooth plane
    inclined at 30° to the horizontal, as shown
    in the diagram. The string is taut and lies

    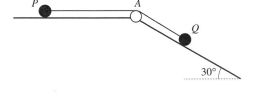

    in a vertical plane perpendicular to the line of intersection of the table and the inclined
    plane. The particles are released from rest and in the subsequent motion each particle has
    an acceleration of magnitude 1.9 m s^{-2}, provided P has not reached A. Find the tension in
    the string and the coefficient of friction between P and the table.

    One second after the system is released from rest the string breaks, and P subsequently
    comes to rest before reaching A. At the instant when the string breaks P is 0.8 m away
    from A. Find the distance from A at which P comes to rest.   (OCR)

12 A metal block M, of mass 2 kg, is held at rest on a smooth horizontal table. The block M is connected to a wooden block W, of mass 0.1 kg, by a light inextensible string which passes over a smooth light pulley fixed at the edge of the table. The block W hangs vertically, as shown in the diagram. Block M, which is 0.6 m from the pulley, is now released. Modelling the blocks as particles and ignoring air resistance, find

(a) the tension in the string in the ensuing motion,

(b) the speed of W immediately before M reaches the pulley. (OCR)

13 Two trucks A and B, of masses 1000 kg and 800 kg respectively, are connected by a horizontal coupling. An engine pulls the trucks along a straight horizontal track by exerting a horizontal force of magnitude

X newtons on truck A (see diagram). The resistances to the motion of truck A, excluding the tension in the horizontal coupling, may be modelled by a constant horizontal force of magnitude 300 N; for truck B the magnitude may be modelled by a constant horizontal force of magnitude 100 N.

(a) Given that the trucks are moving with constant speed, find

   (i) the tension in the horizontal coupling between the trucks,

   (ii) the value of X.

(b) Given instead that $X - 800$, find the common acceleration of the trucks. (OCR)

14 Two trucks A and B, of masses 6000 kg and 4000 kg respectively, are connected by a horizontal coupling. An engine pulls the trucks along a straight horizontal track,

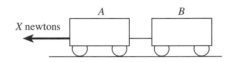

exerting a constant horizontal force of magnitude X newtons on truck A (see diagram). The resistance to motion for truck A may be modelled by a constant horizontal force of magnitude 360 N; for truck B the resistance may be modelled by a constant horizontal force of magnitude 240 N. Given that the tension in the coupling is T newtons and that the acceleration of the trucks is $a \text{ m s}^{-2}$, show that $T = \frac{2}{5}X$, and express a in terms of X. Given that the trucks are slowing down, obtain an inequality satisfied by X.

The model is changed so that the resistance for truck B is modelled by a constant force of magnitude 200 N. The resistance for truck A remains unchanged. For this changed model find the range of possible values of X for which the force in the coupling is compressive (i.e. the force in the coupling acting on B is directed from A to B). (OCR)

15 A load P, of mass 200 kg, is suspended by the vertical cable of a crane. Another load Q, of mass 120 kg, is suspended from P by another vertical cable. Both cables may be considered as light and inextensible, and any resistances to motion may be neglected. Find the tension in the vertical cable supporting the load P,

(a) when the loads are hanging in equilibrium,

(b) when the loads accelerate vertically upwards at 0.4 m s^{-2}. (OCR, adapted)

16 A van of mass 1200 kg is towing a car of mass 800 kg up a slope inclined at 8° to the horizontal. The resistance to the motion of the van may be modelled by a single force of magnitude 500 N acting parallel to the slope. For the car the resistance may be modelled by a single force of magnitude 200 N acting parallel to the slope. The van is travelling at constant speed. Stating one assumption that you have made, find, in either order,

(a) the tension in the tow-rope between the van and the car,

(b) the driving force acting on the van.

The driving force acting on the van is now increased to 4000 N. Find the time taken for the van to increase its speed from 10 m s^{-1} to 14 m s^{-1}.   (OCR)

17 A small smooth ring R, of mass 0.6 kg, is threaded on a light inextensible string. One end of the string is attached to a fixed point A and the other end is attached to a ring B, of mass 0.2 kg, which is threaded on a fixed rough horizontal wire which passes through A (see diagram). The system is in equilibrium, with B about to slip and with the part AR of the string making an angle of 60° with the wire.

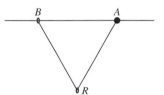

(a) Explain, with reference to the fact that ring R is smooth, why the part BR of the string is inclined at 60° to the wire.

(b) Show that the normal contact force between B and the wire has magnitude 4.9 N, correct to two significant figures.

(c) Find the coefficient of friction between B and the wire.   (OCR)

18 A smooth bead B of mass 0.6 kg is threaded on a light inextensible string whose ends are attached to two identical rings, each of mass 0.4 kg. The rings can move on a fixed straight horizontal wire. The system rests in equilibrium with each section of the string making an angle $\theta°$ with the vertical, as shown in the diagram.

(a) Find the magnitude of the normal contact force exerted on each ring by the wire.

(b) Find, in terms of θ, the magnitude of the frictional force on each ring.

Given that the coefficient of friction between each ring and the wire is 0.3, find the greatest possible value of θ for the system to be in equilibrium.   (OCR)

8 Momentum

This chapter introduces two new ideas, impulse and momentum, which are useful when you are interested in change in the velocity of an object. When you have completed the chapter, you should

- know the definitions of impulse and momentum, and the units in which they are measured
- understand and be able to use the impulse–momentum equation
- know that momentum is conserved in a collision, and apply the principle to calculate velocities.

8.1 The impulse–momentum equation

Example 8.1.1
A spacecraft of mass 8 tonnes is travelling at 15 km s^{-1}. Controllers want to increase its velocity to 15.1 km s^{-1} in the same direction. This is done by firing the motors so that they produce a constant thrust of F newtons for a period of t seconds. Find the connection between F and t.

In basic SI units the mass of the spacecraft is 8000 kg, and its velocity increases from $15\,000 \text{ m s}^{-1}$ to $15\,100 \text{ m s}^{-1}$.

If the force is constant, so is the acceleration. The velocity increases by 100 m s^{-1} in t seconds, so the acceleration is $\dfrac{100}{t} \text{ m s}^{-2}$. By Newton's second law,

$$F = 8000 \times \frac{100}{t}, \quad \text{so} \quad Ft = 800\,000.$$

Notice that, in this example, you can only expect to find a connection between F and t. You can't calculate either quantity without knowing the other. The effect on the velocity of the spacecraft is the same whether the motors produce a thrust of 8000 newtons for 100 seconds, or $80\,000$ newtons for 10 seconds, or $100\,000$ newtons for 8 seconds.

The quantity Ft is called the **impulse** of the constant force F newtons over the time period of t seconds. The SI unit of impulse is the 'newton second', abbreviated to N s. In the example, the spacecraft receives an impulse of $800\,000$ N s from its motors.

The effect of an impulse on a moving object can be found algebraically by combining the equations $F = ma$ and $v = u + at$. You can rearrange the second equation to get $a = \dfrac{v-u}{t}$. Then, substituting this in the first equation,

$$F = m \times \left(\frac{v-u}{t}\right), \quad \text{which can be rearranged to give} \quad Ft = mv - mu.$$

The expression on the left of this equation is the impulse of the force F over the time t. The right side includes two expressions of the form 'mass $\times$ velocity', one with the initial velocity u and the other with the velocity v after time t.

For an object of mass m moving with velocity v, the quantity mv is called the **momentum**. Because momentum terms appear in the same equation as the impulse term, both quantities are measured by the same unit. So an object of mass m kg, moving with velocity v m s^{-1}, has momentum mv N s.

For the spacecraft the initial momentum is $8000 \times 15\,000$ N s, and the final momentum is $8000 \times 15\,100$ N s. So during the manoeuvre the momentum increases from $120\,000\,000$ N s to $120\,800\,000$ N s, that is by $800\,000$ N s.

The equation $Ft = mv - mu$ is called the **impulse–momentum** equation. The expression mu is the initial momentum, which is the momentum of the object when it is moving with its initial velocity. The expression mv is the momentum after time t.

> The impulse received by an object is equal to the increase in the momentum of the object in the direction of the impulse.

Example 8.1.2
Find the impulse needed to drive a golf ball of mass 45 grams from the tee with a velocity of 40 m s^{-1}.

> In basic SI units the mass of the ball is 0.045 kg, so it leaves the tee with momentum 0.045×40 N s, which is 1.8 N s. Since the ball has no initial momentum, the impulse required is 1.8 N s.

As with the rocket motor, this impulse of 1.8 N s could be produced in many ways. For example, a force of 100 newtons acting for 0.018 seconds, or a force of 180 newtons acting for 0.01 seconds, would have the same effect on the golf ball. Some players stroke the ball gently and then follow through, others hit the ball harder but less smoothly.

It is important to remember that velocity can be either positive or negative. In many games the ball changes its direction of motion after it is hit. You must then decide which direction to take as positive, and attach a negative sign to impulses or velocities in the opposite direction.

Example 8.1.3
A tennis player receives a service ball travelling at 50 m s^{-1}, and returns it along the same line with a speed of 30 m s^{-1}. If the mass of the ball is 60 grams, find the impulse given to the ball by the racket.

> Choose the direction the player is facing to be positive. Then the initial momentum has the negative value $0.06 \times (-50)$ N s. The momentum of the returned ball is 0.06×30 N s. So the impulse given to the ball is $(1.8 - (-3))$ N s, which is 4.8 N s.

Example 8.1.4

In the 'snatch', a weight-lifter lifts a barbell of mass 150 kg from the floor to a position above his head in one continuous movement at a speed of 0.8 m s^{-1}. Describe the muscular effort involved.

> The technique is to give the barbell its upward velocity as quickly as possible. It acquires momentum of $150 \times 0.8 \text{ N s}$, which is 120 N s. So producing this speed requires an impulse of 120 N s.
>
> In this calculation the weight of the barbell, 1470 N, has not been taken into account. Its effect is relatively small, since the barbell gains speed very quickly. For example, if the upward jerk lasts for 0.01 seconds, the extra impulse required to overcome the weight is $1470 \times 0.01 \text{ N s}$, which is 14.7 N s.
>
> Once the barbell has got its speed, the weight-lifter wants to keep it up. This requires producing a steady force equal to the weight, that is a force of 1470 N.

The argument in this last example that, if an impulse is applied over a very short time, ordinary forces such as weight have little effect, is often used in applying the impulse-momentum principle.

Exercise 8A

1 Find the momentum of
   (a) a rugby player of mass 90 kg running at 6 m s^{-1},
   (b) an elephant of mass 6 tonnes charging at 10 m s^{-1},
   (c) a racing car of mass 2.5 tonnes travelling at 300 km per hour,
   (d) a bullet of mass 20 grams moving at 400 m s^{-1},
   (e) a meteorite of mass 20 kg as it enters the earth's atmosphere at 8 km s^{-1}.

2 A snooker ball of mass 0.15 kg is given a speed of 2.4 m s^{-1}. Calculate the impulse it receives from the cue.

3 A sprinter of mass 60 kg launches herself from the starting-block at a speed of 5 m s^{-1}. Calculate the impulse needed to achieve this.

4 A spaceship of mass 8 tonnes at lift-off achieves a speed of 7.2 km s^{-1}. Calculate the impulse imparted to it by the rocket motors.

5 A squash ball of mass 24 grams is served with an impulse of 1.2 N s. How fast is it going when it leaves the racket?

6 A flea of mass 40 mg jumps vertically and rises to a height of 50 cm. Calculate the impulse at lift-off.

7 A car of mass 1.4 tonnes reduces speed from 30 m s^{-1} to 20 m s^{-1} in 7 seconds. Calculate the average braking force.

8 A 40-tonne truck increases speed by 5 km per hour. Find the increase in its momentum. If the greatest driving force that the engine can produce is 3 kN, find the least time in which this increase in speed can be achieved.

9 A cricket ball of mass 160 grams is bowled at 15 m s^{-1}, and is hit straight back to the bowler at 25 m s^{-1}. What is the impulse on the ball? If the ball is in contact with the bat for 0.04 seconds, what is the force on the bat (assumed constant) during the hit?

10 A football of mass 450 grams is moving horizontally at head height with a speed of 2 m s^{-1}. A player scores a goal by heading it back along the same line at 8 m s^{-1}. Calculate the impulse on his head.

11 A table-tennis ball of mass $2\frac{1}{2}$ grams crosses the table at a speed of 4 m s^{-1}, and is smashed back along the same line with an impulse of 0.04 N s. What is the speed of the ball on its return?

12 A tennis ball of mass 60 grams is dropped on the floor from a height of 1.6 metres, and rebounds to a height of 1.2 metres. Calculate the impulse it receives when it hits the ground.

8.2 Collisions

An important application of momentum is when two objects moving along the same line collide with each other. Consider for example a shot in snooker in which the white ball hits the black (Fig. 8.1). When they collide, each ball exerts a contact force on the other. Suppose that the impulse of the force from the white ball on the black has magnitude I N s. Then, by Newton's third law, the black ball exerts on the white an impulse of magnitude I N s in the opposite direction.

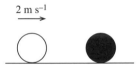

2 m s^{-1}

Fig. 8.1

The effect of the collision is that the black ball gains momentum of I N s, but the white ball loses momentum of the same amount. This means that the total momentum of the two balls is the same after the collision as before.

Suppose for example that the black ball is initially at rest, and that the white ball is moving at 2 m s^{-1}. Suppose also that after the collision the black ball moves at 1.4 m s^{-1}. Then, taking the mass of each ball as 0.15 kg, the white ball initially has momentum 0.3 N s, and the black has none. After the collision 0.21 N s of this momentum has been transferred to the black ball, so only 0.09 N s is left for the white.

This means that the velocity of the white ball is reduced to $\dfrac{0.09}{0.15}$ m s^{-1}. So the white ball has a velocity of 0.6 m s^{-1} after the collision.

This general principle applies whenever two objects collide.

> **Conservation of momentum**   If two objects moving along
> the same line collide with each other, the total momentum of
> the two objects is the same after the collision as it was before.

Example 8.2.1

In an experiment to estimate the speed of a bullet, a shot is fired into a box of sand
mounted on a trolley. The mass of the bullet is 20 grams, and the mass of the box and
trolley is 5 kg. After firing, the box with the bullet embedded in it moves off at a speed
of 1.8 m s^{-1}. How fast was the bullet moving before it hit the box?

If the speed of the bullet was u m s^{-1}, its initial momentum was $0.02u$ N s. When the
bullet has entered the box, both are moving at 1.8 m s^{-1}, so that the total momentum is
$(5+0.02)\times 1.8$ N s. Since the total momentum is the same before and after,

$$0.02u = 5.02\times 1.8, \quad \text{so} \quad u = 451.8.$$

The speed of the bullet was 450 m s^{-1}, correct to 2 significant figures.

Example 8.2.2

Two wagons are moving in the same direction along a horizontal track. The front
wagon, of mass 500 kg, is moving at 3 m s^{-1}. The rear wagon, of mass 800 kg, is
moving at 5 m s^{-1}. As a result of the collision the speed of the rear wagon is reduced to
4 m s^{-1}. Find the speed of the front wagon after the collision.

It is best to begin by putting all the
information on a diagram (Fig. 8.2). A
good method is to show the velocities
before the collision above the picture,
and the velocities after the collision
below. The impulses are shown with
open triangle arrows.

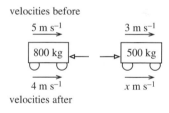

Fig. 8.2

Denote the speed of the front wagon after
the collision by x m s^{-1}. The conservation of the total momentum of the two
wagons is expressed by the equation

$$800\times 5+500\times 3 = 800\times 4+500x,$$

which gives $x = \dfrac{4000+1500-3200}{500} = \dfrac{2300}{500} = 4.6$.

The front wagon moves at 4.6 m s^{-1} after the collision.

Example 8.2.3

Two children sit on swings facing each other. Ann has mass 40 kg, Ben has mass
30 kg. Their swings are pulled away from each other and released, so that the children
meet when their swings are vertical. Ann is then moving at 2 m s^{-1}, and Ben is moving

at 3 m s^{-1}. When they meet, they push each other away with their feet. Ann is then moving at 1.6 m s^{-1}. How fast is Ben moving?

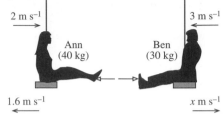

Fig. 8.3 shows the velocities and the impulses. Denote the velocity of Ben on the rebound by $x \text{ m s}^{-1}$. In writing the equation for the conservation of momentum you have to be careful about the signs. Taking the way Ann is facing to be positive,

Fig. 8.3

$$40 \times 2 + 30 \times (-3) = 40 \times (-1.6) + 30x,$$

which gives $x = \dfrac{80 - 90 + 64}{30} = \dfrac{54}{30} = 1.8$.

Ben is pushed away with a speed of 1.8 m s^{-1}.

Exercise 8B

1 In a game of croquet a player hits her ball at 6 m s^{-1} directly towards her opponent's stationary ball. After the collision the hitter's ball continues with its speed reduced to 1 m s^{-1}. The two balls have the same mass. Find how fast the opponent's ball moves.

2 A punt of mass 800 kg moving at 3 m s^{-1} rams into the back of another punt of mass 1000 kg moving at 1 m s^{-1} in the same direction. The speed of the ramming punt is reduced to $1\frac{1}{2} \text{ m s}^{-1}$ by the collision. How fast is the rammed punt then moving?

3 Two trucks are in line on the same rail track. A truck of mass 600 kg moving at 7 m s^{-1} catches up a truck of mass 400 kg moving at 2 m s^{-1}. When the trucks collide they couple together and move on as a single unit. How fast are they then moving?

4 In an ice-dancing manoeuvre, a male dancer skates directly towards his partner, who is stationary, and lifts her clear of the ice. He approaches her at a speed of 3 m s^{-1}, and their masses are 70 kg and 50 kg respectively. Find their common speed after the manoeuvre.

5 A block of mass 3 kg travelling at 5 m s^{-1} catches up another block of mass 7 kg travelling at 2 m s^{-1} along the same line and in the same direction.
   (a) If after the collision the second block has increased its speed to 3 m s^{-1}, what is the speed of the first block?
   (b) You are given that the difference between the speeds of the two blocks after the collision cannot be greater than the difference of the speeds before the collision. Deduce that the speed, $v \text{ m s}^{-1}$, of the first block after the collision must satisfy the inequalities $0.8 \leqslant v \leqslant 2.9$.

6 Ike and Jim are sitting in toy trucks; the masses are 60 kg and 40 kg respectively. The trucks are moving at 8 m s^{-1} along a track, with Ike's behind Jim's. Ike pushes Jim's truck away with a pole, and Jim moves off 2 m s^{-1} faster than Ike. What is Jim's new speed?

7   A block of mass 4 kg travelling at 15 m s^{-1} collides with another block of mass 3 kg travelling at 8 m s^{-1} in the opposite direction. Find the velocity of the 3 kg block after the collision if the 4 kg block

   (a) comes to rest after the collision,

   (b) changes direction and rebounds with a speed of 3 m s^{-1},

   (c) continues to move in the same direction with its speed reduced to 3 m s^{-1}.

Explain why the 4 kg block could not continue to move in the same direction with a speed of 6 m s^{-1} after the collision. What is the largest speed at which it could continue in the same direction?

8   A cannon of mass 500 kg fires a cannonball of mass 5 kg. The cannon is mounted on wheels, so that it can recoil backwards when the shot is fired.

   (a) What is the total momentum of the cannon and the cannonball before firing?

   (b) If the cannonball is fired horizontally, and leaves the muzzle of the cannon moving at 200 m s^{-1}, with what speed does the cannon recoil?

9   A solid sphere of mass 5 kg travelling at 5 m s^{-1} collides with a hollow sphere travelling at 4 m s^{-1} in the opposite direction. After the collision both spheres change their direction of motion, and their speeds are 1 m s^{-1} and 6 m s^{-1} respectively. Find the mass of the hollow sphere.

10 A black ball and a white ball hang side-by-side from the ceiling by strings of equal length. The black ball has mass 100 grams, and the white ball has mass 200 grams. The black ball is pulled aside and then released, so that it strikes the white ball moving at 4 m s^{-1}.

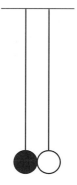

   (a) The black ball is brought to rest as a result of the collision. With what speed does the white ball start to move?

   (b) The white ball now swings aside, and then swings back to hit the black ball with the same speed as it started. After this second collision, both balls are moving in the same direction, and the speed of the black ball is 1 m s^{-1} greater than the speed of the white ball. Find the speeds of the two balls after the second collision.

Miscellaneous exercise 8

1   An unloaded railway wagon A, of mass 800 kg, and a loaded wagon B, of mass 3000 kg, are free to move on a straight horizontal track. Wagon A is travelling at a speed of 8 m s^{-1} when it runs into B, which is stationary, causing B to start to move with a speed of 2 m s^{-1}. Calculate the speed of A immediately after the impact.   (OCR)

2   Particles A and B are moving vertically upwards under gravity, in the same straight line, with B above A. The mass of A is 0.03 kg and the mass of B is 0.05 kg. Immediately before the particles collide, A has a speed of 4.5 m s^{-1} and B has a speed of 3.1 m s^{-1}. The speed of B is increased to 4.0 m s^{-1} by the collision. Calculate the speed of A immediately after the collision.   (OCR)

3 A loaded railway wagon A, of mass 2000 kg, is travelling on a straight horizontal track, with a speed of 7.7 m s^{-1}, when it collides with an empty stationary wagon B. As a result of the collision A continues in the same direction with a speed of 5.6 m s^{-1}. By modelling the wagons as particles,

   (a) find the magnitude of the momentum of B after the collision,

   (b) show that the mass of B cannot exceed 750 kg.   (OCR)

4 Two particles, of masses x kg and 0.1 kg, are moving towards each other in the same straight line and collide directly. Immediately before the impact, the speeds of the particles are 2 m s^{-1} and 3 m s^{-1} respectively.

   (a) Given that both particles are brought to rest by the impact, find x.

   (b) Given instead that the particles move with equal speeds of 1 m s^{-1} after the impact, find the three possible values of x.   (OCR)

5 Particles of mass $5m$ and m are moving directly towards each other, and immediately before they collide the particles have speeds u and $2u$ respectively. Immediately after they collide the particle of mass m has speed $2u$ in the opposite direction to that in which it was initially travelling. Find the speed of the particle of mass $5m$ immediately after the collision.   (OCR)

6 Two particles A and B, with masses m_1 and m_2 respectively, move in the same straight line and collide. Immediately before the collision the particles are moving towards each other, A with speed 3 m s^{-1} and B with speed 2 m s^{-1}. Immediately after the collision both particles are moving in the same direction, one with speed 3 m s^{-1} and the other with speed 2 m s^{-1}.

   (a) Draw a diagram showing the particles and their velocities before and after the collision.

   (b) Find the ratio $m_1:m_2$.   (OCR)

7 Three particles A, B and C have masses 0.2 kg, m kg and 0.3 kg respectively. The particles are free to move on a smooth horizontal table. Initially the particles lie in a straight line, with B and C at rest and A moving directly towards B with speed $u\text{ m s}^{-1}$. After A's collision with B, the speed of A is $\frac{1}{2}u\text{ m s}^{-1}$ in the same direction as before. When B collides with C, the particles B and C coalesce and begin to move with speed $\frac{1}{4}u\text{ m s}^{-1}$. Find the value of m, and find also, in terms of u, the speed of B before it collides with C.   (OCR)

8 (a) Two punts A and B together with their passengers and equipment are of equal mass 930 kg. They are drifting slowly past each other with speeds $p\text{ m s}^{-1}$ and $q\text{ m s}^{-1}$ in opposite directions. As they draw alongside each other, one of A's passengers, of mass 70 kg, steps across to punt B, the speed and direction of punt A remaining unchanged. Show that the speed of punt B is reduced to $r\text{ m s}^{-1}$ where $r = \frac{1}{100}(93q - 7p)$.

   (b) Before the punts pass each other completely the same passenger steps back to punt A. This time the speed and direction of B remain unchanged. Find the speed, $v\text{ m s}^{-1}$, of punt A after the second change in terms of p and r, and show that $v = \frac{1}{100}(93p - 7q)$.

   (c) By considering the total momentum of the system, explain why, if the punts have equal speeds before the incident, then they also have equal speeds afterwards. Verify that your earlier answers confirm this.   (OCR)

9

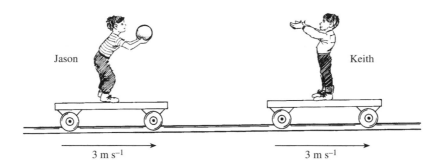

Two boys, Jason and Keith, are travelling on small trucks which are both coasting at 3 m s^{-1} in the same direction along a straight horizontal track. Each boy and the truck he is standing on have a total mass of 120 kg. Jason, on the trailing truck, has a medicine ball of additional mass 5 kg, which he is going to throw to Keith. The trucks are taken to have small frictionless wheels of negligible mass and air resistance is neglected.

(a) Find the total momentum of Jason, his truck and the medicine ball.

(b) Jason throws the ball forwards so that it travels through the air with a horizontal component of 9 m s^{-1} towards Keith. Find the velocity of Jason after he has thrown the ball.

(c) Keith catches the ball. Find out how much faster than Jason he is travelling after he has caught it. (OCR)

9 Combining and splitting forces

This chapter deals with force as an example of a vector quantity, and shows how forces may be combined or taken apart. When you have completed it, you should

- understand the terms 'resultant' and 'component'
- be able to find the resultant of two or more forces
- be able to find the components of a force in two given directions
- appreciate that when a force is split into perpendicular components their magnitudes are equal to the resolved parts of the force in the given directions
- be familiar with the notation of vector addition and with the representation of forces by column vectors or in terms of basic unit vectors.

9.1 Combining forces geometrically

You have now met a number of different mechanics concepts, such as displacement, velocity, acceleration, momentum, force and impulse. What these all have in common is that to describe them you have to give both a magnitude and a direction. They are all examples of **vector quantities**.

Contrast this with mass, which is completely described by its magnitude, and which has no direction associated with it. Mass is an example of a **scalar quantity**.

When you want to show that a symbol stands for a vector quantity, it is usual to write it with a wavy line under the letter. Thus, a force of 10 N on a bearing of 20° might be denoted by the symbol $\underset{\sim}{P}$. In print, in place of the wavy line, the symbol is written in bold, as **P**.

You are already used to showing vector quantities in diagrams as arrows. This is fine for indicating the direction, but you also need a way of showing the magnitude. A simple way of doing this is with the length of the arrow. Choose a scale, such as 1 centimetre to 5 newtons; then the force **P** would be represented by an arrow of length 2 cm pointing on a bearing of 20°, as in Fig. 9.1. Another force, **Q**, of 15 N on a bearing of 80°, would be represented by an arrow of length 3 cm. Now suppose that **P** and **Q** act

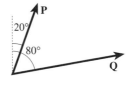

Fig. 9.1

on a particle at the same time. In which direction will the particle accelerate?

To answer this, you want to find a single force which has the same effect on the particle as **P** and **Q** together. This is done by taking the two arrows representing the forces, and placing them so that the head of **P** coincides with the tail of **Q**, as in Fig. 9.2. Then join the tail of **P** to the head of **Q** with a third arrow. This arrow then represents (on the same scale) the single force **R** which has the same effect as **P** and **Q** together. The force **R** is called the **resultant** of **P** and **Q**.

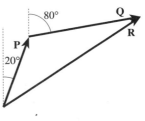

Fig. 9.2

If you draw this to scale, you will find that the length of the third arrow is about 4.4 cm, and that it makes an angle of about 37° with the **P** arrow. Now 4.4 cm represents 4.4×5 N, or 22 N. So the resultant of **P** and **Q** is a force of magnitude 22 N on a bearing of 57°.

To see why this works, look at Fig. 9.3. The lines *AB*, *BC* and *AC* correspond to the three arrows in Fig. 9.2. Draw a line *AL* in any direction you like, and draw *BM* and *CN* perpendicular to *AL*, and *BK* parallel to AL. Then you can see that

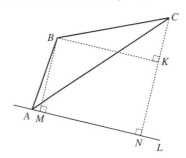

$$AN = AM + MN = AM + BK.$$

Fig. 9.3

Now *AB*, which has length 2 cm, represents the force **P**, of magnitude 10 newtons. So *AM*, of length $2\cos\angle BAL$ cm, represents a force of magnitude $10\cos\angle BAL$ newtons. You will recognise this as the resolved part of **P** in the direction *AL*. In just the same way, *BK* and *AN* represent the resolved parts of **Q** and **R** in the direction *AL*. So the equation $AM + BK = AN$ shows that the effect of **P** and **Q** (taken together) in the direction *AL* is equal to the effect of **R** in that direction.

Since *AL* was drawn in any direction you like, the same argument shows that the effect of **P** and **Q** together in any direction is the same as the effect of **R** in that direction.

> **The triangle law for combining forces.** If two forces **P** and **Q** are represented by arrows (on some scale) and the arrow representing **R** is obtained from these as in Fig. 9.2, then the single force **R** has exactly the same effect on a particle as the two forces **P** and **Q** acting together.

A figure like Fig. 9.2 is called a **force diagram**.

To find **R** by calculation rather than by scale drawing, you have to use trigonometry. In that case you do not need to choose a scale; you can simply use the magnitudes of the forces as if they were the lengths of the sides of the triangle.

Example 9.1.1
Find the resultant **R** of the two forces **P** and **Q** in Fig. 9.1 by calculation.

It is convenient to use the letters *P*, *Q* and *R*, printed in italic but not bold, to stand for the magnitudes of **P**, **Q** and **R**. (In handwriting, you would use *P*, *Q* and *R* without a wavy line underneath.) In Fig. 9.4 these are used as the lengths of the sides of a triangle *XYZ*, so that $XY = 10$, $YZ = 15$ and $XZ = R$. Also the angle between the directions of **P** and **Q** is $80° - 20° = 60°$, so $\angle XYZ = 180° - 60° = 120°$.

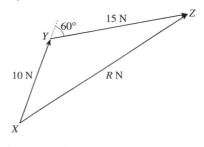

Fig. 9.4

Using the cosine rule,

$$R^2 = 10^2 + 15^2 - 2 \times 10 \times 15 \times \cos 120°$$
$$= 100 + 225 - 300 \times (-0.5)$$
$$= 475, \quad \text{so} \quad R = \sqrt{475} = 21.79\ldots.$$

To find the direction of **R**, you can use the sine rule to calculate $\angle YXZ$.

$$\frac{15}{\sin \angle YXZ} = \frac{R}{\sin 120°} \quad \text{gives} \quad \sin \angle YXZ = \frac{15 \sin 120°}{21.79\ldots},$$

so $\sin \angle YXZ = 0.596\ldots$,   and $\angle YXZ = 36.58\ldots°$.

(Alternatively you could use the cosine rule a second time, in the form $15^2 = 10^2 + R^2 - 2 \times 10 \times R \times \cos \angle YXZ$.)

The resultant is therefore about 22 N on a bearing of approximately $20° + 37°$, which is $57°$.

An important special case is when two forces **P** and **Q** are at right angles to each other. The force diagram then takes the form of Fig. 9.5. From this you can calculate $R = \sqrt{P^2 + Q^2}$ and $\tan \angle YXZ = \dfrac{Q}{P}$.

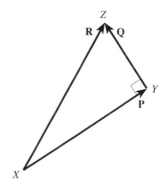

> The resultant of two forces with magnitudes P and Q in perpendicular directions is a force of magnitude $\sqrt{P^2 + Q^2}$ which makes an angle $\tan^{-1}\dfrac{Q}{P}$ with the direction of the force P.

Fig. 9.5

This calculation is easy if your calculator has a rectangular–polar conversion key. Enter the values of P and Q, and you can read off the magnitude of the resultant and the angle.

9.2 Splitting a force into components

Suppose that you are trying to shift a heavy object but don't have the strength to do it by yourself. You get a friend to help, and hope that your combined efforts will produce the resultant force needed. How much force will you each have to exert?

This is the reverse of the problem in Section 9.1. You know **R**, and you want to find **P** and **Q**. The forces **P** and **Q** are called **components** of **R**.

If you know the directions in which these components act, it is easy to construct the force diagram in reverse. Draw the arrow to represent **R** on the chosen scale, and then draw lines through the tail and head of that arrow, one in each of the given directions, far enough so that they intersect. Then insert arrowheads on the two lines so that they form two vectors which combine to give **R**.

Again you can do the calculation using trigonometry. You know all the angles of the triangle and the magnitude of one side, so you can use the sine rule to find the other two sides.

Example 9.2.1

Two people are pushing a piano across a stage. This needs a force of 240 N. One person pushes at $20°$ to the left of the desired direction of motion, the other pushes at $30°$ to the right of it. How hard must each person push?

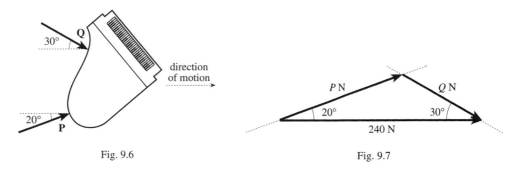

Fig. 9.6   Fig. 9.7

Fig. 9.6 illustrates the actual situation, and Fig. 9.7 is the triangle construction for calculating the forces. Two of the angles of the triangle are $20°$ and $30°$, so the third angle is $130°$. By the sine rule,

$$\frac{P}{\sin 30°} = \frac{Q}{\sin 20°} = \frac{240}{\sin 130°}.$$

This gives $P = \dfrac{240 \sin 30°}{\sin 130°} = 156.6...$ and $Q = \dfrac{240 \sin 20°}{\sin 130°} = 107.1....$

The two people must push with forces of about 157 N and 107 N respectively.

Example 9.2.2

A ship is towed along a narrow channel by cables attached to two tugs. The more powerful tug produces a force of 800 kN; its cable is at $10°$ to the direction of the channel. The other tug is to produce as small a force as possible. What should be the direction of the second tug's cable, and how large is the net forward force on the ship?

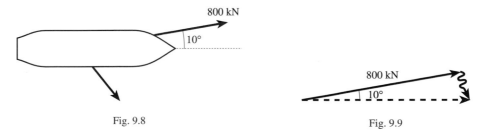

Fig. 9.8   Fig. 9.9

Fig. 9.8 illustrates the ship and the two cables, and Fig. 9.9 is the beginning of the construction of the force diagram. The arrow representing the force in the second cable is drawn with a wavy line, since its direction is unknown. But the arrow representing the resultant force has to lie along the broken line, parallel to the direction of the channel.

For the force in the second cable to be as small as possible, it must be drawn perpendicular to the direction of the channel. The triangle can then be completed as in Fig. 9.10. From this you can calculate the magnitude of the resultant; it is $800\cos 10°$ kN, or $787.8\dots$ kN.

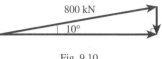

Fig. 9.10

The second tug's cable should be at right angles to the direction of the channel, and the net forward force on the ship is then about 788 kN.

An important special case is when a force is split into two components in perpendicular directions. This is illustrated in Fig. 9.11. If the directions make angles of $A°$ and $(90-A)°$ with the resultant force $\mathbf{R}$, then the magnitudes of the two components are $R\cos A°$ and $R\sin A°$, which is $R\cos(90-A)°$.

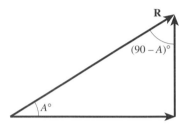

Notice that these expressions are the same as the resolved parts of the force in the two directions. This is an important result.

Fig. 9.11

If a force is split into components in two perpendicular directions, the magnitude of each component is the resolved part of the force in that direction.

When you read mechanics books or articles, you will notice that authors sometimes use the word 'component' instead of the more correct 'resolved part'. Strictly, a phrase like 'the vertical component of $\mathbf{R}$' shouldn't be used without specifying the direction of the other component. But if you do come across it, you should assume that the other component is at right angles (in this case, horizontal), in which case the words 'component' and 'resolved part' are interchangeable.

You can find perpendicular components of a force very quickly if your calculator has a polar–rectangular conversion key. Simply enter the values of R and the angle A, and you can read off the magnitudes of the two components.

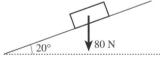

Fig. 9.12

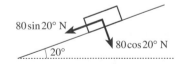

Fig. 9.13

In solving problems it is sometimes helpful to show two perpendicular components of a force separately on a diagram, rather than just the single force. For example, if you are dealing with an object of weight 80 N on a slope inclined at $20°$ to the horizontal, you could replace the weight (Fig. 9.12) by two components (Fig. 9.13), of $80\cos 20°$ N perpendicular to the slope and $80\sin 20°$ N down the slope. These two figures are precisely equivalent ways of showing the same information.

Exercise 9A

1 Use scale drawing to find the resultant of the forces P and Q in the following cases. Confirm your answer in each case by calculation.

(a) P has magnitude 15 N and bearing $25°$, Q has magnitude 10 N and bearing $75°$.

(b) P has magnitude 20 N and bearing $30°$, Q has magnitude 15 N and bearing $115°$.

(c) P has magnitude 25 N and bearing $45°$, Q has magnitude 20 N and bearing $200°$.

(d) P has magnitude 10 N and bearing $65°$, Q has magnitude 5 N and bearing $310°$.

2 A car is being pushed by two people. The magnitude and direction of the horizontal force exerted by each is shown in the diagram. Find the resultant of the two forces.

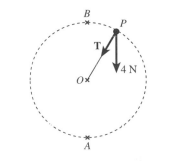

3 A particle P of weight 4 N is attached to one end of a light inextensible string. The other end of the string is attached to a fixed point O. With the string taut P travels in a circular path in a vertical plane. The string exerts a force **T** on the particle in the direction PO as shown in the diagram. The resultant of **T** and the weight of P is denoted by **R**.

(a) The magnitude of **T** is 28 N when P is at A, the lowest point of the circular path. State the direction of **R** when P is in this position, and find its magnitude.

(b) The magnitude of **T** is 4 N when P is at B, the highest point of the circular path. State the direction of **R** when P is in this position, and find its magnitude.

(c) The magnitude of **T** is 16 N when OP is horizontal. Find the magnitude and direction of **R**.

4 Use scale drawing to find the magnitude of the resultant of the forces **P** and **Q** in the following cases. Confirm your answer in each case by calculation.

(a) **P** has magnitude 20 N and bearing $30°$, **Q** has bearing $65°$ and the resultant has bearing $45°$.

(b) **P** has magnitude 25 N and bearing $35°$, **Q** has bearing $125°$ and the resultant has bearing $60°$.

(c) **P** has magnitude 15 N and bearing $50°$, **Q** has bearing $210°$ and the resultant has bearing $100°$.

(d) **P** has magnitude 30 N and bearing $75°$, **Q** has bearing $330°$ and the resultant has bearing $35°$.

5

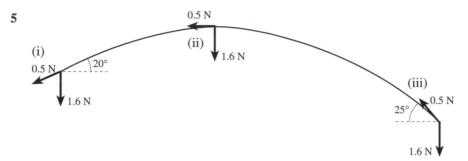

A cricket ball has weight 1.6 N. At any instant between being struck by the bat and reaching the ground the ball is subject to a resistive force of constant magnitude 0.5 N. The diagram shows the directions in which it acts

(i)   immediately after leaving the bat,

(ii) at the highest point of its flight,

(iii) immediately before reaching the ground.

The resultant of the resistive force and the weight of the cricket ball is denoted by **R**. Find the magnitude and direction of **R** in each of the three cases.

Assuming that the resistive force always acts in a direction opposite to that in which the cricket ball is moving, state at which stage of the flight

(a) the magnitude of the resultant is greatest,

(b) the angle between the resultant and the vertical is greatest.

6 A child has weight 450 N. Whilst on a fairground ride the child is subject to a force **P** acting at 35° to the upward vertical, as shown in the diagram. Given that the resultant of **P** and the child's weight acts horizontally,

(a) find the magnitude of this resultant,

(b) state the direction of the child's acceleration,

(c) find the magnitude of the child's acceleration.

7 A package of weight 6 N slides down a smooth chute which is inclined at 50° to the horizontal. The chute exerts a force **C** on the package, which acts in a direction at right angles to the chute, as shown in the diagram. Given that the resultant of **C** and the weight of the package acts in a direction down the chute, find

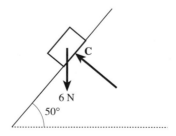

(a) the magnitude of this resultant,

(b) the magnitude of the acceleration of the package.

8 Horizontal forces **P** and **Q** act on a particle of mass 0.8 kg which is free to move on a horizontal plane. **P** has magnitude 0.5 N and bearing 020°, and **Q** has magnitude 0.7 N and bearing 100°. Find the distance travelled by the particle while its speed increases from rest to 4 m s^{-1}.

9 Use scale drawing to find the magnitude of the resultant of the forces **P** and **Q** in the following cases. Confirm your answer in each case by calculation.

(a) **P** has magnitude 15 N and bearing 35°, **Q** has magnitude 20 N and the resultant has bearing 50°.

(b) **P** has magnitude 20 N and bearing 40°, **Q** has magnitude 25 N and the resultant has bearing 75°.

(c) **P** has magnitude 10 N and bearing 55°, **Q** has magnitude 15 N and the resultant has bearing 110°.

(d) **P** has magnitude 25 N and bearing 80°, **Q** has magnitude 30 N and the resultant has bearing 40°.

10 A rock-climber has weight 550 N. A rope attached to her waist-belt passes through a ring which is fixed at a point higher up the cliff. She loses her foothold and starts to move in a direction at 20° to the horizontal. The tension in the rope at this instant is 560 N. Calculate the angle that the rope makes with the vertical.

11 Find the magnitudes of the components **P** and **Q** of the force **R** in the following cases.

(a) **R** has magnitude 20 N due north, **P** and **Q** have bearings 40° and 320°.

(b) **R** has magnitude 25 N due east, **P** and **Q** have bearings 110° and 310°.

(c) **R** has magnitude 30 N due south, **P** and **Q** have bearings 75° and 225°.

(d) **R** has magnitude 35 N due west, **P** and **Q** have bearings 220° and 300°.

12 A force **F** acts in an easterly direction. It has components **P** and **Q**; **P** is known and the magnitude of **Q** is to be as small as possible. Describe the component **Q** when

(a) **P** has magnitude 20 N and bearing 50°,

(b) **P** has magnitude 20 N and bearing 120°.

13 An object can slide on a path inclined at 15° to the horizontal. It is acted on by a force of magnitude 50 N, acting at an angle of 5° to the upward vertical, as shown in the diagram. Find the components of the force

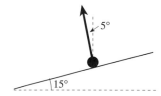

(a) in directions parallel to and at right angles to the path,

(b) in horizontal and vertical directions,

(c) in directions parallel to the path and horizontally,

(d) in directions at right angles to the path and horizontally,

(e) in directions parallel to the path and vertically,

(f) in directions at right angles to the path and vertically.

14

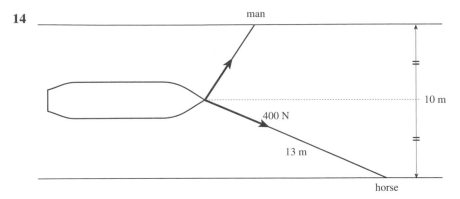

A barge moves in a straight line parallel to and midway between the banks of a canal of width 10 m. A horse on one bank and a man on the other bank pull the barge with taut horizontal tow-ropes. The length of the tow-rope pulled by the horse is 13 m and the tension in it is 400 N, as shown in the diagram. Assuming the resultant of the two tensions is in the direction of motion of the barge, state the direction in which the man must pull to exert the least effort. Find the corresponding tension.

15   A particle of mass 0.2 kg moves in a straight line AB on a horizontal surface, under the influence of horizontal forces $\mathbf{P}$ and $\mathbf{Q}$. The direction of $\mathbf{P}$ makes an angle of 30° with AB. The distance AB is 1.5 m and the speed of the particle is $1\,\text{m s}^{-1}$ at A and $2\,\text{m s}^{-1}$ at B. If the magnitude of $\mathbf{Q}$ is as small as possible, find the magnitude of $\mathbf{P}$.

9.3   Combining forces by perpendicular components

The process of splitting and combining forces in perpendicular directions suggests another method of calculating the resultant of two or more forces.

> **Step 1**   Choose two directions at right angles.
>
> **Step 2**   Split each force into components in these directions.
>
> **Step 3**   For each direction, find the sum of the components you have calculated.
>
> **Step 4**   Find the resultant of the two sums.

Example 9.3.1
Use this procedure to calculate the resultant of $\mathbf{P}$ and $\mathbf{Q}$ in Fig. 9.1 (page 126).

The solution shows the procedure in use with two different choices of directions.

Choice 1   Choose the directions to be north and east, as shown in Fig. 9.14. The calculation is set out in Table 9.15; the first two lines of figures correspond to Step 2, and the third line is Step 3.

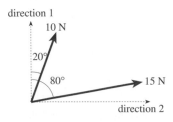

Fig. 9.14

Force	Component in	
	direction 1 (north)	direction 2 (east)
P	$10\cos 20° = 9.39\ldots$	$10\sin 20° = 3.42\ldots$
Q	$15\cos 80° = 2.60\ldots$	$15\sin 80° = 14.77\ldots$
R	$12.00\ldots$	$18.19\ldots$

Table 9.15

The resultant of $12.00\ldots$ N north and $18.19\ldots$ N east is a force of magnitude

$\sqrt{12.00\ldots^2 + 18.19\ldots^2}$ N, or 22 N to

the nearest whole number. It acts at an

angle $\tan^{-1}\dfrac{18.19\ldots}{12.00\ldots}$, or $57°$ to the

nearest degree, to the north direction.

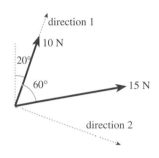

Fig. 9.16

Choice 2 The calculation is simpler if you choose one of the directions to be parallel to one of the forces, say **P**. This is shown in Fig. 9.16, and the calculation is set out in Table 9.17.

Force	Component in	
	direction 1 (∥ to **P**)	direction 2 (⊥ to **P**)
P	10	0
Q	$15\cos 60° = 7.5$	$15\sin 60° = 12.99\ldots$
R	17.5	$12.99\ldots$

Table 9.17

The resultant of 17.5 N parallel to **P** and $12.99\ldots$ N perpendicular to **P** is a force of

magnitude $\sqrt{17.5^2 + 12.99\ldots^2}$ N, or 22 N, at an angle $\tan^{-1}\dfrac{12.99\ldots}{17.5}$, or $37°$, to the

direction of **P** (both to the nearest whole number). So the bearing is $(20 + 37)° = 57°$.

With this method you need to take care when calculating the direction of the resultant. Using $\tan^{-1}$ to find the angle leaves you with two possible ways in which the resultant could point. If the components of **R** in directions 1 and 2 are denoted by R_1 and R_2, then the angle which the resultant makes with direction 1 could be either $\tan^{-1}\dfrac{R_2}{R_1}$ or $\tan^{-1}\dfrac{R_2}{R_1} \pm 180°$.

Draw for yourself diagrams with the four possible sign combinations:

$$R_1 > 0, R_2 > 0; \quad R_1 > 0, R_2 < 0; \quad R_1 < 0, R_2 > 0; \quad R_1 < 0, R_2 < 0.$$

You will see that in the first two cases the resultant makes an acute angle with direction 1.

The angle is therefore given by $\tan^{-1}\dfrac{R_2}{R_1}$, since by definition the angle $\tan^{-1}x$ lies between $-90°$ and $90°$. But in the last two cases the resultant makes an obtuse angle with direction 1, so the angle is $\tan^{-1}\dfrac{R_2}{R_1}\pm180°$.

The rule is therefore that if $R_1>0$ (as it is in Example 9.3.1), the angle is $\tan^{-1}\dfrac{R_2}{R_1}$; but if $R_1<0$ you have to add or subtract $180°$.

It is not worthwhile remembering this rule. In a numerical example it is easy to check with a sketch whether you have chosen the correct angle. But it is important to remember that you have to make the decision.

The advantage of the component method is greatest when you want to find the resultant of several forces. The next example solves such a problem by scale drawing and by the component method.

Example 9.3.2
The following four forces act on a particle (see Fig. 9.18). Find their resultant $\mathbf{V}$.

P   6 N in the x-direction
Q   8 N at $50°$ to the x-direction
S   12 N in the negative y-direction
U   10 N at $160°$ to the x-direction

Method 1   The force diagram is drawn in Fig. 9.19 on a scale of 1 cm to 4 N. It contains a chain of four arrows, **P**, **Q**, **S** and **U**. The resultant **V** is represented by the arrow from the tail of **P** to the head of **U**.

To see why, draw in the broken arrows **R** and **T**. **R** is the resultant of **P** and **Q**. **T** is the resultant of **R** and **S**; that is, of **P**, **Q** and **S**. **V** is the resultant of **T** and **U**; that is, of **P**, **Q**, **S** and **U**.

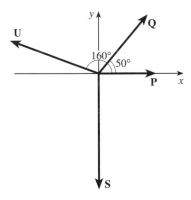

Fig. 9.18

By measurement the arrow labelled **V** has length 0.75 cm and is at an angle of $55°$ below the x-axis. So the resultant is about 3 N and at an angle of $-55°$ to the x-axis.

Method 2   Table 9.20 shows the components of the forces and of their resultant.

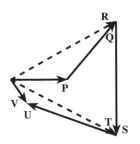

Fig. 9.19

Force	Component in	
	x-direction	y-direction
P	6	0
Q	$8\cos 50° = 5.14...$	$8\sin 50° = 6.12...$
S	0	−12
U	$10\cos 160° = -9.39...$	$10\sin 160° = 3.42...$
R	1.74...	−2.45...

Table 9.20

The resultant of $1.74...$ N in the x-direction and $-2.45...$ N in the y-direction has magnitude $\sqrt{1.74...^2 + (-2.45...)^2}$ N, or 3.01 N, and makes an angle $\tan^{-1}\dfrac{-2.45...}{1.74...}$, or $-55°$, with the x-axis (both values to the nearest whole number).

In solving this example, the first method is fine, but you will often want greater accuracy than you can achieve with scale drawing. You don't need to include in the diagram the intermediate resultant forces **R** and **T**. The figure formed by **P**, **Q**, **S**, **U** and the resultant **V** is called a **force polygon**.

However, if you wanted to calculate the resultant accurately with this method you would have to use the sine and cosine rules in three triangles, one after the other. This would be very laborious. The second method, using components, is the only sensible way to find the resultant by calculation when there are forces in more than two directions.

9.4 Using algebraic notation

The process of finding a resultant **R** of two forces **P** and **Q** is called **vector addition**, and is expressed by the equation $\mathbf{R} = \mathbf{P} + \mathbf{Q}$. This is of course a different operation from addition of numbers, though there are many similarities between the two. Notice that the magnitude of the resultant is not the sum of the magnitudes of the components. For instance, in Example 9.1.1 (working in newtons) $P = 10$ and $Q = 15$, but $R = 21.79...$, not 25.

If you use the component method for finding the resultant, the most obvious perpendicular directions to take are those of the x- and y-axes, as in Method 2 of Example 9.3.2. In that case, it is usual to represent a force as a column of two numbers, called a **column vector**. A force with components X in the x-direction and Y in the y-direction is denoted by $\begin{pmatrix} X \\ Y \end{pmatrix}$.

Putting these two ideas together, you could write out the solution in Method 2 of Example 9.3.2 in algebraic form.

$$\mathbf{V} = \mathbf{P} + \mathbf{Q} + \mathbf{S} + \mathbf{U} = \begin{pmatrix} 6 \\ 0 \end{pmatrix} + \begin{pmatrix} 8\cos 50° \\ 8\sin 50° \end{pmatrix} + \begin{pmatrix} 0 \\ -12 \end{pmatrix} + \begin{pmatrix} 10\cos 160° \\ 10\sin 160° \end{pmatrix}$$

$$= \begin{pmatrix} 6 \\ 0 \end{pmatrix} + \begin{pmatrix} 5.14... \\ 6.12... \end{pmatrix} + \begin{pmatrix} 0 \\ -12 \end{pmatrix} + \begin{pmatrix} -9.39... \\ 3.42... \end{pmatrix}$$

$$= \begin{pmatrix} 6 + 5.14... + 0 + (-9.39...) \\ 0 + 6.12... + (-12) + 3.42... \end{pmatrix} = \begin{pmatrix} 1.75 \\ -2.45 \end{pmatrix}, \text{ to 3 significant figures.}$$

There is nothing essentially new here that is not in Table 9.20. You may use whichever layout you prefer. However, more advanced mechanics uses vector operations other than addition. The advantages of using column vector notation then become apparent. So you may like to get some practice in using it now in simple applications.

9.5 Unit vectors

Yet another way of writing forces in component form is to introduce the vectors $\mathbf{i}$ and $\mathbf{j}$, which are vectors of magnitude 1 in the x- and y-directions. That is, $\mathbf{i}$ is the column vector $\begin{pmatrix} 1 \\ 0 \end{pmatrix}$, and $\mathbf{j}$ is $\begin{pmatrix} 0 \\ 1 \end{pmatrix}$.

These vectors do not have units, but they can be multiplied by quantities which do have units. For example, a force of 6 N in the x-direction would be denoted by $6\mathbf{i}$ N. A force with components X N in the x-direction and Y N in the y-direction is written $(X\mathbf{i} + Y\mathbf{j})$ N.

In unit vector notation, working in newtons, Method 2 of Example 9.3.2 would be written

$$\begin{aligned} \mathbf{V} &= (6\mathbf{i}) + (5.14\ldots\mathbf{i} + 6.12\ldots\mathbf{j}) + (-12\mathbf{j}) + (-9.39\ldots\mathbf{i} + 3.42\ldots\mathbf{j}) \\ &= (6 + 5.14\ldots - 9.39\ldots)\mathbf{i} + (6.12\ldots - 12 + 3.42\ldots)\mathbf{j} \\ &= 1.75\mathbf{i} - 2.45\mathbf{j}, \text{ to 3 significant figures.} \end{aligned}$$

Again, the only thing that is new is the notation itself. The mechanics ideas are just the same as in Table 9.20 and in Section 9.4.

Example 9.5.1
Describe the forces $-3\mathbf{i}$ N, $5\mathbf{j}$ N and $(6\mathbf{i} - 8\mathbf{j})$ N, and their resultant. Draw the corresponding force diagram, and rewrite the calculation in column-vector notation.

$-3\mathbf{i}$ N is a force of 3 N in the negative x-direction.

$5\mathbf{j}$ N is a force of 5 N in the positive y-direction.

$(6\mathbf{i} - 8\mathbf{j})$ N is a force of magnitude $\sqrt{6^2 + (-8)^2}$, or 10 N, at an angle $\tan^{-1}\frac{-8}{6}$, or $-53°$ (to the nearest degree), with the x-axis.

The resultant is

$$(-3\mathbf{i}) + (5\mathbf{j}) + (6\mathbf{i} - 8\mathbf{j}) = (-3 + 6)\mathbf{i} + (5 - 8)\mathbf{j}$$
$$= 3\mathbf{i} - 3\mathbf{j}.$$

This is a force of magnitude $\sqrt{3^2 + (-3)^2}$ N, which is $\sqrt{18}$ N, or $3\sqrt{2}$ N, and it makes an angle $\tan^{-1}(-1)$, or $-45°$, with the x-axis. The force diagram is shown in Fig. 9.21.

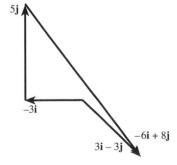

Fig. 9.21

In column-vector notation the corresponding calculation is

$$\begin{pmatrix} -3 \\ 0 \end{pmatrix} + \begin{pmatrix} 0 \\ 5 \end{pmatrix} + \begin{pmatrix} 6 \\ -8 \end{pmatrix} = \begin{pmatrix} -3 + 0 + 6 \\ 0 + 5 - 8 \end{pmatrix} = \begin{pmatrix} 3 \\ -3 \end{pmatrix}.$$

████████████████   **Exercise 9B**   ████████████████

1 Rework Exercise 9A Question 1 using the splitting and combining method, taking components in directions north and east.

2 Repeat Question 1, taking components parallel to and at right angles to **P**.

3 Rework Exercise 9A Question 2 using the splitting and combining method, taking components parallel and at right angles to the direction in which the car is facing.

4 Find the magnitude and direction of the resultant of the four forces $\begin{pmatrix} -5 \\ 12 \end{pmatrix}$ N, $\begin{pmatrix} -18 \\ -8 \end{pmatrix}$ N, $\begin{pmatrix} 4 \\ 9 \end{pmatrix}$ N and $\begin{pmatrix} 4 \\ -5 \end{pmatrix}$ N.

5 Express each of the three forces shown in the diagram in column-vector form. Find the resultant of the three forces in column-vector form, and hence find the magnitude and direction of the resultant.

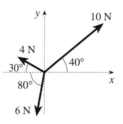

6 The diagram represents a model aircraft of mass 2 kg. Its engine produces a force of $\begin{pmatrix} 24 \\ 7 \end{pmatrix}$ N, and the force of the air on its wings is $\begin{pmatrix} -19.2 \\ 14.4 \end{pmatrix}$ N.

Find the magnitude and direction of the acceleration of the aircraft.

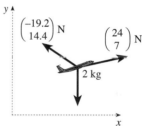

7 In the first diagram, the resultant of the four forces is $\begin{pmatrix} 7 \\ 24 \end{pmatrix}$ N. By expressing this in the notation of vector addition, find the values of X and Y.

New directions are now chosen parallel and perpendicular to the resultant force, as shown in the second diagram. Rewrite the equation of vector addition in column vectors relative to the new directions, and check that this equation is satisfied by the values of X and Y that you have found.

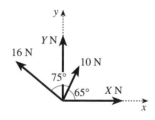

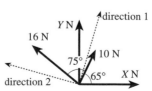

8 A particle of mass 2.6 kg moves in a straight line on a horizontal surface under the influence of horizontal forces $\begin{pmatrix} X \\ 0.2 \end{pmatrix}$ N and $\begin{pmatrix} 0.7 \\ 0.3 \end{pmatrix}$ N. The velocity of the particle increases from 2 m s^{-1} to 3.5 m s^{-1} in 3 seconds. Find the two possible values of X.

9 A particle of weight W N moves up an inclined track under the action of a pull of magnitude P N at $20°$ to the track. The track is at $15°$ to the horizontal. The normal contact force has magnitude C N. Taking axes parallel and perpendicular to the track, find the resultant force on the particle, in terms of W, P and C, in column-vector form.

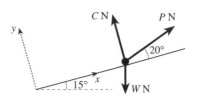

Given that the resultant force is parallel to the track, express C and the magnitude of the resultant force in terms of P and W.

10 Find the magnitude and the direction of the resultant of the three forces $(2\mathbf{i} + 7\mathbf{j})$ N, $(8\mathbf{i} - 5\mathbf{j})$ N and $(-5\mathbf{i} + 10\mathbf{j})$ N.

11 Rewrite the solution to Question 4 using unit vectors $\mathbf{i}$ and $\mathbf{j}$ instead of column vectors.

12 Rewrite the solution to Question 5 using unit vector notation.

13 Rewrite the solution to Question 6 using unit vector notation.

14 A load of weight 285 N is supported by two ropes. They exert on the load tension forces of $(84\mathbf{i} + 288\mathbf{j})$ N and $(-40\mathbf{i} + 30\mathbf{j})$ N, where $\mathbf{i}$ and $\mathbf{j}$ are unit vectors in the horizontal and vertical directions. Find the magnitude of the resultant force on the load, and the angle which its direction makes with each of the ropes.

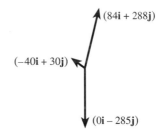

15 Solve Question 8 using unit vectors $\mathbf{i}$ and $\mathbf{j}$ instead of column vectors.

16 A particle of mass m moves in a straight line on a horizontal surface under the influence of horizontal forces $m(2x\mathbf{i} - \mathbf{j})$, $m(\mathbf{i} + x\mathbf{j})$ and $m(x\mathbf{i} + 2x\mathbf{j})$. The particle has an initial velocity of 1.5 m s^{-1}, and travels 7 m in 2 seconds. Find the two possible values of x.

Miscellaneous exercise 9

1 Two forces, of magnitudes 5 N and 7 N, act on a body. The angle between the forces is $55°$. The resultant has magnitude R and acts at an angle $\theta°$ to the 5 N force, as shown in the diagram. Calculate R and θ.   (OCR)

2 Forces of magnitudes 50 N and P N act on a particle in the directions shown in the diagram. The resultant of the two forces is at right angles to the direction of the force of magnitude 50 N. Find P.   (OCR)

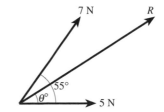

3 Two forces, each of magnitude 5 N, act at the point P, as shown in the diagram. Their resultant also has magnitude 5 N. By drawing a vector triangle to represent the two forces and their resultant, find θ. (OCR)

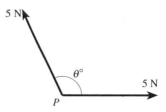

4 Two forces, acting in a vertical plane, have a horizontal resultant of magnitude R newtons. One the forces has magnitude 6 N and acts at an angle $\theta°$ above the horizontal. The other force has magnitude 4 N and acts at an angle of 30° below the horizontal, as shown in the diagram.

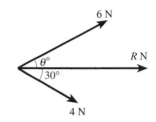

   (a) Find the value of θ.

   (b) Calculate the value of R. (OCR)

5 Two horizontal forces **P** and **Q** act at a point. The force **P** has magnitude 7.6 N and acts due north. The resultant of **P** and **Q** has magnitude 15.4 N and acts due east. Calculate the magnitude and direction of **Q**. (OCR)

6 Two forces of magnitudes 5 N and 6 N act at the point O. The angle between the two forces is $\theta°$. The resultant of the two forces has magnitude 5 N.

   (a) Draw a diagram to represent this information.

   (b) Calculate the value of θ. (OCR)

7 Two forces **P** and **Q** have magnitudes 3 N and 6 N respectively and act at the point O. The angle between **P** and **Q** is acute. The resultant of **P** and **Q** is **R**, and **R** makes an angle of 20° with **Q**, as shown in the diagram. Find, in either order,

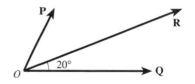

   (a) the angle between **P** and **Q**,

   (b) the magnitude of **R**. (OCR)

8 Each of two forces has magnitude X N, and the resultant of the two forces has magnitude 12 N. When the magnitude of one of the forces is increased by 70%, the magnitude of the resultant of the two forces becomes 21 N. Find X and the angle between the two forces.

9 A force **F** of magnitude 12 N has components **P** and **Q**. The sum of the magnitudes of **P** and **Q** is 18 N. The direction of **Q** is at right angles to **F**. Find the magnitude of **Q**.

10 Forces **X**, **Y** and **Z** have magnitudes 10 N, $5(\sqrt{3}-1)$ N and $5(\sqrt{3}+1)$ N. The forces **Y** and **Z** act in the same direction, as shown in the diagram. The resultant of **X** and **Y** and the resultant of **X** and **Z** have the same magnitude. Find $\theta°$, the angle between **X** and **Y**.

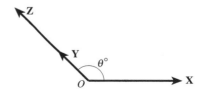

11 A particle of mass $0.7\,\text{kg}$ is free to move on a horizontal surface under the influence of horizontal forces of magnitudes $1\,\text{N}$ and $1.7\,\text{N}$. The particle starts from rest and reaches a speed of $3\,\text{m s}^{-1}$ in a distance of $1.5\,\text{m}$. Find the angle between the directions of the forces.

12 Three constant horizontal forces, with magnitudes and directions as shown in the diagram, act on a small block. Find the magnitude and direction of the resultant of these three forces.

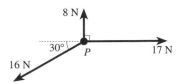

The block is moving on a rough horizontal plane under the action of the three forces. Given that the mass of the block is $2\,\text{kg}$, and that its acceleration has magnitude $0.3\,\text{m s}^{-2}$, calculate the coefficient of friction between the block and the plane.   (OCR)

13 Three forces, with magnitudes and directions as shown in the diagram, act in a horizontal plane at the point A. The resultant of the three forces has magnitude $14\,\text{N}$ and acts in the direction of the force of magnitude X newtons. Find θ and X.

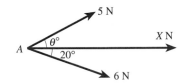

        (OCR)

14 Two loads X and Y, of weights $800\,\text{N}$ and $400\,\text{N}$ respectively, are connected by a rope which passes over a pulley A. The forces acting on X, Y and A are as shown in the diagram. Find the magnitude and direction of the resultant force acting on each of X, Y and A.

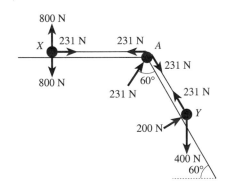

15 A concrete pyramid of weight $300\,\text{N}$ is being lifted vertically upwards. The forces on the pyramid are a pulling force of magnitude $320\,\text{N}$, exerted by a wire which passes over a fixed pulley, and a restraining force of magnitude $F\,\text{N}$ exerted by a rope being pulled by a man. The directions of the forces are as shown in the diagram. The values of F, θ and ϕ vary as the pyramid moves upwards, but the direction of the resultant force is always vertical. Find the value of F and the magnitude of the resultant, stating whether the resultant acts upwards or downwards, when

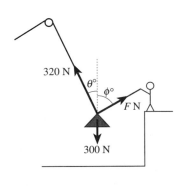

(a) $\theta = 15$ and $\phi = 53$,   (b) $\theta = 19$ and $\phi = 90$,   (c) $\theta = 26$ and $\phi = 127$.

10 Forces in equilibrium

This chapter uses vector ideas to provide an alternative method of calculating the forces on objects in equilibrium. When you have completed it, you should

- understand how the equilibrium of two or three forces can be expressed in vector notation
- be able to represent the equilibrium of three forces with a triangle of forces
- understand how the standard model of friction can be recast in terms of a total contact force and the angle of friction.

10.1 Two forces in equilibrium

Fig. 10.1 shows two people pulling a Christmas cracker. The person on the right pulls with a force **P**, the person on the left with a force **Q**. Until it breaks, the cracker remains at rest. The weight of the cracker is negligible compared with the pulling forces.

Fig. 10.1

The two people are pulling with forces of equal magnitude, so the force diagram for the resultant of **P** and **Q** has the form of Fig. 10.2. Since the tail of **P** coincides with the head of **Q**, the resultant force is zero. This is expressed algebraically by the equation **P** + **Q** = **0**, where **0** denotes the zero vector. Alternatively, you can write **Q** = −**P**, where the symbol −**P** stands for the force with the same magnitude as **P** but in the opposite direction.

Fig. 10.2

10.2 Three forces in equilibrium

Consider the following two problems.

A crate is being unloaded from a ship on to a quay down a ramp inclined at 5° to the horizontal. It is placed on a wheeled trolley, so that friction is negligible. The total mass of the trolley and crate is 80 kg. The crate is held steady by a member of the crew, who supports it with a force at 30° to the horizontal, as shown in Fig. 10.3. How large a force must he exert?

Fig. 10.3

In a military exercise a soldier of mass 80 kg is lowered over a river by a rope from a helicopter. She catches a lifeline which is used to pull her towards the river bank, as

shown in Fig. 10.4. When the rope is at 5°
to the vertical, the lifeline is at 30° to the
horizontal. How large is the tension in the
lifeline?

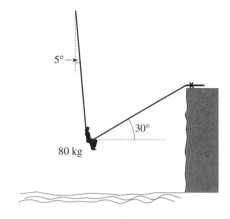

Fig. 10.4

At first sight these appear to be quite different
problems, but you will see from Fig. 10.5 that,
when the crate and the soldier are modelled as
particles acted on by forces, the two models are
identical. It is unimportant that in the first
problem the force **U** is provided by the push
from the crewman's hand and the force **V** is the
normal contact force from the ramp, but that in
the second case **U** and **V** are the tensions in the
lifeline and the helicopter cable. Also, what
matters is not the point at which each force is
applied, but only the line along which it acts,
which in this model must pass through the point
representing the particle. This is called the **line
of action** of the force.

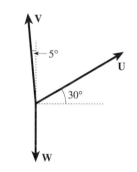

Fig. 10.5

It would be possible to complete the solution by
resolving in two directions, but this is not easy
unless you choose the two directions rather
cleverly. A simpler method is to use vector ideas
and to calculate the forces by trigonometry.

So in both problems you have a weight **W** of
784 N supported by two forces, **U** at 30° to the
horizontal and **V** at 5° to the vertical. The
resultant of **U** and **V** must therefore be equal
and opposite to the weight. Algebraically,

$$\mathbf{U} + \mathbf{V} = -\mathbf{W}, \quad \text{or} \quad \mathbf{U} + \mathbf{V} + \mathbf{W} = \mathbf{0}.$$

This equation is represented by Fig. 10.6. This is
an example of a **triangle of forces**.

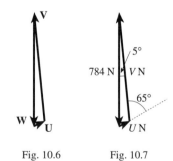

Fig. 10.6   Fig. 10.7

Triangle of forces   If three forces **X**, **Y** and **Z** are in
equilibrium, then the corresponding vectors can be
represented by the sides of a closed triangle in which at each
vertex the head of one vector arrow meets the tail of another.

You can now find the magnitude, U N, of the force **U**, either by scale drawing or by
applying the sine rule to the triangle of forces. From Fig. 10.7, this gives

$$\frac{U}{\sin 5°} = \frac{784}{\sin 115°}, \quad \text{so} \quad U = \frac{784 \sin 5°}{\sin 115°} = 75.3\ldots.$$

So the crewman can steady the crate by pushing with a force of about 75 N, and the tension in the lifeline is also about 75 N.

Example 10.2.1

Three strings are knotted together at one end, and parcels of weights 5 N, 7 N and 9 N are attached to the other ends. The first two strings are placed over smooth horizontal pegs, and the third parcel hangs freely, as shown in Fig. 10.8. The system is in equilibrium. Find the angles which the first two strings make with the vertical between the knot and the pegs.

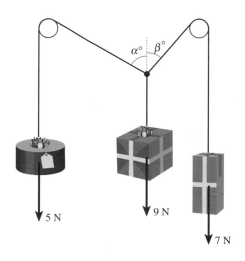

Since the pegs are smooth, the tensions in the strings at the knot are 5 N, 7 N and 9 N as shown in Fig. 10.9, and these forces are in equilibrium. The three vectors therefore form a closed triangle of forces, as in Fig. 10.10.

Fig. 10.8

You can complete the solution either by scale drawing or by trigonometry. If you use scale drawing, begin by drawing the 9 N arrow to your chosen scale, since you know its direction. Then find the third vertex of the triangle as the intersection of arcs with radii proportional to 5 N and 7 N on the same scale.

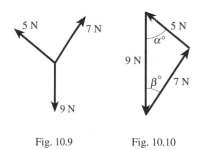

Fig. 10.9   Fig. 10.10

To calculate the angles $\alpha°$ and $\beta°$ which the 5 N and 7 N strings make with the vertical by trigonometry, use the cosine rule in the forms

$$7^2 = 5^2 + 9^2 - 2 \times 5 \times 9 \times \cos \alpha°$$

and $\quad 5^2 = 7^2 + 9^2 - 2 \times 7 \times 9 \times \cos \beta°.$

These equations give $\cos \alpha° = \frac{57}{90}$ and $\cos \beta° = \frac{105}{126}$, so that $\alpha = 50.7\ldots$ and $\beta = 33.5\ldots.$

The 5 N and 7 N strings make angles of about $51°$ and $34°$ with the vertical respectively.

Example 10.2.2
A trough is formed from two rectangular planks at
angles of 30° and 40° to the horizontal, joined
along a horizontal edge. A cylindrical log of
weight 400 N is placed in the trough with its axis
horizontal. Calculate the magnitudes P N and
Q N of the normal contact forces from each plank
on the log
(a) using a triangle of forces,
(b) by resolving.

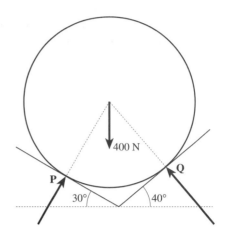

Fig. 10.11 shows the forces on the log. The
log has no tendency to slip, so there is
equilibrium without any frictional force, and
the contact forces act along radii of the log.

Fig. 10.11

(a) The forces **P** and **Q** are at 30° and
40° to the vertical, so the triangle of forces
has the form of Fig. 10.12. By the sine rule,

$$\frac{P}{\sin 40°} = \frac{Q}{\sin 30°} = \frac{400}{\sin 110°},$$

so $P = \dfrac{400 \sin 40°}{\sin 110°} = 273.6\ldots$

and $Q = \dfrac{400 \sin 30°}{\sin 110°} = 212.8\ldots.$

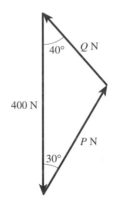

Fig. 10.12

The forces **P** and **Q** have magnitude
274 N and 213 N respectively, correct to 3
significant figures.

(b) If you resolve horizontally and vertically you get two simultaneous equations
for P and Q, with unpleasant coefficients, which are awkward to solve. But you
can get the answers directly by resolving parallel to each of the planks.

Since **P** is at 60° to the horizontal, it is at $(60 - 40)° = 20°$ to the right plank.
The weight is at $(90 - 40)° = 50°$ to the right plank.

$R(\parallel$ to right plank) $P \cos 20° = 400 \cos 50°.$

Since $\cos 20° = \sin 70° = \sin 110°$ and $\cos 50° = \sin 40°$,

$$P = \frac{400 \sin 40°}{\sin 110°}, \text{ as before.}$$

*Check for yourself that resolving parallel to the left plank leads to the same expression
for Q as that found from the triangle of forces.*

The reason why you get simpler equations by resolving parallel to the planks is that, in each case, one of the forces does not come into the equation. For example, **Q** acts at right angles to the right plank, so its resolved part parallel to the right plank is zero. The only unknown force in the equation is therefore P N.

This is a useful general rule.

> If two forces of unknown magnitude act on a particle in equilibrium, they can be found directly by resolving in directions perpendicular to each force.

Notice that in Example 10.2.2 this involves resolving in two directions which are not perpendicular to each other. Although many problems are best solved by resolving in two perpendicular directions, it is sometimes better to use non-perpendicular directions.

The next example uses a geometrical trick: a triangle similar to the triangle of forces is constructed in the diagram.

Example 10.2.3*

A coordinate grid is marked on a vertical wall. Small smooth pegs are driven into the wall at the points $(-3, 11)$ and $(9, 7)$ and a hoop of weight W and radius $\sqrt{130}$ rests on the pegs with its centre at the origin. Find the magnitudes of the contact forces at the pegs in terms of W.

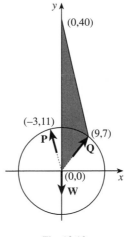

Fig. 10.13

Since the pegs are smooth, contact forces of magnitudes P and Q act along the radii, as shown in Fig. 10.13. Therefore, in the triangle of forces, one arrow must point in the negative y-direction and the other two have gradients $-\frac{11}{3}$ and $\frac{7}{9}$.

If you draw a line with gradient $-\frac{11}{3}$ through the point $(9, 7)$, you can verify that it cuts the y-axis at the point $(0, 40)$. So a triangle with vertices $(0, 0)$, $(9, 7)$ and $(0, 40)$ is similar to the triangle of forces, with sides proportional to P, Q and W.

The lengths of the sides of this triangle are $\sqrt{(-9)^2 + 33^2} = 3\sqrt{130}$, $\sqrt{9^2 + 7^2} = \sqrt{130}$ and 40. Therefore

$$\frac{P}{3\sqrt{130}} = \frac{Q}{\sqrt{130}} = \frac{W}{40},$$

so $P = \frac{3}{40}\sqrt{130}W$ and $Q = \frac{1}{40}\sqrt{130}W$.

Exercise 10A

1 An object is in equilibrium under the action of three horizontal forces **P**, **Q** and **R**. Use a triangle of forces to find the magnitudes of **Q** and **R** respectively in each of the following cases.

  (a) **P** has magnitude 10 N and bearing 90°, **Q** and **R** have bearings 210° and 340° respectively.

  (b) **P** has magnitude 20 N and bearing 20°, **Q** and **R** have bearings 90° and 240° respectively.

Confirm your answers by resolving in directions perpendicular to **R** and to **Q**.

2 A cable car is connected to a cable by two rigid supports which make angles of 75° and 35° with the upward vertical, as shown in the diagram. Find the tensions in the supports when the cable car is stationary and the total weight of the cable car and its passengers is 8000 N.

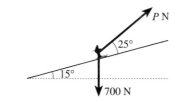

3 An object of mass 5 kg is held at rest on a smooth plane, inclined at an angle of 20°, by a force of magnitude P N acting directly up the plane.

  (a) State the direction of the force exerted by the plane on the object, and find its magnitude.

  (b) Hence state the magnitude and direction of the force exerted by the object on the plane.

  (c) Find the value of P.

4 A skier of weight 700 N is pulled at constant speed up a smooth slope, of inclination 15°, by a force of magnitude P N acting at 25° upwards from the slope, as shown in the diagram. Find the value of P.

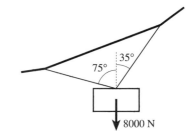

5 A small sign of weight 6 N is suspended by two chains AC and BC, as shown in the diagram.

A and B are attached to fixed points which are 60 cm apart and at the same horizontal level. The lengths of AC and BC are 40 cm and 30 cm. Calculate the tensions in the chains.

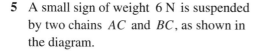
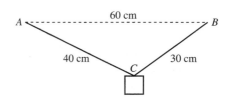

6 Part of the floor of a workshop in which large gun barrels are forged is inclined at $10°$ to the horizontal. This is to facilitate the safe storage of steel ingots. A cylindrical ingot of mass 7000 kg is stored as shown in the diagram. The magnitudes of the forces exerted on the ingot by the wall and the floor are R_W N and R_F N respectively. Find the values of R_W and R_F.

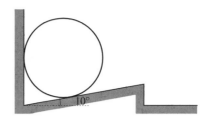

If the sloping part of the floor was inclined at $\alpha°$ $(0 < \alpha < 45)$ instead of at $10°$, show that

(a) $R_W < 68\,600 < R_F$, whatever the value of α,

(b) R_W and R_F both increase with α.

7 A body is in equilibrium under the action of three horizontal forces **P**, **Q** and **R**. Find the angle between the direction of **P** and the direction of **Q**, and the angle between the direction of **P** and the direction of **R**, in each of the following cases.

(a) **P**, **Q** and **R** have magnitudes 16 N, 24 N and 25 N respectively.

(b) **P**, **Q** and **R** have magnitudes 7 N, 20 N and 25 N respectively.

8 A child of weight 300 N is seated on a swing which is supported by the tension in the rope of magnitude 320 N. The child and the swing are held at rest by a restraining force of magnitude 130 N, as shown in the diagram. Find the angles that

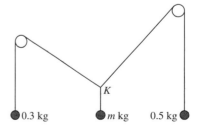

(a) the rope,   (b) the restraining force,

make with the upward vertical.

9 A tanker is being steered at constant speed along a channel by two tugs. The cables from the tugs have tensions of $45\,000$ N and $20\,000$ N and the motion of the tanker is resisted by a drag force of $52\,000$ N, Find the angle between each cable and the direction of motion of the tanker.

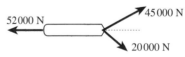

10 The diagram shows three strings, which are tied in a knot K. Two of the strings pass over smooth pulleys and have particles of mass 0.3 kg and 0.5 kg attached to them at the ends opposite to K. The other string has a particle of mass m kg attached to it at the end opposite to K. The system is at rest.

(a) In the case $m = 0.7$, find the angle made by the sloping part of each string with the upward vertical.

(b) Give a reason why $m < 0.8$.

(c) In the case when $m = 0.4$, show that part of one of the strings is horizontal.

(d) If the pulleys were at the same horizontal level, give a reason why $m > 0.4$.

11 A particle of mass m hangs by a thread from a hook. It is pulled aside with the thread at an angle of $\alpha°$ the vertical by a force. In what direction should the force be applied for its magnitude to be as small as possible? Find an expression for its magnitude in this case in terms of m, g and α.

12 A particle is in equilibrium under the action of three horizontal forces $\mathbf{P}$, $\mathbf{Q}$ and $\mathbf{R}$. The magnitudes of $\mathbf{P}$, $\mathbf{Q}$ and $\mathbf{R}$ are $25\,\text{N}$, $Q\,\text{N}$ and $R\,\text{N}$ respectively, and the cosine of the angle between $\mathbf{P}$ and $\mathbf{Q}$ is -0.96. Show that $R^2 = (Q-24)^2 + 7^2$. Hence find

   (a) the least possible value of R,

   (b) the corresponding angle between $\mathbf{Q}$ and $\mathbf{R}$.

13 A hoop of diameter $1.5\,\text{m}$ and weight $11.7\,\text{N}$ hangs on two smooth horizontal pegs P and Q. The forces exerted on the hoop by P and Q have magnitudes $12\,\text{N}$ and $7.5\,\text{N}$ respectively. Find the directions of these forces.

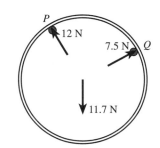

The x- and y-axes are taken to be horizontal and vertical respectively, and the origin O is the centre of the hoop. Find the (x, y) coordinates of P and Q.

14 A barge moves, at constant speed, in a straight line midway between the parallel banks of a canal. The banks are $8\,\text{m}$ apart. A horse on one bank and a man on the other bank exert pulling forces on the barge, through taut horizontal tow-ropes. The length of the tow-rope pulled by the horse is $16.25\,\text{m}$. A horizontal drag force

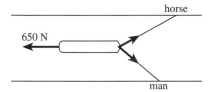

of magnitude $650\,\text{N}$ acts on the barge in a direction opposite to its motion, as shown in the diagram. State the angle between the tow-ropes which minimises the effort exerted by the man. Find the magnitudes of the corresponding pulling forces.

10.3 More forces in equilibrium

There is no difficulty in extending the triangle of forces to situations in which there are more than three forces. If four forces are in equilibrium, then the arrows representing them form a closed quadrilateral, and so on. The problem arises when you want to do calculations with the sides and angles of the quadrilateral, since this usually involves splitting the quadrilateral into two triangles.

This means, in effect, beginning by combining two of the forces into a single force, and then using a triangle of forces. The next section shows how this can be a useful technique in problems involving friction.

10.4*The angle of friction

Whenever you have a frictional force, there is always a normal contact force at right angles to it. The normal force and the friction can therefore be combined to give a resultant called the **total contact force**, as shown in Fig. 10.14.

Fig. 10.14   Fig. 10.15

Fig. 10.15 is the force diagram. The friction and the normal force have magnitudes F and R, and θ is the angle between the total contact force and the normal, so that $\tan\theta = \dfrac{F}{R}$.

This fraction is familiar! One of the properties of the frictional force is that $\dfrac{F}{R} \leqslant \mu$, the coefficient of friction. You can now write this property in the form $\tan\theta \leqslant \mu$, or $\theta \leqslant \tan^{-1}\mu$.

The angle $\tan^{-1}\mu$ is called the **angle of friction**. It is usually denoted by the Greek letter λ (lambda). The friction property can then be restated in terms of the angle λ instead of the coefficient μ.

> When one surface tends to slide over another, the angle between the total contact force and the normal is less than or equal to the angle of friction λ. When friction is limiting, the angle is equal to λ.
>
> The value of λ is $\tan^{-1}\mu$, a constant which depends on the nature and materials of the surfaces.

Replacing the normal reaction and the frictional force by the total contact force reduces the number of forces by one. This often makes it possible to use one of the methods described in the first part of this chapter.

Example 10.4.1   (see Experiment 5.3.2)   *[Safety!]*
Place a book on a table. Slowly tilt the table until the book starts to slide, and measure the angle of inclination of the table to the horizontal when this happens. If this angle is θ, show that the coefficient of friction is equal to $\tan\theta$.

Fig. 10.16 shows the only two forces acting on the book, its weight and the total contact force from the table. If the table is tilted at an angle θ, the weight is at an angle θ to the normal. Since the contact force acts in the direction opposite to the weight, it too makes an angle θ to the normal.

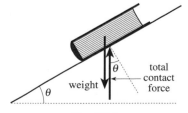

Fig. 10.16

In limiting equilibrium $\theta = \lambda$, so $\tan\theta = \tan\lambda = \mu$.

Example 10.4.2   (see Example 5.5.1)

A block of weight 20 N is at rest on a horizontal surface. When a force of magnitude
12 N is applied to the block at an angle of 30° above the horizontal, it is on the point of
moving. Find the coefficient of friction between the block and the surface.

In Fig. 10.17 the friction and normal reaction are combined as a total contact
force. This reduces the number of forces on the object to three, so equilibrium can
be expressed by a triangle of forces (Fig. 10.18). Since the object is on the point of
moving, friction is limiting, so the contact force is at an angle $\lambda°$ to the vertical.

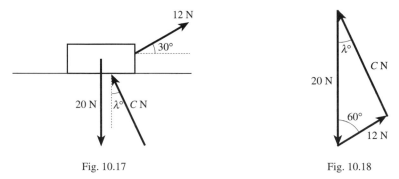

Fig. 10.17   Fig. 10.18

Denote the magnitude of the contact force by C N. By the cosine rule,

$$C^2 = 20^2 + 12^2 - 2 \times 20 \times 12 \times \cos 60° = 400 + 144 - 240 = 304.$$

The sine rule then gives

$$\frac{C}{\sin 60°} = \frac{12}{\sin \lambda°}, \quad \text{so} \quad \sin \lambda° = \frac{12 \sin 60°}{\sqrt{304}}.$$

This gives $\lambda = 36.5\ldots$, so that $\mu = \tan \lambda° = 0.74$, correct to 2 significant figures.

The coefficient of friction between the object and the surface is about 0.74.

Example 10.4.3

A rough path climbs at an angle α to the horizontal. A gardener drags a heavy sack of
weight W up the path at constant speed with a rope inclined at an angle β to the path,
as shown in Fig. 10.19. For what value of β will the tension in the rope be smallest?

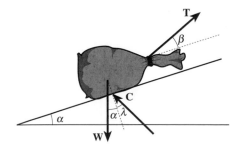

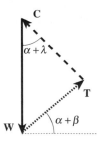

Fig. 10.19   Fig. 10.20

Since the sack is moving, friction is limiting. The contact force **C** is at an angle λ to the normal, so it is at an angle $\alpha + \lambda$ to the vertical. At a steady speed the forces are in equilibrium, so a triangle of forces can be drawn, as in Fig. 10.20.

In this triangle the side representing **W** is completely known. You also know the direction of the side representing **C**, but its length depends on the choice of β. The aim is to make the length of the side representing the tension **T** as small as possible.

This will happen when the angle between **T** and **C** is a right angle. So to minimise the tension in the rope, you should make $\beta = \lambda$. That is, the rope should be at an angle λ to the path.

Exercise 10B*

1 An object of weight 50 N is at rest on a horizontal plane. An upward force of magnitude 20 N is applied to the object in a direction making an angle of 30° with the horizontal, as shown in the diagram. Given that the object is on the point of sliding, find

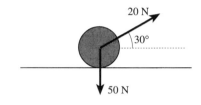

(a) the magnitude of the total contact force between the object and the plane,

(b) the angle of friction,

(c) the coefficient of friction.

2 A crate of mass 100 kg is to be moved from rest along horizontal ground. The angle of friction for the contact between the crate and the ground is 35°. Find the magnitude of the force necessary to just move the crate when this force is

(a) a push applied at 25° downwards from the horizontal,

(b) a pull applied at 25° upwards from the horizontal.

3 A log of weight W rests on horizontal ground. When it is pulled with a force of magnitude F at an angle of $\alpha°$ above the horizontal, the log is on the point of moving. The angle of friction for the contact between the log and the ground is $\gamma°$.

(a) Show that $\dfrac{F}{W} = \dfrac{\sin \gamma°}{\cos(\gamma - \alpha)°}$.

(b) Find the ratio $\dfrac{F}{W}$ when $\gamma = 25$ and $\alpha = 20$.

(c) Show that $\dfrac{F}{W}$ is least when $\alpha = \gamma$.

4   A parcel of mass 6 kg rests on a plane
    inclined at 40° to the horizontal. The parcel
    is held in limiting equilibrium by a force of
    magnitude 15 N acting at 20° upwards from
    the plane, as shown in the diagram. Find

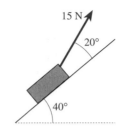

(a) the magnitude of the total contact force,

(b) the direction of the total contact force,

(c) the coefficient of friction between the parcel and the plane.

5   An adjustable inclined plane can be set at any angle to the horizontal between 0 and 90°.
    With the angle of inclination set at 15°, a block of weight 12 N is pulled up the incline at
    constant speed by a force parallel to the plane of magnitude 7 N. Find the direction of the
    total contact force acting on the block. Hence find the angle of inclination of the plane at
    which the block can rest, in the absence of any applied force, whilst on the point of sliding
    down the plane.

6   A ring of mass 2 kg is threaded on a fixed
    horizontal rod. It is pulled by a force of
    magnitude P N at an angle to the rod. The
    ring is on the point of moving along the rod.
    The coefficient of friction between the ring
    and the rod is 0.7. Find

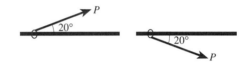

(a) the angle the total contact force makes with the upward vertical,

(b) the value of P when the pulling force acts at an angle of 20° above the horizontal,

(c) the value of P when the pulling force acts at an angle of 20° below the horizontal.

7   The diagram shows a man of weight
    800 N using a power-saw to make a cut
    into a tree-trunk at an angle of 20°
    downwards from the horizontal. The
    magnitude of the force exerted on the man
    and his saw by the tree-trunk, in the
    vertical plane perpendicular to the cut, is
    denoted by P N. The contact force exerted
    on the man by the horizontal ground is
    denoted by **C**.

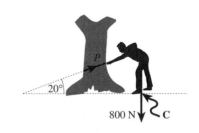

Find the magnitude and direction of **C** when

(a) $P = 200$,   (b) $P = 300$.

In each case, state the magnitude and direction of the force exerted by the man and his saw
on

(i) the tree-trunk,   (ii) the horizontal ground.

Give a reason why the magnitude of the force exerted by the man and his saw on the tree-
trunk cannot exceed $\dfrac{800}{\cos 70°}$ N.

Miscellaneous exercise 10

1   A small smooth ring R of mass 0.1 kg is threaded on a
    light string. The ends of the string are fastened to two
    fixed points A and B. The ring hangs in equilibrium with
    the part AR of the string inclined at $40°$ to the
    horizontal, as shown in the diagram. Show that the part
    RB of the string is also inclined at $40°$ to the
    horizontal, and find the tension in the string.   (OCR)

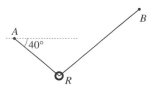

2   A basket of fish of weight 200 N is being unloaded from
    a truck. Two light wires AB and AC are attached to the
    basket at A. Initially, the wire AB is at an angle of $30°$
    to the vertical and the wire AC is horizontal. The basket
    is in equilibrium. The tensions in the wires AB and AC
    are T N and P N respectively.

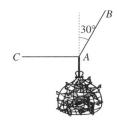

(a) Use a triangle of forces to calculate the values of T and P.

(b) Determine in each of the following cases whether the magnitudes of the tensions in
     AB and AC are greater than, the same as or less than the values of T and P you
     calculated in part (a). In each case the basket is in equilibrium.

    (i) AC is horizontal; AB is inclined at an angle greater than $30°$ to the vertical.

    (ii) AB is inclined at $30°$ to the vertical; CA is not horizontal and C is below the
         level of A.

(c) In a new situation, AB is inclined at $30°$ to the vertical and AC is at an angle of $θ°$
     with the horizontal, with C above the level of A. Discuss briefly what happens to the
     magnitudes of the tensions in AB and AC as the basket is held in equilibrium for
     different values of $θ$. Hence determine the least possible value for the tension in AC.
     What are the corresponding values for the tension in AB and for $θ$?   (MEI, adapted)

3   Two light, inextensible strings are attached to a
    small case of mass 12 kg at B. One string is fixed
    to a point A. The other string passes over a small
    smooth pulley at C and is held at D. The points
    A and C are at the same height and AB and BC
    are at $45°$ and $30°$, respectively, to the
    horizontal. The string section CD is at $θ°$ to the
    horizontal. The system is in equilibrium.

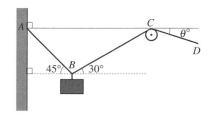

(a) By considering a triangle representing the forces acting at B, calculate the tensions in
     the string sections AB and BC.

(b) The position of D is moved so that $θ$ increases but B remains in the same position.
     What effect does this have on the tension in the string section CD?

(c) The end D of the string section CD is now pulled so that the mass at B rises. It is
     then held in equilibrium. Describe what effect this has on the tensions in the string
     sections AB and BC. Explain why the system cannot be in equilibrium with B on the
     same level as A and C.   (MEI, adapted)

4 A small Christmas decoration is suspended by light strings AP and PB. The point A is on a vertical wall and the point B is on a ceiling. The strings AP and PB are at $30°$ to the vertical. The decoration, of weight $4\,\text{N}$, hangs in equilibrium from P. Show that there is the same tension in the strings AP and PB and calculate this tension.   (MEI, adapted)

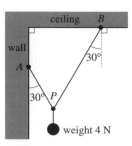

5 Two decorations are suspended between the wall and ceiling in Question 4 using light strings AP, PQ and QC. The strings AP, QP and CQ are respectively at $30°$, $60°$ and $\theta°$ to the vertical. The decorations hanging in equilibrium from P and Q have weights of $4\,\text{N}$ and $3\,\text{N}$ respectively.

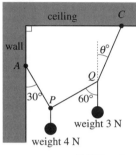

   (a) By considering the equilibrium of the forces at P, show that the tension in the string PQ is $2\,\text{N}$.

   (b) Calculate the tension in the string CQ and the angle $\theta°$.   (MEI, adapted)

6 A light inextensible string is attached to two fixed points A and B, where AB is horizontal. Two objects P and Q, of masses $2\,\text{kg}$ and $3\,\text{kg}$ respectively, are attached to the string. They rest in equilibrium, with the part of the string between P and Q horizontal and the part of the string between B and Q making an angle of $60°$ with the horizontal, as shown in the diagram.

   (a) Show that the tension in the part of the string between B and Q is $33.9\,\text{N}$, correct to three significant figures.

   (b) Find the tension in the string joining P and Q.

The part of the string between A and P makes an angle of $\theta°$ with the horizontal. Find the tension in this part of the string, and show that θ is approximately 49.   (OCR, adapted)

7 A small smooth ring R, of mass $0.3\,\text{kg}$, is threaded on a light inextensible string whose ends are attached to two fixed points A and B which are at the same horizontal level. A force of magnitude X newtons is applied to the ring in a direction parallel to AB, as shown in the diagram. When the ring is in equilibrium with both parts of the string taut, angle $BAR = 30°$ and angle $ABR = 40°$. Find the tension in the string and the value of X.   (OCR)

8 A particle of mass $0.6\,\text{kg}$ is held in equilibrium on a rough plane, inclined at $30°$ to the horizontal, by means of a horizontal force of magnitude $5\,\text{N}$. Given that the equilibrium is limiting with the particle about to slip up a line of greatest slope of the plane, find the coefficient of friction between the particle and the plane.   (OCR)

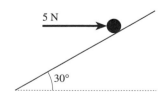

9   A light inextensible string which passes over a
    fixed smooth peg A is fastened at one end to a
    small ring R of mass 0.1 kg and at the other
    end to a particle P of mass 0.3 kg. The ring is
    threaded on a fixed rough vertical wire and the
    system rests in equilibrium with the part AR of
    the string inclined at an angle of $60°$ to the
    vertical and the part AP of the string vertical,
    as shown in the diagram. Draw a clear diagram showing all the forces acting on the particle
    and on the ring, and state the tension in the string.

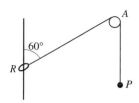

    Given that the equilibrium is limiting, explain why the ring is on the point of moving
    upwards and calculate the coefficient of friction between the ring and the wire.

    Find the magnitude of the resultant force exerted on the peg by the string.   (OCR)

10 The diagram shows a block of weight W in
    contact with a plane inclined at $30°$ to the
    horizontal, and another block of weight W in
    contact with a plane inclined at $60°$ to the
    horizontal. The blocks are connected by a light
    inextensible string which passes over a smooth
    pulley at the top of the planes. The system is at
    rest with the tension in the string equal to
    $W(\sqrt{3}-1)$, and the blocks on the point of
    moving. Find the magnitude and direction of
    the contact force acting on each block, and hence show that the coefficient of friction
    between block and plane is the same for each contact.

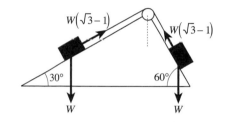

11 Three strings AB, BC and CD, each of length 1 m, are knotted together at B and C. The
    ends A and D are pinned to a horizontal beam at a distance of 2 m apart, and weights of
    20 N are hung at B and C. Use triangles of forces to calculate the tensions in each of the
    three strings.

    The weight at B is now replaced by a heavier one, so that the figure is no longer
    symmetrical, and the string AB makes an angle of $70°$ with the horizontal. Use either
    scale drawing or trigonometry to find the new values of

    (a) the distance of B from D,

    (b) the angle ABD,

    (c) the angle CBD.

    Use a triangle of forces to calculate the tension in BC. Then use another triangle of forces
    to calculate the new value of the weight hung at B.

11 General motion in a straight line

This chapter extends the study of kinematics to include objects moving with acceleration which is not constant. When you have completed it, you should

- know how to use differentiation and integration to find expressions for acceleration, velocity and displacement as functions of time.

11.1 Velocity and acceleration

So far you have mostly met examples of objects moving with constant acceleration. And as acceleration is proportional to the force applied, the forces have also been constant.

But forces are often not constant. For example, on a bicycle you can't exert as much force on the pedals when you are going fast as you can at low speeds. If you are driving on an icy road, it is wise to apply the brakes gently to start with and then gradually increase the pressure. If the force is variable, then so is the acceleration. How can you deal with this mathematically?

When the idea of acceleration was introduced in Section 1.3, it was described as the rate at which velocity increases. The clue lies in the word 'rate'. In P1 Section 9.3, it is shown that the rate at which a variable y increases with respect to an independent variable x is measured by the derivative $\dfrac{dy}{dx}$. In this mechanics application you want the rate at which the velocity v increases with respect to the time t, so this is measured by the derivative $\dfrac{dv}{dt}$.

Notice that this fits in with the rule you have already used for motion with constant acceleration, that the acceleration is the gradient of the velocity–time graph.

Example 11.1.1
A car starts to accelerate as soon as it leaves a town. After t seconds its velocity v m s^{-1} is given by the formula $v = 14 + 0.45t^2 - 0.03t^3$, until it reaches maximum velocity. Find a formula for the acceleration. How fast is the car moving when its acceleration becomes zero?

The acceleration a is found by differentiating the formula for v, so

$$a = \frac{dv}{dt} = 0.9t - 0.09t^2.$$

This can be factorised as $a = 0.09t(10 - t)$, so the acceleration becomes zero when $t = 10$. This is when the car reaches its maximum velocity. After that the model no longer applies.

To find the maximum velocity, substitute $t = 10$ in the formula for v. This gives $v = 14 + 0.45 \times 100 - 0.03 \times 1000 = 14 + 45 - 30 = 29$.

The car reaches a maximum velocity of 29 m s^{-1} after 10 seconds.

Notice that in this example the acceleration is also zero when $t = 0$, but this is not relevant to the question asked. You can easily see that at time $t = 0$, $v = 14$. That is, the initial velocity of the car as it leaves the built-up area is 14 m s^{-1}.

Sketch for yourself the velocity–time graph for this example. Notice that when the acceleration is zero there is a stationary point on the graph.

11.2 Displacement and velocity

Just as acceleration is the rate of increase of velocity with respect to time, so velocity is the rate of increase of displacement.

If the displacement is constant, then the object is not moving, and the velocity is zero. The more rapidly the displacement changes, the faster the object is moving.

So if x denotes the displacement of the object from a fixed point of the line along which it is moving, the velocity is measured by the derivative $\dfrac{dx}{dt}$.

Example 11.2.1

A space probe is launched by rockets. For the first stage of its ascent, which is in a vertical line and lasts for 40 seconds, the height x metres after t seconds is modelled by the equation $x = 50t^2 + \frac{1}{4}t^3$. How high is the probe at the end of the first stage, and how fast is it then moving?

To find the height, you substitute 40 for t in the equation for x, which gives

$$x = 50 \times 1600 + \tfrac{1}{4} \times 64\,000 = 96\,000.$$

To find a formula for the velocity you must differentiate, to get

$$v = \frac{dx}{dt} = 100t + \tfrac{3}{4}t^2.$$

Substituting 40 for t in this equation gives

$$v = 100 \times 40 + \tfrac{3}{4} \times 1600 = 4000 + 1200 = 5200.$$

So at the end of the first stage the probe is at a height of $96\,000$ m and moving at 5200 m s^{-1}. This is more conveniently expressed in kilometre units: the height is then 96 km, and the velocity is 5.2 km s^{-1}.

Since velocity is the derivative of displacement, and acceleration is the derivative of velocity, it follows that acceleration is the second derivative of displacement.

For an object moving in a straight line, if x denotes the displacement from a fixed point O of the line at time t, v denotes the velocity and a the acceleration, then

$$v = \frac{dx}{dt} \quad \text{and} \quad a = \frac{dv}{dt} = \frac{d^2x}{dt^2}.$$

The velocity is represented by the gradient of the (t, x) graph.

The acceleration is represented by the gradient of the (t, v) graph.

Notice that there has been a small change of notation from Chapter 1, where the letter s was used for displacement. The reason is that s and x may stand for different quantities. In Chapter 1, s was the displacement from the position of the object when $t = 0$, so that $s = 0$ when $t = 0$. But it is sometimes more convenient to measure the displacement x from some other point of the line. For example, to describe the complete motion of a spacecraft, it may be better to measure the displacement x from the centre of the earth rather than from the launch point. Or, if someone throws a stone upwards from the top of a cliff and you are standing on the beach, you may prefer to measure the height of the stone above the beach rather than from the top of the cliff.

Example 11.2.2

A remote-controlled toy racing car moves along a straight track laid on the floor. It starts at a point O and for the next 6 seconds its displacement x cm is modelled by the formula $x = t^3(t - 4)(t - 7)$, where t is the time in seconds. Describe the motion of the car in detail.

The displacement is 0 when $t = 0$ and when $t = 4$. The formula also gives $x = 0$ when $t = 7$, but this can be ignored, because the model only holds for values of t from 0 to 6. Also, x is positive when t is between 0 and 4, and negative when t is between 4 and 6. So the car starts out in the positive direction, comes back through O after 4 seconds and after that is on the negative side of O. This is shown in the displacement–time graph in Fig. 11.1.

To investigate this in more detail you need a formula for the velocity, so you have to differentiate. Multiplying out the expression for x gives

$$x = t^5 - 11t^4 + 28t^3,$$

so

$$v = 5t^4 - 44t^3 + 84t^2,$$

which you can factorise as

$$v = t^2(5t - 14)(t - 6).$$

This shows that other interesting values of t are 0, 2.8 and 6, when the velocity is zero. Also, v is positive when t is between 0 and 2.8, and negative when t is between 2.8 and 6. This is shown on the velocity–time graph in Fig. 11.2.

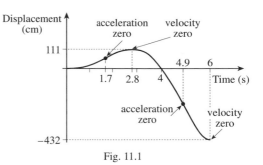

Fig. 11.1

The times at which the velocity is zero correspond to the stationary points on the displacement–time graph. (This is why such points are called 'stationary'.) By substituting $t = 2.8$ and $t = 6$ in the original formula for x, you can find the maximum distances from O in the positive and negative directions respectively. The values of x are $2.8^3 \times (-1.2) \times (-4.2) = 110.6\ldots$ and $6^3 \times 2 \times (-1) = -432$. These are marked on Fig. 11.1.

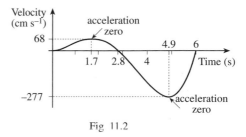

Fig. 11.2

Fig. 11.2 suggests that it would also be interesting to find the maximum and minimum values of the velocity. These occur when $\dfrac{dv}{dt} = 0$, which is when the acceleration is zero. You already know the formula for v, so you can work out

$$a = \frac{dv}{dt} = 20t^3 - 132t^2 + 168t = 4t(5t^2 - 33t + 42).$$

This shows that $a = 0$ when $t = 0$ and when $t = \dfrac{33 \pm \sqrt{33^2 - 4 \times 5 \times 42}}{2 \times 5}$, which is when $t = 1.72\ldots$ and $t = 4.87\ldots$. Substituting these values of t into the formula for v gives $v = 68.3\ldots$ and $v = -277.3\ldots$. These are marked on Fig. 11.2.

You can now describe the motion of the car in detail. It starts off from O in the positive direction, and reaches a maximum velocity of about 68 cm s^{-1} after about 1.7 seconds. Then it decelerates, coming to rest after 2.8 seconds at a maximum displacement of about 111 centimetres from O. Its velocity then becomes negative, and the car moves back towards O, passing through O after 4 seconds and continuing onto the negative side of O. You can calculate, by substituting $t = 4$ in the formula for v, that it is then moving with a velocity of $\left(4^2 \times (5 \times 4 - 14) \times (4 - 6)\right)$ cm s^{-1}, or -192 cm s^{-1}, which is a speed of 192 cm s^{-1} in the negative direction.

After about 4.9 seconds the car reaches its minimum velocity of about -277 cm s^{-1}, or 277 cm s^{-1} in the negative direction, and then starts to slow down. (But notice that this shows in Fig. 11.2 as a positive acceleration, not a deceleration! The velocity, which is negative, is increasing, but the speed is decreasing.) After 6 seconds, the largest value of t for which the formulae hold, the car has come to rest with a displacement of -432 centimetres; that is, at a distance of 432 centimetres from O in the negative direction.

The force applied on the car through the control mechanism must match the acceleration, which means that the controller has to anticipate the change of direction. So the force has to be switched from positive to negative when t is about 1.7 seconds, even though the car will not start to move backwards until $t = 2.8$. Similarly, to get the car to stop when $t = 6$, the force must be switched back to positive when t is about 4.9.

There is one last thing to notice. At the times when the velocity of the car is a maximum or minimum, after about 1.7 and 4.9 seconds, $\dfrac{dv}{dt} = 0$, so $\dfrac{d^2x}{dt^2} = 0$.

These correspond to the points of inflexion marked on the displacement–time graph, which are the points where the displacement–time graph is steepest. Between $t = 0$ and $t = 1.7$, and between $t = 4.9$ and $t = 6$, where the acceleration is positive, the displacement–time graph bends upwards; between $t = 1.7$ and $t = 4.9$, where the acceleration is negative, the graph bends downwards.

Exercise 11A

In Questions 1 to 16, x metres is the displacement at time t seconds of a particle moving in a straight line, v is the velocity in m s^{-1} and a is the acceleration in m s^{-2} Only zero and positive values of t should be considered.

1 Given that $x = t^3 + 4t + 6$, find expressions for v and a in terms of t. Find the displacement, velocity and acceleration when $t = 2$.

2 Given that $x = 3 + 20t - t^4$, find expressions for v and a in terms of t. Find the displacement, velocity and acceleration when $t = 1$ and when $t = 3$.

3 Given that $x = t^3 + 5t$, find the displacement, velocity and acceleration when $t = 3$.

4 Given that $x = t(t - 2)(t - 5)$, find the displacement, velocity and acceleration when $t = 0$.

5 Given that $x = 36 - \dfrac{4}{t}$, find the velocity and acceleration when $t = 2$.

6 Given that $v = 3\sqrt{t}$, find the velocity and acceleration when $t = 4$.

7 Given that $x = 16 - 2t^3$, find the time when the displacement is zero. Find the velocity and acceleration at this instant.

8 Given that $x = 120 - 15t - 6t^2 + t^3$, find the time when the velocity is zero. Find the displacement at this instant.

9 Given that $x = 2 + 48t - t^3$, find the displacement when the velocity is zero.

10 Given that $v = t^2 - 12t + 40$, find the velocity when the acceleration is zero.

11 Given that $x = t^3 + 4t^2 + 3$, find the displacement and the velocity when the acceleration is 20 m s^{-2}.

12 Given that $x = 10t - \dfrac{16}{\sqrt{t}}$, find the displacement and the acceleration when the velocity is 11 m s^{-1}.

13 Given that $v = 32 - \dfrac{18}{t^2}$, find the acceleration when the velocity is 30 m s^{-1}.

14 Given that $x = 2t^4 + 8t$, find the displacement and the acceleration when the velocity is 35 m s^{-1}.

15 Given the $x = 4t^3 - 7t^2 + 10$, and that the particle has mass 5 kg, find an expression for the resultant force acting on the particle in terms of t.

16 Given that $v = 4t(8 - t)$, and that the particle has mass 3 kg,

    (a) find the maximum velocity,

    (b) sketch the (t, v) graph for $0 \leqslant t \leqslant 8$,

    (c) find the resultant force acting on the particle when $t = 2$.

17 A car is accelerating from rest. At time t seconds after starting, the velocity of the car is $v \text{ m s}^{-1}$, where $v = 6t - \frac{1}{2}t^2$, for $0 \leqslant t \leqslant 6$.

    (a) Find the velocity of the car 6 seconds after starting.

    (b) Find the acceleration of the car when its velocity is 10 m s^{-1}.

18 A train leaves a station and travels in a straight line. After t seconds the train has travelled a distance x metres, where $x = \left(320t^3 - 2t^4\right) \times 10^{-5}$. This formula is valid until the train comes to rest at the next station.

    (a) Find when the train comes to rest, and hence find the distance between the two stations.

    (b) Find the acceleration of the train 40 seconds after the journey begins.

    (c) Find the deceleration of the train just before it stops.

    (d) Find when the acceleration is zero, and hence find the maximum velocity of the train.

19 An insect flies in a straight line from one flower to another. The two flowers are 270 cm apart and the flight takes 3 seconds. At time t seconds after the flight begins, the insect is x cm from the first flower. Two alternative models are proposed:

    (A) $x = 60t^2 - 10t^3$,   (B) $x = 40t^3 - 10t^4$.

For each of these models,

    (a) show that the model fits the given information about the flight,

    (b) find the maximum velocity of the insect,

    (c) sketch the (t, v) graph.

Comment on the differences between the two models. Which do you consider to be the better model?

20 A flare is launched from a balloon and moves in a vertical line. At time t seconds, the height of the flare is x metres, where $x = 1664 - 40t - \dfrac{2560}{t}$ for $t \geqslant 5$.

The flare is launched when $t = 5$.

(a) Find the height and the velocity of the flare immediately after it is launched.

(b) Find the acceleration of the flare immediately after it is launched, when its velocity is zero, and when $t = 25$.

(c) Find the terminal speed of the flare.

(d) Find when the flare reaches the ground.

(e) Sketch the (t, v) graph and the (t, x) graph for the motion of the flare.

11.3 The reverse problem

Section 11.2 shows how to find the acceleration, and therefore the force, if you know the displacement–time formula. But more often you want to work the other way round; that is, you know the force and want to find how fast an object is moving, and how far it has travelled, after a given time.

For this you need to use integration rather than differentiation. The rules given in Section 11.2 can be turned round as follows.

> For an object moving in a straight line, if a denotes the acceleration as a function of the time t,
>
> $$v = \int a \, dt \quad \text{and} \quad x = \int v \, dt.$$

Remember that integration involves an arbitrary constant. You can usually find this by knowing the initial velocity, which was denoted by u in Chapter 1, and the initial displacement; these are the values of v and of x when $t = 0$.

Example 11.3.1

A train of mass 500 tonnes is travelling on a straight track at 48 m s^{-1} when the driver sees an amber light ahead. He applies the brakes for a period of 30 seconds with a force given by the formula $4t(30 - t) \text{ kN}$, where t is the time in seconds after the brakes are applied. Find how fast the train is moving after 30 seconds, and how far it has travelled in that time.

Begin by applying Newton's second law to find a formula for the acceleration of the train (which is in fact a deceleration, since the train is slowing down). To keep the numbers small, use units of tonnes for the mass and kilonewtons for the force. (Since 1 tonne $= 1000$ kg and 1 kN $= 1000$ N, the units are still consistent.) Then

$$-4t(30 - t) = 500a, \quad \text{so} \quad a = -\tfrac{1}{125}t(30 - t) = \tfrac{1}{125}t^2 - \tfrac{6}{25}t.$$

Integrating to find v,

$$v = \int \left(\tfrac{1}{125} t^2 - \tfrac{6}{25} t \right) dt = \tfrac{1}{375} t^3 - \tfrac{3}{25} t^2 + k.$$

It is given that $v = 48$ when $t = 0$, so substitute these values giving

$$48 = 0 - 0 + k, \quad \text{so} \quad k = 48.$$

The formula for v is therefore

$$v = \tfrac{1}{375} t^3 - \tfrac{3}{25} t^2 + 48.$$

Integrating a second time to find x,

$$x = \int \left(\tfrac{1}{375} t^3 - \tfrac{3}{25} t^2 + 48 \right) dt = \tfrac{1}{1500} t^4 - \tfrac{1}{25} t^3 + 48t + c.$$

If x denotes the displacement from the instant when the brakes are first applied, then $x = 0$ when $t = 0$. Substitute these values giving

$$0 = 0 - 0 + 0 + c, \quad \text{so} \quad c = 0.$$

The formula for x is therefore

$$x = \tfrac{1}{1500} t^4 - \tfrac{1}{25} t^3 + 48t.$$

To find the final speed and the distance travelled, substitute $t = 30$ in the expressions for v and x. This gives

$$v = \tfrac{27\,000}{375} - \tfrac{3 \times 900}{25} + 48 = 72 - 108 + 48 = 12$$

and

$$x = \tfrac{810\,000}{1500} - \tfrac{27\,000}{25} + 48 \times 30 = 540 - 1080 + 1440 = 900.$$

The train slows down to a speed of 12 m s^{-1}, and travels 900 metres during the time that the brakes are on.

In this example, if you only want the distance the train travels while the brakes are on, and are not interested in the (t, x) formula, you could finish off the calculation by using a definite integral. The distance is

$$\int_0^{30} \left(\tfrac{1}{375} t^3 - \tfrac{3}{25} t^2 + 48 \right) dt = \left[\tfrac{1}{1500} t^4 - \tfrac{1}{25} t^3 + 48t \right]_0^{30}$$

$$= (540 - 1080 + 1440) - (0 - 0 + 0) = 900.$$

Since the definite integral gives the area under the velocity–time graph, this shows that the displacement is represented by this area.

> For an object moving in a straight line, with the velocity v given as a
> function of the time t, the displacement between times t_1 and t_2 is given by
>
> $$\int_{t_1}^{t_2} v\,dt.$$
>
> This displacement is represented by the area under the (t, v) graph for the
> interval $t_1 \leqslant t \leqslant t_2$.

Example 11.3.2

For the car in Example 11.1.1, with velocity given by the formula
$v = 14 + 0.45t^2 - 0.03t^3$, find the distance travelled while the car accelerates to its
maximum velocity.

It was shown that the car reaches its maximum velocity at time $t = 10$, so the
distance travelled is

$$\int_0^{10} \left(14 + 0.45t^2 - 0.03t^3\right) dt = \left[14t + 0.15t^3 - 0.0075t^4\right]_0^{10}$$
$$= (140 + 150 - 75) - (0 + 0 - 0) = 215.$$

The car travels 215 metres in the 10 seconds that it takes to reach its maximum
velocity of 29 m s^{-1}.

11.4 The constant acceleration formulae

Motion with constant acceleration is simply a special case of general motion in a straight
line, so you can get the formulae in Chapter 1 by the integration method in Section 11.3.

First, since $\dfrac{dv}{dt} = a$, where a is now a constant number,

$$v = \int a\,dt = at + k.$$

To find k, use the fact that the initial velocity is u, so that $v = u$ when $t = 0$. Therefore
$u = a \times 0 + k$, which gives $k = u$. The velocity–time formula is therefore $v = at + u$,
which is usually written as

$$v = u + at.$$

A second integration gives the displacement formula. Since u and a are both constant,

$$x = \int v\,dt = \int (u + at)\,dt = ut + \tfrac{1}{2}at^2 + c.$$

Now the quantity s in the constant acceleration equations is the displacement from the
initial position at time $t = 0$, so that

$$s = \text{displacement at time } t - \text{displacement at time } 0$$

$$= \left(ut + \tfrac{1}{2}at^2 + c\right) - \left(u \times 0 + \tfrac{1}{2}a \times 0^2 + c\right)$$

$$= \left(ut + \tfrac{1}{2}at^2 + c\right) - (0 + 0 + c)$$

$$= ut + \tfrac{1}{2}at^2.$$

Once you have the (t, v) and the (t, s) equations, you can find the other three equations in Section 1.5 algebraically, by eliminating a, t or u. This is Question 21 in Exercise 11B.

11.5* A shorthand notation

Expressions like $\dfrac{dx}{dt}$, $\dfrac{dv}{dt}$ and $\dfrac{d^2x}{dt^2}$ occur so often in mechanics that people often use a shorter notation when writing them. In this notation a dot is written over the top of a letter to denote the derivative with respect to time. Thus $\dfrac{dx}{dt}$ is written as $\dot{x}$ (pronounced 'x dot'), and $\dfrac{dv}{dt}$ as $\dot{v}$. A second derivative with respect to time is written with two dots, so that $\dfrac{d^2x}{dt^2}$ becomes $\ddot{x}$ (pronounced 'x double-dot').

In this notation the equation for Newton's second law becomes $F = m\ddot{x}$. For example, the first equation in Example 11.3.1 would be written

$$-4t(30 - t) = 500\ddot{x},$$

and the motion would be described by

$$\ddot{x} = \dot{v} = \tfrac{1}{125}t^2 - \tfrac{6}{25}t.$$

In fact, this notation did not begin life as a shorthand; it is very similar to the notation which Isaac Newton invented when he introduced his theory of 'fluxions'. The $\dfrac{dx}{dt}$ notation was invented by the German mathematician Gottfried Leibniz, who was working on the ideas of calculus at the same time as Newton but from a different point of view.

You do not need to use the dot notation yet, but if you intend to go on to more advanced mechanics you will find it very useful later. In that case, you may like to practise using it in the next exercise.

Exercise 11B

In Questions 1 to 20, x metres is the displacement at time t seconds of a particle moving in a straight line, v is the velocity in m s^{-1} and a is the acceleration in m s^{-2}. Only zero and positive values of t should be considered.

1 Given that $v = 3t^2 + 8$ and that the displacement is 4 m when $t = 0$, find an expression for x in terms of t. Find the displacement and the velocity when $t = 2$.

2   Given that $a = 10 - 6t^2$, and that the velocity is 4 m s^{-1} and the displacement is 12 m when $t = 1$, find expressions for v and x in terms of t. Find the displacement, velocity and acceleration when $t = 0$.

3   Given that $v = 6\sqrt{t}$ and that the displacement is 30 m when $t = 4$, find the displacement, velocity and acceleration when $t = 1$.

4   Given that $a = 2 - \dfrac{6}{t^3}$, and that the velocity is 6 m s^{-1} and the displacement is zero when $t = 1$, find the displacement, velocity and acceleration when $t = 3$.

5   Given that $v = 9 - t^2$ and that the displacement is 2 m when $t = 0$, find the displacement when the velocity is zero.

6   Given that $a = 3t - 12$, and that the velocity is 30 m s^{-1} and the displacement is 4 m when $t = 0$, find the displacement when the acceleration is zero.

7   Given that $v = t^2 + 10t$ and that the displacement is 6 m when $t = 0$, find the displacement when the acceleration is 16 m s^{-2}.

8   Given that $a = 4 - 2t$, and that the velocity is 5 m s^{-1} when $t = 0$, find the acceleration when the velocity is zero.

9   Given that $v = 3t^2 + 4t + 3$, find the distance travelled between $t = 0$ and $t = 2$.

10 Given that $v = 12 - 8t^3$, find the distance travelled between $t = 0$ and $t = 1$.

11 Given that $v = 4 + 3\sqrt{t}$, find the distance travelled between $t = 1$ and $t = 4$.

12 Given that $v = \dfrac{3}{t^2}$, find the distance travelled between $t = 2$ and $t = 10$.

13 Given that $v = t^2 - 20$, find the distance travelled between $t = 0$ and $t = 4$.

14 Given that $v = \dfrac{1}{t^2} - 2$, find the distance travelled between $t = 1$ and $t = 5$.

15 Given that $a = 4t - 1$ and that the velocity is 5 m s^{-1} when $t = 0$, find the distance travelled between $t = 0$ and $t = 3$.

16 Given that $a = 12 - 3\sqrt{t}$ and that the velocity is 15 m s^{-1} when $t = 1$, find the distance travelled between $t = 1$ and $t = 25$.

17 Given that $v = 3(t - 3)(t - 5)$, find the distance travelled
    (a) between $t = 0$ and $t = 3$,
    (b) between $t = 3$ and $t = 5$,
    (c) between $t = 5$ and $t = 6$.

Hence find the total distance travelled between $t = 0$ and $t = 6$.

Sketch the (t, v) graph and the (t, x) graph (assume that the displacement is zero when $t = 0$).

How far is the particle from its starting point when $t = 6$?

18 Given that $a = \dfrac{1}{t^2}$ and that the velocity is 4 m s^{-1} when $t = 1$, find the velocity when $t = 100$. State the terminal speed of the particle.

19 Given that $a = -\dfrac{4}{t^3}$, and that the velocity is 2 m s^{-1} and the displacement is zero when $t = 1$, find the displacement when $t = 4$. Show that the velocity is always positive but the displacement never exceeds 2 m.

20 Given that $v = 13 + 5t$, find the distance travelled as the velocity increases from 13 m s^{-1} to 33 m s^{-1}. Show that the acceleration is constant, and verify that the formula $v^2 = u^2 + 2as$ gives the same result.

21 A particle moves in a straight line with constant acceleration a. In Section 11.4 integration was used to obtain the equations $v = u + at$ and $s = ut + \frac{1}{2}at^2$.

   (a) Eliminate a from these equations to show that $s = \frac{1}{2}(u + v)t$.

   (b) Obtain the equations $v^2 = u^2 + 2as$ and $s = vt - \frac{1}{2}at^2$.

22 A car starts from rest and for the first 4 seconds of its motion the acceleration $a \text{ m s}^{-2}$ at time t seconds after starting is given by $a = 6 - 2t$.

   (a) Find the maximum velocity of the car.

   (b) Find the velocity of the car after 4 seconds, and the distance travelled up to this time.

23 A truck, with initial velocity 6 m s^{-1}, brakes and comes to rest. At time t seconds after the brakes are applied the acceleration is $a \text{ m s}^{-2}$, where $a = -3t$. This formula applies until the truck stops.

   (a) Find the time taken for the truck to stop.

   (b) Find the distance travelled by the truck while it is decelerating.

   (c) Find the greatest deceleration of the truck.

24 A force of $\left(36 - t^2\right)$ newtons acts at time t seconds on a particle of mass 2 kg. When $t = 0$ the particle has velocity 2 m s^{-1} in the direction of the force. Find the velocity of the particle when $t = 6$ and find the distance travelled between $t = 0$ and $t = 6$.

25 A trailer of mass 250 kg, initially at rest, is pushed along a horizontal straight line. After t seconds the forwards force is $150(4 - t)$ newtons, for $0 \leqslant t \leqslant 4$, and there is a constant resistive force of 75 N acting backwards. For $t > 4$ there is no forwards force but the resistive force continues to act.

   (a) Find the maximum velocity of the trailer.

   (b) Find when the trailer comes to rest, and find the total distance travelled.

   (c) Sketch the (t, v) graph and the (t, x) graph for the motion of the trailer.

26 A load is being lifted by a crane and moves in a vertical straight line. Initially the load is on the ground and after t seconds its velocity v m s^{-1} (measured upwards) is given by $v = \frac{3}{5}t(t-3)(t-4)$ for $0 \leqslant t \leqslant 4$.

(a) Sketch the (t, v) graph for the motion of the load.

(b) State when the magnitude of the acceleration is greatest, and calculate this greatest acceleration.

(c) State when the load is at its highest point, and find the acceleration at this instant.

(d) Find the height of the load above the ground when $t = 3$ and when $t = 4$.

(e) Sketch a graph showing the height of the load for $0 \leqslant t \leqslant 4$.

(f) Find the total distance moved by the load.

Miscellaneous exercise 11

1 A particle starts from O and moves along a straight line. At time t seconds its displacement from O is x cm and its velocity is $\left(10t - t^2\right)$ cm s^{-1}.

(a) Find x in terms of t.

(b) Find an expression for the acceleration of the particle in terms of t.

(c) Find the distance covered and the velocity at the moment when the acceleration is zero.

(d) Find the average velocity of the particle during the first 3 seconds. Show that this is less than the actual velocity after 1.5 seconds. (OCR)

2 A particle is travelling on the x-axis. Its velocity v m s^{-1} is given by $v = 6(2 - t)(2t - 9)$ where t is the time in seconds.

(a) Find the time at which the speed of the particle in the positive direction is greatest. Calculate the speed at this time.

(b) The figure, which is not to scale, shows the velocity–time graph for the motion of the particle in the time interval $0 \leqslant t \leqslant 5$. Write down the values of t and v at each of the points A, B, C and D.

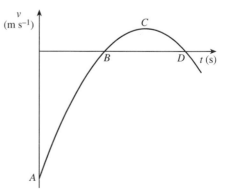

(c) At $t = 0$, the particle is 61 m from O in the positive direction. Calculate the position of the particle when it is first instantaneously at rest.

(d) Determine how many times the particle passes through the origin O.

(e) Give a brief description of the motion of the particle between the points B and D shown in the figure. (MEI)

3 The (t, v) graph for a motorcyclist travelling on a straight course is shown in the figure, for $0 \leqslant t \leqslant 60$, where t is the time measured in seconds and v is the velocity measured in m s^{-1}. Show that the total distance travelled during the 60 seconds is greater than 800 m.

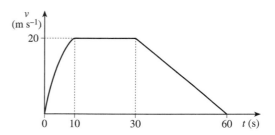

Explain how you could use the (t, v) graph to estimate the time at which the motorcyclist was accelerating at 2 m s^{-2}. (OCR)

4 A loaded fork-lift truck starts from rest and travels in a straight line from a point A to a point B. It is unloaded at B before returning directly to A, coming to rest at A. The (t, x) graph for the motion is as shown in the diagram, where x metres is the displacement from A after t seconds. The coordinates of the points marked $O, P, Q, R, S,$

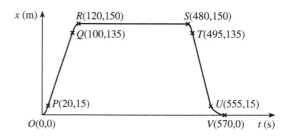

T, U and V are as shown on the diagram, and PQ, RS and TU are all straight line segments. Find the speed of the truck at each of the following times:

   (a) $\ t = 60$,   (b) $\ t = 300$,   (c) $\ t = 525$.

Making the assumption that the acceleration or retardation of the truck is constant in each of the time intervals $0 < t < 20$, $100 < t < 120$, $480 < t < 495$ and $555 < t < 570$,

   (d) sketch the (t, v) graph for the motion of the truck for $0 < t < 570$,

   (e) calculate the acceleration of the truck during the interval $0 < t < 20$.   (OCR)

5 A particle moving in a straight line has displacement x metres after t seconds for $0 \leqslant t \leqslant 5$, where $x = t^3 - 12t^2 + 21t + 18$.

   (a) Find the displacement, velocity and acceleration when the time is zero.

   (b) Find the time, velocity and acceleration when the displacement is zero.

   (c) Find the time, displacement and acceleration when the velocity is zero.

   (d) Find the time, displacement and velocity when the acceleration is zero.

6 A particle moving on the x-axis has displacement x metres from the origin O after t seconds for $0 \leqslant t \leqslant 5$, where $x = t^2(t - 2)(t - 5)$.

   (a) For what values of t is the particle on the positive side of O?

   (b) For what values of t is the particle moving towards O?

   (c) For what values of t is the force on the particle directed towards O?

7 The displacement, x metres, of a particle moving on the x-axis at a time t seconds after it starts to move is given by $x = t^5$ for $0 \leq t \leq 1$, and by $x = \dfrac{4}{t} - \dfrac{3}{t^k}$ for $t \geq 1$.

(a) Verify that both formulae give the same value for x when $t = 1$.

(b) Find the value of k for which there is no sudden change of velocity when $t = 1$.

For the rest of the question, take k to have the value you found in part (b).

(c) Show that the particle stays on the same side of O throughout the motion.

(d) What is the greatest distance of the particle from O?

(e) For what values of t is the force on the particle acting in the positive direction?

8 A battery-operated toy dog starts at a point O and moves in a straight line. Its motion is modelled by the velocity–time graph in the figure.

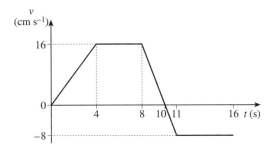

(a) Calculate the displacement from O of the toy

(i) after 10 seconds,

(ii) after 16 seconds.

(b) Write down expressions for the velocity of the toy at time t seconds in the intervals $0 \leq t \leq 4$ and $4 \leq t \leq 8$.

(c) Obtain expressions for the displacement from O of the toy at time t seconds in the intervals $0 \leq t \leq 4$ and $4 \leq t \leq 8$.

(d) An alternative model for the motion of the toy in the interval $0 \leq t \leq 10$ is $v = \frac{2}{3}\left(10t - t^2\right)$ where v is the velocity in cm s^{-1}. Calculate the difference in the displacement from O after 10 seconds as predicted by the two models.   (MEI)

9 A cyclist is travelling along a straight road. The (t, v) graph in the figure, where t is measured in seconds and v is measured in m s^{-1}, consists of three line segments and models the first 250 seconds of the cyclist's journey. The cyclist has a constant speed of V m s^{-1} in the interval $60 \leq t \leq 160$.

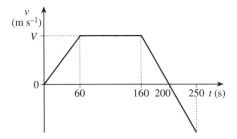

(a) Find an expression, in terms of V, for the distance travelled, in metres, by the cyclist in the first 200 seconds.

(b) Given that the average speed of the cyclist in the interval $0 \leq t \leq 200$ is 6.75 m s^{-1}, find V.

(c) Hence find the distance of the cyclist from his starting point at the end of the 250 seconds.   (OCR)

10 The figure shows the (t, v) graph for a miniature train as it moves along a straight track. At time $t = 0$ the train passes a point A and is moving at 3 m s^{-1}. The farthest point from A reached by the train in the 2-minute period is P. Find

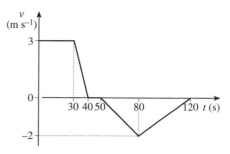

(a) the value of t at the instant that the train reaches P,

(b) the magnitude of the acceleration of the train in the time interval $50 < t < 80$,

(c) the distance of the train from A at the end of the 2-minute period.   (OCR)

Revision exercise 2

1   A sphere of mass 3 kg moving at 8 m s^{-1} collides with a sphere of mass 2 kg moving at 5 m s^{-1} in the opposite direction. After the collision the first sphere continues to move in its original direction with its speed reduced to 2 m s^{-1}. What happens to the other sphere?

2   Find the resultant of forces of 2 N due north, 3 N on a bearing of 120° and 4 N on a bearing of 220°.

Check your answer by showing that the sum of the resolved parts of the three forces perpendicular to the resultant is zero.

3   A water-skier of mass 60 kg holds a horizontal cable which trails behind a speedboat of mass 480 kg. The resistance of the water to the boat is 700 N, and the resistance to the skier is 90 N. If the engine produces a forward thrust of 1600 N, find the acceleration and the tension in the cable.

4   An object of weight 25 N is supported by two strings. The tensions in the strings are 20 N and X N. Find the angle between the strings when

   (a) $X = 20$,   (b) $X = 25$,   (c) $X = 30$.

5   A particle of mass 0.2 kg is at rest on a smooth surface. It is acted on by two constant forces, of magnitude 0.3 N and 0.5 N at an angle of 110° to each other. Find which direction it moves in, and how long it takes to move 10 m from its original position.

6   A flat truck of mass 400 kg is running smoothly on rails alongside a platform at a constant speed of 3 m s^{-1}. A person of mass 80 kg standing on the platform steps sideways on to the truck as it passes. Explain why the speed of the truck is reduced. Find the new speed.

A few seconds later the person steps sideways back on to the platform. What is the impulse of the force of friction in a direction parallel to the rails?

7   A long shelf has small light pulleys set into it at either end. A string passes over both pulleys, and loads of mass 0.6 kg and 0.8 kg are attached at the two ends.

   (a)   Find the acceleration with which the heavier load descends.

   (b)   It is desired to reduce the acceleration to 0.4 m s^{-2}. This is done by cutting the string in the middle and inserting a block between the two parts. The block slides on the shelf. If friction is neglected in the calculation, calculate the mass of the block.

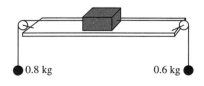
0.8 kg   0.6 kg

   (c)   If friction is taken into account, calculate how large the coefficient of friction must be for the acceleration to be reduced to zero.

   (d)   Explain why, however heavy the block is, the acceleration cannot be reduced to zero in this way if the surfaces are smooth.

8   A sphere of weight 50 N hangs by a light chain from the roof of a hall. A person standing on the floor uses a pole pushed at $30°$ to the vertical to push the sphere sideways. The chain is then at an angle of $20°$ to the vertical. Find the force from the pole on the sphere, and the tension in the chain.

9   A particle is placed on a plane inclined at an angle α to the horizontal. It rests in equilibrium under the action of its weight W, the normal contact force N and a frictional force F. Express N and F in terms of W and α.

Each force is now split into components horizontally and parallel to the plane. Find the magnitude of the components in each direction. Check your answer by showing that the sum of the components of the three forces in each direction is zero.

10   Three separate trucks, of mass 400 kg, 500 kg and 300 kg, are in line in that order on a railway track. Initially the second and third trucks are at rest, and the 400 kg truck is moving towards them at a speed of 12 m s^{-1}. Each time that a moving truck hits a stationary truck at a speed u m s^{-1}, the difference in the speeds of the two trucks after the collision is $\frac{1}{2}u$ m s^{-1}. Find the speeds of the trucks after two collisions have taken place. Will there be any more collisions?

11   A block of mass M is placed on a track inclined at $45°$ to the horizontal. A string attached to the block runs up parallel to the track, passes over a smooth rail at the top, and carries at its other end a counterweight of mass m which hangs vertically. The coefficient of friction between the block and the track is 0.6. Find an expression for the tension T in the string in terms of m, M and g, distinguishing the various situations that can occur for different values of m and M.

State the direction of the resultant force on the rail, and find an expression for its magnitude in terms of T.

12   A model railway engine of mass 2 kg runs on a straight horizontal track. Its displacement, x cm, from a point O on the track after t seconds is given, for $0 \leqslant t \leqslant 8$, by the formula

$$x = 3t^4 - 44t^3 + 144t^2 + 25.$$

Find an expression for the velocity of the engine in terms of t. Use this to sketch (t, v) and (t, x) graphs. Show that there is an integer value of t in the interval $0 < t < 8$ for which $x = 0$.

Describe the motion of the engine during the interval. Find an expression for the force needed to produce this motion, and describe how this force varies during the interval.

13   Ron, Sam and Tim are playing with a rope. Ron and Sam tie the rope round Tim's waist, and pull on the two ends with forces of 30 N and 40 N at an angle of $50°$ to each other. Find the magnitude and direction of the force on Tim.

The weights of the boys are 250 N, 200 N and 350 N respectively. The boys are all wearing identical trainers. What is the least value of the coefficient of friction if none of their feet are to slip?

14   Two small wooden discs, of mass 30 grams and 20 grams, are placed on a polished table, 1 metre apart. The coefficient of friction is $\frac{1}{2}$. The heavier disc is struck so that it starts to move at a speed of 4.2 m s^{-1} towards the lighter disc. After the impact the speed of the heavier disc is halved. How far from their starting points do the discs come to rest?

15 (a) If $x = p^2 t^2$, where p is a positive constant and $t > 0$, express the velocity v and the acceleration a in terms of t. Prove that $v = 2p\sqrt{x}$. Hence show that $a = v\dfrac{dv}{dx}$.

(b) If $x = \dfrac{p}{t}$, find expressions for v and a in terms of t, and for v in terms of x. Is it still true that $a = v\dfrac{dv}{dx}$?

16 An angler of mass 80 kg standing on a jetty is slowly reeling in a 15 kg fish at the end of a line. The tip of the rod is 8 m above the water level, and there are 17 m of line between the tip of the rod and the hook. As the fish comes in at constant speed there is a horizontal resistive force from the water of 105 N. Calculate the tension in the line.

Draw diagrams to show the forces on

(a) the fish,   (b) the angler and rod (considered as a single object).

Find the magnitude of each force. The mass of the rod can be neglected.

17 A skip of mass 2 tonnes has to be dragged along a track. The coefficient of friction is $\frac{5}{7}$. A cable attached to the skip runs horizontally to a winch powered by an electric motor. Using the controls on the motor, the tension in the cable is gradually increased, so that after t seconds its value is $400t$ newtons, until it reaches its maximum value of 16 000 newtons. This maximum tension is then maintained until the skip is moving at a speed of 3.5 m s^{-1}. The tension is then reduced instantaneously so that the skip continues to move at this speed.

(a) How long does it take before the skip starts to move?

(b) How fast is the skip moving when the tension in the cable reaches its greatest value?

(c) How long does it take after that for the skip to reach its greatest speed, and how far has it then moved altogether?

(d) What is the tension in the cable when the skip is moving at its greatest speed?

(e) Just before the skip reaches its destination the cable is disconnected. How much further after that will the skip move?

(f) Draw sketches of the (t, x), (t, v) and (t, a) graphs to illustrate the motion of the skip.

18 Forces of 7 N in the x-direction and 5 N in the y-direction, together with a third force of magnitude 6 N, have a resultant at an angle of $45°$ with the positive x-axis. If the third force makes an angle $\theta°$ with the positive x-axis, measured anticlockwise, show that $\sin\theta° - \cos\theta° = \frac{1}{3}$.

Use a graphic calculator to show that the functions $\sin\theta° - \cos\theta°$ and $\sqrt{2}\sin(\theta - 45)°$ have the same graph. Hence find two possible values for θ.

Draw a polygon of forces to show why there are two possible directions for the third force.

19 A string passes over a rough cylindrical rail, and objects of mass 10 kg and m kg attached to the ends hang vertically on either side. Because of friction between the string and the rail, when the objects are in motion the tension in the string on the descending side is twice the tension on the ascending side. Find the acceleration of the system in the cases

(a) $m = 2$,   (b) $m = 24$,   (c) $m = 12$.

Mock examination 1

Time 1 hour 20 minutes

Answer all the questions.

Graphic calculators are permitted.

1 Two spheres, one black and one white, hang side by side from the ceiling by vertical strings, just touching each other. The black sphere has mass 1 kg, and the white sphere has mass 4 kg. The black sphere is then pulled aside and let go, so that it hits the white sphere with a speed of 3 m s^{-1}. After the collision the spheres separate from each other with equal speeds of v m s^{-1} in opposite directions. Calculate the value of v. [2]

Both spheres swing out and back, and collide again when their strings are vertical. They are now moving towards each other with speed v m s^{-1}. After this second collision both spheres move in the same direction, and the black sphere is moving 5 times as fast as the white sphere. How fast are the spheres then moving? [4]

2

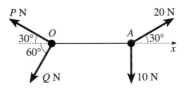

A string OA lies in equilibrium along a portion of the positive x-axis, with one end at the origin. Forces act at A of magnitude 10 N in the negative y-direction and 20 N at 30° anticlockwise from the positive x-direction, as shown in the figure. Show that the resultant of these two forces acts in the positive x-direction, and find the tension in the string. [3]

The forces at O are P N and Q N making angles of 150° and 240° anticlockwise from the positive x-direction. Find P and Q. [3]

You may if you like use the values $\cos 30° = \frac{1}{2}\sqrt{3}$, $\cos 60° = \frac{1}{2}$ *and leave* $\sqrt{3}$ *in your answers.*

3 A stone drops into the sea from the edge of a cliff 80 m high. Neglecting air resistance, calculate the time that it takes to reach the water, and the speed with which it enters the water. [4]

In fact the fall of the stone is affected by air resistance. State, giving reasons, whether the actual time and speed will be larger or smaller than those you have calculated. [3]

4

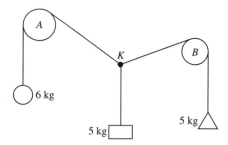

Three strings are tied together at a knot K. Objects of mass 5 kg, 5 kg and 6 kg are attached to the other ends of the strings. The string carrying one of the 5 kg objects hangs vertically from K. The other strings, carrying the 6 kg object and the other 5 kg object, pass over smooth pegs A and B, as shown in the figure. Calculate the angles which these last two strings make with the vertical at the ends which are tied to K when the system is in equilibrium.   [5]

Find also the direction and magnitude of the resultant force on the peg A.   [4]

5 A car of mass 1200 kg travelling at 20 m s^{-1} experiences air resistance of 150 N. How large must the forward driving force be for the car to accelerate at 0.5 m s^{-2}?   [3]

A caravan of mass 800 kg is now attached to the car. At 20 m s^{-1} the air resistance on the caravan is 500 N. If the driving force is the same as it was before the caravan was attached, calculate the acceleration of the car and caravan. Find also the force in the towbar.   [7]

6 A suitcase of mass 16 kg is placed on a ramp inclined at 15° to the horizontal. The coefficient of friction between the suitcase and the ramp is 0.4. Determine whether the suitcase can rest in equilibrium on the ramp without additional support.   [4]

A person tries to push the suitcase up the ramp using a horizontal force. Find the magnitude of the force which must be exceeded for the suitcase to start moving.   [7]

7 A particle is moving on a straight line. Its velocity, v m s^{-1}, at a time t seconds after it passes through the origin O is given, for $0 \leqslant t \leqslant 5$, by the equation

$$v = t^2 - 6t + 8.$$

(i) Draw a sketch of the (t, v) graph, and give a brief description of the motion.   [4]

(ii) Find the displacement, x m, of the particle from O after t seconds. Does the particle ever return to O in the interval $0 \leqslant t \leqslant 5$? Give a reason for your answer.   [4]

(iii) Draw a sketch of the graph of the acceleration of the particle in the interval $0 \leqslant t \leqslant 5$. What can you say about the direction of the acceleration in this interval?   [3]

Mock examination 2

Time 1 hour 20 minutes

Answer all the questions.

Graphic calculators are permitted.

1 Three forces act on a particle in a horizontal plane. One force acts due east with magnitude $10\,\text{N}$, and a second force acts south-west with magnitude $6\,\text{N}$. The third force acts on a bearing of $330°$, and the direction of the resultant is due north. Calculate the magnitude of the third force and the magnitude of the resultant. [5]

2 A van travelling at a constant speed of $25\,\text{m s}^{-1}$ passes a red traffic light. Four seconds later a police car, travelling at $10\,\text{m s}^{-1}$ and accelerating at $2\,\text{m s}^{-2}$, passes the same light. Write expressions for the distance of each vehicle from the light t seconds after the police car passes it. [2]

Find the time that it takes for the police car to catch up with the van, and how fast it is then travelling. [3]

3 A person walking at constant speed drags a $25\,\text{kg}$ sack of potatoes along a horizontal path, using a rope tied round the neck of the sack. The rope makes an angle of $25°$ with the horizontal, and there is frictional resistance from the ground of $120\,\text{N}$. Calculate

   (i) the tension in the rope, [3]

   (ii) the coefficient of friction between the sack and the ground. [5]

4

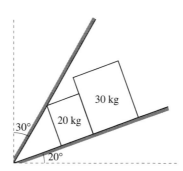

The figure shows a corner of the loft space in a house. The roof slopes at $30°$ to the vertical, and the floor slopes at $20°$ to the horizontal. Rectangular crates, of mass $20\,\text{kg}$ and $30\,\text{kg}$, stand on the floor in contact with each other, and the lower top edge of the $20\,\text{kg}$ crate is in contact with the roof. There are no frictional forces. Draw diagrams to show the forces on each of the crates, and calculate the magnitude of the normal contact force from the roof on the $20\,\text{kg}$ crate. [9]

5 In a circus act two clowns, Biggo and Littlo, have mass 74 kg and 24 kg respectively. They stand facing each other on platforms at a height of 10 m above the floor. In front of each clown is one end of a rope, which is hung over a fixed smooth rail high above the floor. At the same instant the clowns step off their platforms and grab the end of the rope in front of them. How fast is Biggo moving when he lands on the floor?   [6]

As he lands, Biggo continues to hold on to the rope, and to pull downwards on it with a force of 180 N. How high is Littlo above the floor when he comes to rest?   [4]

6

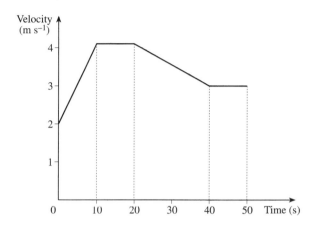

The figure shows the (t, v) graph for a person running to catch a bus.

(i)   Write a brief description of the run.   [3]

(ii) Calculate how far the person has run after 10, 20, 30, 40 and 50 seconds.   [4]

(iii) Make a sketch of the (t, x) graph on graph paper.   [2]

(iv) The person has a mass of 80 kg. Calculate the frictional force between her shoes and the ground during the first 10 seconds.   [2]

7 Two particles A and B have mass 1 kg and 8 kg respectively. They are initially 80 m apart, and they are set in motion at the same instant. At a time t seconds later the displacements in metres of the particles from a point O on the line are $x_A = t^3$ and $x_B = 80 - t^2$ respectively. Verify that the particles collide after 4 seconds, and find their velocities at this time.   [4]

As a result of the collision the particle A's velocity is reversed in direction and its magnitude is halved. Calculate the velocity of B after the collision.   [3]

The accelerations of the particles are given by the same formulae after the collision as before. Show that after the collision the displacement of A is given by

$$x_A = t^3 - 72t + 288,$$

and find an expression for the displacement of B. Show that, when $t = 5$, the particles are 11 m apart.   [5]

Answers

Most non-exact numerical answers are given correct to 3 significant figures.

1 Velocity and acceleration

Exercise 1A (page 3)

1   200 s

2   72 km south

3   21.2 hours

4   16.8 miles south

5   (a)   52 m.p.h. north-west, 65 m.p.h. south-east
    (b)   23.1 m s^{-1} north-west,
          28.9 m s^{-1} south-east

6   About $5\frac{1}{2}$ minutes

7   8.2×10^{13} km

8   $33\frac{1}{3}$ m s^{-1}

Exercise 1B (page 7)

1   4 m s^{-2}, 125 m

2   $7\frac{1}{2}$ m s^{-1}

3   1.6 m s^{-2}, 60 m s^{-1}; 15.5 s

4   6 s, $1\frac{2}{3}$ m s^{-2}

5   30 s, 2 m s^{-2}

6   20 m s^{-1}, 1500 m

7   25 s, 175 m

Exercise 1C (page 10)

1   (a)   11   (b)   16   (c) $-\frac{3}{2}$ (d)   45
    (e)   102   (f)   1.2   (g)   14   (h) $2\frac{1}{2}$
    (i)   24   (j) $-26\frac{2}{3}$ (k)   20   (l)   2
    (m) $1\frac{1}{3}$ (n)   25

2   40 s, $\frac{7}{8}$ m s^{-2}

3   $\sqrt{\frac{1}{5}}s$

4   0.06 m s^{-2}

5   1500 m

6   (a)   2.7 km   (b)   250 s

7   (a) $\sqrt{900 - 20s}$ (b)   10 m s^{-1} (c)   5 m

8   60 m

9   $(5 + 0.8t)$ m s^{-1}, $(5t + 0.4t^2)$ m; 15 s, 17 m s^{-1}

10   $2\frac{1}{2}$ m s^{-2}, 2 m s^{-2}

11   1800 mile hour^{-2}; 40 mile hour^{-1}

12   $\left(\frac{1}{2}t^2 - 4t + 10\right)$ m ; yes

Exercise 1D (page 15)

1   22 s

2   (a)   18 minutes (b)   21 minutes

3   30 m s^{-1}, 675 m; $1\frac{1}{2}$ m s^{-2}; 20 s

4   20 m s^{-1}, 2 m s^{-2}

5   12 m s^{-1}, 44 s

6   (a)   22 s   (b) $53\frac{1}{3}$ m

7   (a)   7 m s^{-1} (b) $\frac{1}{2}$ (c) $\frac{11}{28}$

8   $\frac{1}{36}$ m s^{-2}

9   (a)   50 m s^{-1} (b)   5000 m

10   $5D$ metres

Miscellaneous exercise 1 (page 16)

1   (a)   1.5 m s^{-2} (b)   11.0 m s^{-1}

2   (a)   40 s   (b)   24.85

3   15.0 m s^{-1}

4   $a = \frac{1}{8}, T = 20$

5   2 m s^{-2}, 200 m

6   $\frac{3}{4}t^2$ m, 2 s, 31 m

7   0.2 m s^{-2}; 0.34 m s^{-2}

8   10.8 m

9   0.08 m s^{-2}

10   (a) (i) $\frac{1}{2}$ m s^{-2} (ii) 7200 m
     (b)   460 s; no

2 Force and motion

Exercise 2A (page 23)

1   1.5 m s^{-2}

2   0.625 m s^{-2}

3   9240 N

4   65 kg

5   4 s

6   1.44 m s^{-2}, 0.576 N

7   $0.96m$ N

8   850 kg

9   18.75 m

10   90 m s^{-1}

11   6.4 m s^{-2}, 12.8 N

12   2.47

13   0.12 m s^{-2}, 22.4 s

14 13.5 cm

15 40.5 kN

Exercise 2B (page 27)

1 115

2 4

3 2120 N

4 300 N, 400 N

5 165 N

6 (a) 16 N   (b) 25.6 N

7 45 N, 2 m s^{-2}

8 7.91 m s^{-1}

9 3125 N

10 1.3×10^4 N

11 10.75 N, 2.81 m

12 2625 kg

13 52.2

14 780 N, 1 min 20 s

15 7.5 s

Miscellaneous exercise 2 (page 28)

1 1640

2 11.0 s

3 1400 N

4 10 s

5 750 N, 938 N

6 20 kg

7 4500 N

8 Yes; a force of 92.6 N would be needed for the box to decelerate at the same rate as the car.

9 0.25 m s^{-2}, 25 N

10 4500 N

11 (a) 0.33 m s^{-2} (b) 1160 N, 0.04 m s^{-2}

12 1720 N

13 12 s, $6\frac{2}{3}$

14 (a) 3000 N

15 (a) $\frac{1}{80}$ m s^{-2} (b) $\frac{1}{2}$ m s^{-1}, 40 s

    (c) (i) 15 s   (ii) $13\frac{3}{4}$ m   (iii) 55 s

3 Vertical motion

Exercise 3A (page 34)

1 (a) 29.4 N   (b) 0.098 N   (c) 7840 N

2 17 kg

3 2.2 m s^{-2}

4 17 600 N

5 12 740 N; 0.392 m s^{-2}

6 7.56 N

7 72.6 m s^{-2}

8 1248 N; 0.217 m s^{-2}

9 (a) 10 800 N   (b) 10 584 N

    (c) 10 368 N   (d) 10 800 N

10 1250 N

11 40 kg

12 90 kg; 6.53 m s^{-1}

13 1.58 N

14 39.2 N, 16 kg

15 $s = \dfrac{Mv^2}{2(T - Mg)}$

16 36.3, 870

17 8400 N

Exercise 3B (page 40)

1 2.86 kg

2 (a) 39 200 N   (b) 37 200 N

3 650 N, the drum leaves the ground.

4 (a) 372 N (b) 441 N (c) 372 N

5 135 kg

6 65 800 N

7 0.8 m s^{-2}

8 The scales register the normal contact force between the man and the scales, not the 'weight'; decelerating at 0.436 m s^{-2}.

9 $\frac{2}{3}mg$

10 0.7 m s^{-2}

11 80, 20

12 10.75, 1.60

Miscellaneous exercise 3 (page 41)

1 744 N

2 His weight, 588 N; normal contact force acting vertically upwards, 618 N.

3 4800 N

4 3948 N   (a) 25.2 kg   (b) 7.5 s

5 1400 N

7 $W(3 - 2k)$

8 $\frac{7}{3}mg$; (a) 14 m s^{-1} (b) $4\frac{2}{7}$ s

9 (a) There are forces acting upwards, buoyancy and water resistance.

    (b) 8.5, 0.195 N

10 4 m s^{-2}; 5900 N

11   (a)   Initially accelerates at 10 m s^{-2} for 4 s, then decelerates at 5 m s^{-2} for 6 s before falling to ground with constant speed for 15 s.

      (b)   380 m;

      1332 N; for example, air resistance depends on speed, so acceleration and deceleration are not constant; change from acceleration to deceleration is not instantaneous.

4 Resolving forces

Exercise 4A (page 47)

1   (a)   4 N, 6.93 N; -7.88 N, -1.39 N

      (b)   3.46 N, -2 N; -3 N, 5.20 N

      (c) -4 N, 0 N; 2.05 N, -5.64 N

      (d)   2.5 N, 4.33 N; -2.5 N, 4.33 N

2   (a)   60   (b)   8.66

3 2.89 m s^{-2}

4   35.1 N

5   166 N

6   350, 8180 N

7 5 m s^{-2}, $9.2m$ N

8   8.05 kg, 84.1 N

9   6.12 kg

10 1.23 m s^{-2}

11   968 N, 127 N

12 $\left(49 - \tfrac{1}{2}T\right)$ N

13   (a)   23.8   (b)   32.0 N

14 1.50 m s^{-2}, 408 N

15   1.38

16   11.7°, 521

17   21.9, 822 N

18   170 N, 331 N

Exercise 4B (page 53)

1   (a) $F\cos\theta°$, $F\cos(90-\theta)° = F\sin\theta°$

      (b) $F\cos(90+\theta)° = -F\sin\theta°$, $F\cos\theta°$

      (c) $F\cos\theta°$, $F\cos(\theta-90)° = F\sin\theta°$

      (d) $F\cos\theta°$, $F\cos(90+\theta)° = -F\sin\theta°$

2 4.9 m s^{-2}, 5.42 m s^{-1}

3   2240 N

4 1.02 m s^{-2}

5   6.99 N

6   8.66

7   21.4 N, 62.6 N

8   38.4 N, 676 N

9   (a)   5.74 N   (b)   7.00 N   (c)   6.33 N

      In case (b) a component of the applied force will be added to $10\cos 35°$; in (c) it is subtracted.

10   (a)   4.57 N   (b)   28.6   (c) 1.60 m s^{-2}

11   559 N, 26.6

12   40.2 N, 111 N

13   82.3, 73.3 N

14   (b)   172 N   (c)   12.1 N

15   53.2

16   470, 4620

Miscellaneous exercise 4 (page 56)

1   10.3 N, 28.2 N

2   31.1 N

3   (a)   67.4°   (b)   1.96

4   1.46, 4.26; in the opposite direction to the 4 N force.

5   Yes

6   7.7 N, 14.5 N

7   252 N, 392 N

8   (a) 0.65 m s^{-2} (b)   12.3 s, 49.2 m

9   0.76, 2.20; 3 m s^{-2} in the opposite direction to the 1.2 N force.

10   (a)   8 N   (b)   1.73 kg;   13.9 kg

11   25.7, 21.7 N

12   (a)   There is no force to the left to counterbalance the resolved part of the tension to the right.

      (c)   94.0 N, 750 N   (d)   128 N

      (e) 0.144 m s^{-2}

13   (b)   91.4 N   (c)   29.9 N

      (d)   No, the resolved part of the tension will be greater, so the normal force will be smaller.

14   20.1 N; 88.1 N

15   (a)   98.5 N, 17.4 N

      (b)   Force on the wheels from the track.

      (c)   98.5 N

      (d)   All the forces in the direction of motion are constant, 109 N, 11.25 m.

      (e)   As θ increases $T\cos\theta°$ gets less but $(100 + 44\sin\theta°)$ gets larger and so the truck will decelerate.

5 Friction

Exercise 5A (page 66)

1   (a) $(P-Q)$ N in the direction of the force of magnitude Q N.

      (b) $(Q-P)$ N in the direction of the force of magnitude P N.

2 $80 \leqslant P \leqslant 120$

3 6.93 N

4 0.408, 63 N

5 0.255

6 (a) 4000 N,   (b) 5000 N   (c) 5880 N
    (a), (b) The dinghy remains at rest.
    (c) The dinghy accelerates at $0.15 \mathrm{~m~s}^{-2}$.

7 (a) $(P - 50\sin\alpha°)$ N acting down the plane.
    (b) $(50\sin\alpha° - P)$ N acting up the plane.

8 $8.0 \leqslant P \leqslant 37.0$, where the numbers have been
    rounded down and up respectively to 1 decimal
    place.

9 (a), (b) 0   (c) 0.053 N
    (a), (b) The bowl remains at rest (with limiting
    equilibrium in (b)).   (c) The bowl slides down
    with acceleration $0.106 \mathrm{~m~s}^{-2}$.

10 28.7 cm

11 0.42

12 80

13 32.7 N

14 $4.70 \mathrm{~m~s}^{-2}$; 2.30 m

15 $3.92 \mathrm{~m~s}^{-2}$

16 $0.98 \mathrm{~m~s}^{-2}$

Exercise 5B (page 71)

1 In the direction of motion of the train;
    accelerating; 0.408

2 0.5

3 750 kg

4 12.5 m

5 4.27 N down the plane

6 0.0225

7 0.2

8 0.817

9 (a) $161 \mathrm{~N}$, $21.5 \mathrm{~m~s}^{-1}$
    (b) $230 \mathrm{~N}$, $21.5 \mathrm{~m~s}^{-1}$

10 4.18 m, 1.52 s

11 0.746

12 0.455 N; 1.52 N

13 0.534

14 0.380; $1.61 \mathrm{~m~s}^{-2}$

15 0.183; $3.34 \mathrm{~m~s}^{-2}$

Miscellaneous exercise 5 (page 73)

1 3.76 N; the friction is not limiting.

2 $3.94 \mathrm{~m~s}^{-1}$

3 39.8

4 14 200 N, 1800 N; 0.268

5 0.703

7 0.457

8 831;   (a), because the normal force, and hence
    the frictional force, is less when pulling.

10 0.321

11 25.4 N; 0.249

12 $4.80 \mathrm{~m~s}^{-2}$

13 0.297

14 $2.30 \mathrm{~m}$; $2.70 \mathrm{~m~s}^{-1}$

15 17.7 s

16 $2.70 \mathrm{~m~s}^{-1}$; 587 N

17 3.11 m

6 Motion due to gravity

Exercise 6A (page 78)

1 $29.4 \mathrm{~m~s}^{-1}$, 44.1 m

2 $14 \mathrm{~m~s}^{-1}$

3 11.0 m

4 15 m

5 $17.4 \mathrm{~m~s}^{-1}$

Exercise 6B (page 81)

1 $5.4 \mathrm{~m~s}^{-1}$ upwards, 30.4 m

2 1.6 m

3 $21 \mathrm{~m~s}^{-1}$

4 2.67 s

5 23.7 m

6 0.42 s

7 $9.4 \mathrm{~m~s}^{-1}$ downwards, 15.9 m

8 $15.7 \mathrm{~m~s}^{-1}$

9 3.67 s, $18 \mathrm{~m~s}^{-1}$ downwards

10 $1\frac{1}{7}$ s

11 2.64 s, $13.9 \mathrm{~m~s}^{-1}$ downwards

12 61.9 m

13 u downwards

14 $8.82 \mathrm{~m~s}^{-1}$, 4.0 m

15 (a) 60.0 m   (b) 6 s

Exercise 6C (page 87)

1 (a) $9 \mathrm{~m~s}^{-2}$, $1 \mathrm{~m~s}^{-2}$ (b) 8 m, $\frac{4}{3}$ s
    (c) 4 s, $4 \mathrm{~m~s}^{-1}$;   (b) 14.4 m, 2.4 s
    (c) 2.4 s, $12 \mathrm{~m~s}^{-1}$

2 $66\frac{2}{3}$ m, $28 \mathrm{~m~s}^{-1}$, $9\frac{11}{21}$ s;
    $41\frac{2}{3}$ m, $14 \mathrm{~m~s}^{-1}$, $8\frac{13}{14}$ s

3 50 m s^{-1}, 7.35 m s^{-2}

4 44.1 m, 29.4 m s^{-1}; both smaller; 0.5;
7.8 m s^{-2}

5 $\frac{10}{7} \text{ s}$, 14 m s^{-1}; 10 m s^{-1}, $0.98(10-v) \text{ m s}^{-2}$;
(a) Smaller with air resistance.
(b) Larger with air resistance.

6 $\frac{1}{320} m$; 28 m s^{-1};   (a) 8.42 m s^{-2}
(b) 4.29 m s^{-2}

7 3 m, $\frac{10}{7} \text{ s}$; (a) 11.2 m s^{-2} downwards
(b) 9.8 m s^{-2} downwards;
(i) Less than 3 m (ii) Less than 7 m s^{-1}
(iii) Between 8.4 m s^{-2} and 9.8 m s^{-2}; not more
than 49 m s^{-1}.

Miscellaneous exercise 6 (page 89)

1 $\frac{6}{7} \text{s}$, 8.4 m s^{-1}

2 29 m

3 6.53 s

4 3 s, 12.7 m s^{-1}

5 39.2 m s^{-1} (b) Neither is correct.

6 (a) Weight is opposed by buoyancy and the
resistance of the liquid.
(b) 8.5, 5.1 m s^{-1}
(c) With constant acceleration ball-bearing
would have fallen 0.38 m.

7 490 m

8 $49t^2 \text{ m}$, $19.6(t-1) \text{ m}$, $\left(490-4.9(t-2)^2\right) \text{ m}$, 0;
176.4 m

9 105; 28 m s^{-1}; 29.4 m s^{-2}

10 0.34 m s^{-1}, 2.3 m s^{-1}; 6.6 m s^{-2} deceleration,
4.33 m s^{-2} acceleration; between 10 and 30
seconds.

11 $0.7m$, $0.05m$; $(9.8-0.7v) \text{ m s}^{-2}$,
$\left(9.8-0.05v^2\right) \text{ m s}^{-2}$; model 2

Revision exercise 1
(page 91)

1 0.161 m s^{-1}

2 (a) $\frac{1}{2} \text{ m s}^{-2}$ (b) 40 s

3 $\left(15t+1.25t^2\right) \text{ m}$, $(1.5+2.5t) \text{ m s}^{-1}$;
8 s, 35 m s^{-1}

4 6 s, 4.5 m

5 300 kN; smaller

6 60 N

7 53 kN

8 24 s, 405 m

9 125 N: 130 N

10 14.3 m s^{-1}

11 $\frac{2}{3} \text{ m s}^{-2}$; 408 m, 35 s

12 81.6 m, 5.08 s

13 2.59 s

14 7 N

15 (a) 18.2 N (b) 345 N

16 7 m, 3.86 s

17 17.5 kN; no, the weight is negligible compared
with the other forces

18 10 kg; 59.9 m

19 40.5 s

20 $\frac{1}{3} \leqslant \mu < 1$

22 8 m s^{-1}, 0.082; 1.98 m s^{-2}, 16.2 m

23 (a) 0.8 m s^{-2} (b) 0.32 m s^{-2} (c) 6 m s^{-1}

24 0.30 s

25 $g\sin\alpha°$, $g\sin\beta°$

7 Newton's third law

Exercise 7A (page 99)

1 Weights of 80 N and 100 N respectively, and
vertical contact forces 80 N upwards on the top
crate, 80 N downwards and 180 N upwards on
the bottom crate.

2 (a) 200 N upwards
(b) 200 N downwards
(c) 1200 N upwards

4 705 N

5 (i) 375 N (ii) 750 N

6 42

8 400 N, 500 N; 800 N forwards; it will appear
that the car is being pushed from behind.

9 Weight 5880 N, contact from pile driver
(a) $21\,200 \text{ N}$ (b) $19\,600 \text{ N}$;
force from earth
(a) $27\,560 \text{ N}$ (b) $25\,480 \text{ N}$

10 (a) $16\,950 \text{ N}$ (b) $14\,700 \text{ N}$

12 $P > \mu W$, middle box won't move; $P > 3\mu W$

13 (a) $W\cos\alpha°$ (b) $W\sin\alpha°$ (c) $W\sin\alpha°$
(d) $2W\tan\alpha°$ (e) $\dfrac{W\left(1+\sin^2\alpha°\right)}{\cos\alpha°}$

Exercise 7B (page 107)

1 (a) 9.8 N, 9.8 N
(b) 9.8 N, 14.7 N (up the slope)
(c) 19.6 N, 9.8 N; 9.8 N
(d) 7.35 N, 7.35 N (e) 17.0 N, 2.27 N
(f) 34.6 N, 54.2 N

2 10 kg

3 23.52 N, 1.96 m s^{-2}

4 (a) 1.63 m s^{-2} (b) 2.45 m s^{-2}
   (c) 0.754 m s^{-2} (d) 2.94 m s^{-2}
   (e) 0.455 m s^{-2} (f) 6.03 m s^{-2}

5 2.26 m s^{-2}; 30.2 N, 7.54 N

6 (a) 0.6125 m s^{-2} (b) 1.225 m s^{-2}

7 3:1

8 $0.2m \leqslant M \leqslant m$; $\dfrac{(M-m)g}{M+m}$ if $M > m$,

   $\dfrac{(0.2m - M)g}{M+m}$ if $M < 0.2m$

Exercise 7C (page 111)

1 (a) 0.48 m s^{-2}, 170 N
   (b) 0.08 m s^{-2}, 170 N

2 250 N, 50 N;
   (a) 0.05 m s^{-2} acceleration, 62.5 N
   (b) 0.05 m s^{-2} deceleration, 37.5 N
   (c) 0.156 m s^{-2} deceleration, 10.9 N
   (d) 0.175 m s^{-2}, 6.25 N tension
   (e) 0.2 m s^{-2}, zero
   (f) 0.25 m s^{-2}, 12.5 N thrust

3 $\dfrac{F - (P+Q)}{M+m} + g\sin\alpha°$

4 $4mg$, $3mg$, $2mg$, mg (uppermost to lowermost); $\frac{9}{10}g$,
   (a) zero (all strings)
   (b) $\frac{1}{5}mg$, $\frac{3}{20}mg$, $\frac{1}{10}mg$, $\frac{1}{20}mg$ (uppermost to lowermost)

Miscellaneous exercise 7 (page 112)

1 547 N

2 0.8 m s^{-2}, speeding up

3 36.75 N

4 436 N; 0.20
Children as particles: analysis not affected because of the absence of a turning effect.
Rope light: unrealistic, the weight of the rope could be significant compared with the weight of a child.
Rope inextensible: unrealistic, a characteristic of rope is that it stretches, but reasonable for a first approximation.
Smooth groove: unrealistic, even if the tree is a eucalyptus or similar the frictional forces are likely to be significant.

5 4.43 m s^{-1}, 3 m; 7.67 m s^{-1}

6 1.62 N, 0.180

8 3.02 N, 3.96 m s^{-1}, there is no friction; 4.99 m

9 1.32; 0.540 N

10 2280, 5700

11 18 N, 0.265; 0.106 m

12 (a) 0.933 N   (b) 0.748 m s^{-1}

13 (a) (i) 100 N   (ii) 400 N   (b) 0.222 m s^{-2}

14 $a = \dfrac{X - 600}{10\,000}$, $X < 600$; $X < 60$

15 (a) 3140 N   (b) 3260 N

16 Possible assumptions are: vehicles modelled as particles, tow-rope is light, tow-rope is inextensible, tow-rope is parallel to the slope.
   (a) 1290 N   (b) 3430 N; 14.0 s

17 (a) The tensions in each part of the string are equal, and so, by resolving horizontally for the 0.6 kg ring, angles ABR, RAB are equal.
   (c) 0.346

18 (a) 6.86 N   (b) $2.94\tan\theta°$ N; 35.0

8 Momentum

Exercise 8A (page 119)

1 (a) 540 N s   (b) 60 kN s   (c) 208 kN s
   (d) 8 N s   (e) 160 kN s

2 0.36 N s

3 300 N s

4 5.76×10^7 N s

5 50 m s^{-1}

6 1.25×10^{-4} N s

7 2000 N

8 55.5... kN s, 18.5 s

9 6.4 N s, 160 N

10 4.5 N s

11 12 m s^{-1}

12 0.627 N s

Exercise 8B (page 122)

1 5 m s^{-1}

2 2.2 m s^{-1}

3 5 m s^{-1}

4 1.75 m s^{-1}

5 (a) $2\frac{2}{3}$ m s^{-1}

6 9.2 m s^{-1}

7 (a) 12 m s^{-1} (b) 16 m s^{-1}
(c) 8 m s^{-1}. The 4 kg block can't go faster than the 3 kg block. $5\frac{1}{7} \text{ m s}^{-1}$

8 (a) 0   (b) 2 m s^{-1}

9 3 kg

10 (a) 2 m s^{-1} (b) $2 \text{ m s}^{-1}, 1 \text{ m s}^{-1}$

Miscellaneous exercise 8 (page 123)

1 $\frac{1}{2} \text{ m s}^{-1}$

2 3 m s^{-1}

3 (a) 4200 N s

4 (a) 0.15 (b) $0.4, 0.133, 0.067$

5 $\frac{1}{5}u$

6 (b) $5:1$

7 $m = 0.1, u$

8 (b) $v = \frac{1}{93}(86p - 7r)$
(c) The total momentum is zero at the beginning, so it is zero at the end.

9 (a) 375 N s (b) 2.75 m s^{-1}
(c) 0.49 m s^{-1}

9 Combining and splitting forces

Exercise 9A (page 131)

1 (a) Magnitude 22.8 N, bearing $44.7°$
(b) Magnitude 26.0 N, bearing $65.0°$
(c) Magnitude 10.9 N, bearing $95.9°$
(d) Magnitude 9.10 N, bearing $35.1°$

2 543 N, making an angle $0.029°$ with the direction in which the car is facing.

3 (a) Vertically upwards, magnitude 24 N.
(b) Vertically downwards, magnitude 8 N.
(c) 16.5 N at an angle $14.0°$ downward from the horizontal.

4 (a) 33.5 N (b) 27.6 N
(c) 5.46 N (d) 32.0 N

5 (i) 1.83 N in a direction $14.9°$ backward from the downward vertical.
(ii) 1.68 N in a direction $17.4°$ backward from the downward vertical.
(iii) 1.46 N in a direction $18.1°$ backward from the downward vertical.
(a) Immediately on leaving the bat.
(b) When descending at $18.2°$ to the horizontal.

6 (a) 315 N (b) Horizontal to the left.
(c) 6.86 m s^{-2}

7 (a) 4.60 N (b) 7.51 m s^{-2}

8 6.90 m

9 (a) 34.1 N (b) 38.6 N
(c) 18.3 N (d) 44.5 N

10 $42.6°$

11 (a) $13.1 \text{ N}, 13.1 \text{ N}$ (b) $47.0 \text{ N}, 25 \text{ N}$
(c) $42.4 \text{ N}, 58.0 \text{ N}$ (d) $17.8 \text{ N}, 27.2 \text{ N}$

12 (a) 12.9 N south   (b) 10 N north

13 (a) 8.68 N up the plane, 49.2 N perpendicular to the plane.
(b) 4.36 N to the left, 49.8 N upwards.
(c) 192 N up the plane, 190 N to the left.
(d) 51.6 N perpendicular to the plane, 8.99 N to the right.
(e) 4.51 N down the plane, 51.0 N upwards.
(f) 16.8 N perpendicular to the plane, 33.5 N upwards.

14 At $90°$ to the banks, from south to north; 154 N.

15 0.173 N

Exercise 9B (page 139)

1 (a) Magnitude 22.8 N, bearing $44.7°$
(b) Magnitude 26.0 N, bearing $65.0°$
(c) Magnitude 10.9 N, bearing $95.9°$
(d) Magnitude 9.10 N, bearing $35.1°$

2 (a) Magnitude 22.8 N, bearing $44.7°$
(b) Magnitude 26.0 N, bearing $65.0°$
(c) Magnitude 10.9 N, bearing $95.9°$
(d) Magnitude 9.10 N, bearing $35.1°$

3 543 N, making an angle $0.029°$ with the direction in which the car is facing

4 $17 \text{ N}, 151.9°$ anticlockwise from the positive x-axis.

5 $\begin{pmatrix} 7.66 \\ 6.43 \end{pmatrix} \text{N}, \begin{pmatrix} -3.46 \\ 2 \end{pmatrix} \text{N}, \begin{pmatrix} -1.04 \\ -5.91 \end{pmatrix} \text{N}; \begin{pmatrix} 3.15 \\ 2.52 \end{pmatrix} \text{N};$
$4.04 \text{ N}, 38.6°$ anticlockwise from the x-axis.

6 $2.56 \text{ m s}^{-2}, 20.6°$ above the horizontal

7 $15.03, 4.65$

8 $0.5, -1.9$

9 $\begin{pmatrix} -W\sin 15° + P\cos 20° \\ -W\cos 15° + P\sin 20° + C \end{pmatrix} \text{N}$
$W\cos 15° - P\sin 20°, \ P\cos 20° - W\sin 15°$

10 $13 \text{ N}, 67.4°$ anticlockwise from $\mathbf{i}$

11 $17 \text{ N}, 151.9°$ anticlockwise from $\mathbf{i}$

12 $7.66\mathbf{i} + 6.43\mathbf{j}, -3.46\mathbf{i} + 2\mathbf{j}, -1.04\mathbf{i} - 5.91\mathbf{j},$
$3.15\mathbf{i} + 2.52\mathbf{j}; 4.04 \text{ N}$, direction $38.6°$ anticlockwise from $\mathbf{i}$.

13 $2.56 \text{ m s}^{-2}, 20.6°$ above the horizontal

14 $55 \text{ N}; 36.9°, 106.3°$

15 $0.5, -1.9$

16 $\pm\frac{1}{5}$

Miscellaneous exercise 9 (page 140)

1 10.7 N , 32.5

2 53.9

3 120

4 (a) 19.5   (b) 9.12

5 17.2 N , bearing 116.3°

6 (b) 126.9

7 (a) 63.2° (b) 7.83 N

8 20.0 , 145.1°

9 5 N

10 150°

11 81.2°

12 3.14 N , in the direction of the force of magnitude 17 N ; 0.130

13 24.2 , 3.80

14 231 N horizontally to the right, 115 N downwards parallel to the incline, zero

15 (a) 104 N , 72 N upwards
    (b) 104 N , 3 N upwards
    (c) 176 N , 118 N downwards

10 Forces in equilibrium

Exercise 10A (page 148)

1 (a) 12.3 N, 11.3 N   (b) 25.7 N, 37.6 N

2 4880 N , 8220 N

3 (a) Along the outward normal to the plane, 46.0 N
    (b) 46.0 N in the direction of the inward normal to the plane.   (c) 16.8

4 200

5 5.44 N, 6.05 N

6 12 100 N , 69 700 N

7 (a) 105.6°, 112.4°   (b) 51.1°, 141.5°

8 (a) 23.9° (b) 86.7°

9 22.3°, 58.8°

10 (a) 38.2°, 21.8°
    (b) The length of any one side of the triangle of forces cannot exceed the sum of the lengths of the other two sides (the case $m = 0.8$ is excluded because the pulleys are not in the same vertical line).
    (d) K cannot be above the level of the pulleys.

11 Perpendicular to the thread, $mg \sin \alpha°$

12 (a) 7 (b) 90°

13 36.9° and 73.7° either side of the upward vertical; $(-0.45, 0.6)$, $(0.72, 0.21)$

14 90°; 630 N , 160 N

Exercise 10B (page 153)

1 (a) 43.6 N   (b) 23.4°   (c) 0.433

2 (a) 1120 N   (b) 571 N

3 (b) 0.424

4 (a) 46.4 N
    (b) 9.3° to the upward vertical (c) 0.594

5 33.6° to the upward vertical; 18.6°

6 (a) 35.0° (b) 11.6   (c) 19.6

7 (a) 755 N at 14.4° to the upward vertical,
        (i) 200 N at 20° below the horizontal in to the tree, (ii) 755 N at 20° to the downward vertical
    (b) 752 N at 22.0° to the upward vertical,
        (i) 300 N at 22.0° below the horizontal in to the tree, (ii) 752 N at 14.5° to the downward vertical.
    The force exerted on the man by the ground must act upwards; $P > 800/\cos 70°$ is inconsistent with this.

Miscellaneous exercise 10 (page 155)

1 0.762 N

2 (a) 231, 115
    (b) (i) Both greater   (ii) Both greater
    (c) As θ increases, T decreases, P decreases until $\theta = 30$ and then increases; when $\theta = 30$, $P = 100$ and $T = 173$ N.

3 (a) 105.4 N, 86.1 N   (b) None
    (c) Both increase

4 2.31 N

5 (b) 4.36 N , 23.4°

6 (b) 17.0 N ;   25.9 N

7 2.57 N ; 0.257

8 0.183

9 2.94 N, 0.192; 5.09 N

10 $(3 - \sqrt{3})W/\sqrt{2}$ at 15° downward from the outward normal, $(\sqrt{3} - 1)W/\sqrt{2}$ at 15° downward from the outward normal, $\mu = \tan 15°$ or $2 - \sqrt{3}$ for both contacts.

11 23.1 N, 11.5 N , 23.1 N ;
    (a) 1.905... m (b) 80.45...°
    (c) 17.65...°; 23.50... N , 68.0 N

11 General motion in a straight line

Exercise 11A (page 162)

1   $v = 3t^2 + 4$, $a = 6t$; 22 m, 16 m s^{-1}, 12 m s^{-2}

2   $v = 20 - 4t^3$, $a = -12t^2$; 22 m, 16 m s^{-1},
    -12 m s^{-2}; -18 m, -88 m s^{-1}, -108 m s^{-2}

3   42 m, 32 m s^{-1}, 18 m s^{-2}

4   0 m, 10 m s^{-1} -14 m s^{-2}

5   1 m s^{-1}, -1 m s^{-2}

6   6 m s^{-1}, $\frac{3}{4} \text{ m s}^{-2}$

7   2 s; -24 m s^{-1}, -24 m s^{-2}

8   5 s; 20 m

9   130 m

10   4 m s^{-1}

11   27 m, 28 m s^{-1}

12   32 m, $-\frac{3}{8} \text{ m s}^{-2}$

13   $\frac{4}{3} \text{ m s}^{-2}$

14   $22\frac{1}{8}$ m, 54 m s^{-2}

15   $10(12t - 7)$ N

16   (a) 64 m s^{-1} (c)   48 N

17   (a) 18 m s^{-1} (b) 4 m s^{-2}

18   (a)   120 s, 1380 m   (b) 0.384 m s^{-2}
     (c) 1.15 m s^{-2} (d)   80 s, 20.5 m s^{-1}

19   (b)   (A) 120 m s^{-1}, (B) 160 m s^{-1}; (B), because
     $v = 0$ when $t = 3$.

20   (a)   952 m, 62.4 m s^{-1}
     (b) -41.0 m s^{-2}, -10 m s^{-2}, -0.328 m s^{-2}
     (c) 40 m s^{-1} (d)   40 s

Exercise 11B (page 167)

1   $x = t^3 + 8t + 4$; 28 m, 20 m s^{-1}

2   $v = 10t - 2t^3 - 4$, $x = \frac{1}{2}(23 - 8t + 10t^2 - t^4)$;
    $11\frac{1}{2}$ m, -4 m s^{-1}, 10 m s^{-2}

3   2 m, 6 m s^{-1}, 3 m s^{-2}

4   12 m, $7\frac{1}{3} \text{ m s}^{-1}$, $1\frac{7}{9} \text{ m s}^{-2}$

5   20 m

6   60 m

7   60 m

8   -6 m s^{-2}

9   22 m

10   10 m

11   26 m

12   1.2 m

13   $58\frac{2}{3}$ m

14   7.2 m

15   28.5 m

16   1364.8 m

17   (a)   54 m   (b)   4 m   (c)   4 m
     62 m, 54 m

18   4.99 m s^{-1}, 5 m s^{-1}

19   $1\frac{1}{2}$ m

20   90 m

22   (a) 9 m s^{-1} (b) 8 m s^{-1}, $26\frac{2}{3}$ m

23   (a)   2 s   (b)   8 m   (c) 6 m s^{-2}

24   74 m s^{-1}, 282 m

25   (a) $3\frac{27}{40} \text{ m s}^{-1}$ (b)   16 s, 32 m

26   (b)   0 s, 7.2 m s^{-2} (c)   3 s, -1.8 m s^{-2}
     (d)   6.75 m, 6.4 m   (f)   7.1 m

Miscellaneous exercise 11 (page 170)

1   (a) $5t^2 - \frac{1}{3}t^3$ (b) $(10 - 2t) \text{ m s}^{-2}$
    (c) $83\frac{1}{3}$ m, 25 m s^{-1}
    (d) 12 m s^{-1} $\left(< 12\frac{3}{4} \text{ m s}^{-1}\right)$

2   (a) $3\frac{1}{4}$ s, $18\frac{3}{4} \text{ m s}^{-1}$
    (b)   0, -108; 2, 0; $3\frac{1}{4}$, $18\frac{3}{4}$; $4\frac{1}{2}$, 0
    (c)   31 m from O in the negative direction
    (d)   3   (e)   Begins at rest, accelerates to a
    maximum speed of $18\frac{3}{4} \text{ m s}^{-1}$ and then
    decelerates to rest, moving in the positive
    direction throughout.

3   Find the point of the graph where the tangent is
    parallel to the line joining $(0,0)$ to $(10,20)$.

4   (a) $1\frac{1}{2} \text{ m s}^{-1}$ (b)   0   (c) 2 m s^{-1}
    (e) $\frac{3}{40} \text{ m s}^{-2}$

5   (a)   18 m, 21 m s^{-1}, -24 m s^{-2}
    (b)   3 s, -24 m s^{-1}, -6 m s^{-2}
    (c)   1 s, 28 m, -18 m s^{-2}
    (d)   4 s, -26 m, -27 m s^{-1}

6   (a) $0 < t < 2$ (b) $1\frac{1}{4} < t < 2$ and $4 < t < 5$
    (c) $0.568... < t < 2$ and $2.931... < t < 5$

7   (b)   3   (d) $1\frac{7}{9}$ m
    (e) $0 < t < 1$ and $t > \frac{3}{2}\sqrt{2}$

8   (a)   (i)   112 cm   (ii)   68 cm
    (b) $4t \text{ cm s}^{-1}$, 16 cm s^{-1}
    (c) $2t^2$ cm, $16(t-2)$ cm   (d) $\frac{8}{9}$ cm

9   (a) $150V$ (b)   9   (c)   1070 m

10   (a)   40   (b) $\frac{1}{15} \text{ m s}^{-2}$ (c)   35 m

Revision exercise 2
(page 175)

1   Changes direction with speed 4 m s^{-1}.

2   2.56 N, bearing 179.4°

3 $1.5\,\mathrm{m\,s^{-2}}$, $180\,\mathrm{N}$

4 (a) $102.6°$ (b) $113.6°$ (c) $124.2°$

5 At $74.6°$ to the $0.3\,\mathrm{N}$ force, $2.87\,\mathrm{s}$

6 $2.5\,\mathrm{m\,s^{-1}}$, $200\,\mathrm{N\,s}$

7 (a) $1.4\,\mathrm{m\,s^{-2}}$ (b) $3.5\,\mathrm{kg}$ (c) 0.057

8 $22.3\,\mathrm{N}$, $32.6\,\mathrm{N}$

9 $W\cos\alpha$, $W\sin\alpha$; $\dfrac{W}{\tan\alpha}$, $\dfrac{W\cos\alpha}{\sin\alpha}$, 0;

$\dfrac{W}{\sin\alpha}$, $\dfrac{W\cos\alpha}{\tan\alpha}$, $W\sin\alpha$

10 $2\,\mathrm{m\,s^{-1}}$, $3\frac{1}{2}\,\mathrm{m\,s^{-1}}$, $7\frac{1}{2}\,\mathrm{m\,s^{-1}}$; there are no more collisions.

11 If $m < \frac{1}{5}\sqrt{2}M$, $\dfrac{Mmg}{M+m}\left(1+\frac{1}{5}\sqrt{2}\right)$;

if $\frac{1}{5}\sqrt{2}M \leqslant m \leqslant \frac{4}{5}\sqrt{2}M$, mg;

if $m > \frac{4}{5}\sqrt{2}M$, $\dfrac{Mmg}{M+m}\left(1+\frac{4}{5}\sqrt{2}\right)$;

$22\frac{1}{2}°$ to the vertical, $2T\cos 22\frac{1}{2}°$

12 $12t(t-3)(t-8)\,\mathrm{cm\,s^{-1}}$; $t=5$;

$0.24(3t-4)(t-6)\,\mathrm{N}$

13 $63.6\,\mathrm{N}$ at $28.8°$ to Ron's rope; 0.2

14 $1.2\,\mathrm{m}$, $0.45\,\mathrm{m}$

15 (a) $2p^2t$, $2p^2$

(b) $-\dfrac{p}{t^2}$, $\dfrac{2p}{t^3}$, $-\dfrac{x^2}{p}$, still true

16 $119\,\mathrm{N}$

(a) Weight $147\,\mathrm{N}$, tension $119\,\mathrm{N}$, resistance $105\,\mathrm{N}$, buoyancy $91\,\mathrm{N}$.

(b) Weight $784\,\mathrm{N}$, tension $119\,\mathrm{N}$, normal contact force $840\,\mathrm{N}$, friction $105\,\mathrm{N}$.

17 (a) $35\,\mathrm{s}$ (b) $2.5\,\mathrm{m\,s^{-1}}$ (c) $1\,\mathrm{s}$, $7\frac{1}{6}\,\mathrm{m}$

(d) $14\,000\,\mathrm{N}$ (e) $\frac{7}{8}\,\mathrm{m}$

18 58.6, 211.4

19 (a) $4.2\,\mathrm{m\,s^{-2}}$ (b) $0.89\,\mathrm{m\,s^{-2}}$ (c) $0\,\mathrm{m\,s^{-2}}$

Mock examinations

Mock examination 1 (page 178)

1 1; $\frac{5}{3}\,\mathrm{m\,s^{-1}}$, $\frac{1}{3}\,\mathrm{m\,s^{-1}}$

2 $10\sqrt{3}\,\mathrm{N}$; 15, $5\sqrt{3}$

3 $4.04\,\mathrm{s}$, $39.6\,\mathrm{m\,s^{-1}}$; larger, smaller

4 $53.1°$, $73.7°$; $26.6°$ to the vertical, $105\,\mathrm{N}$

5 $750\,\mathrm{N}$; $0.05\,\mathrm{m\,s^{-2}}$, $540\,\mathrm{N}$

6 The suitcase can rest in equilibrium; $117\,\mathrm{N}$

7 (ii) $x = \frac{1}{3}t^3 - 3t^2 + 8t$, doesn't return to O.
(iii) Negative for $t < 3$, positive for $3 < t < 5$.

Mock examination 2 (page 180)

1 $11.5\,\mathrm{N}$, $5.73\,\mathrm{N}$

2 $(25t+100)\,\mathrm{m}$, $\left(10t+t^2\right)\,\mathrm{m}$; $20\,\mathrm{s}$, $50\,\mathrm{m\,s^{-1}}$

3 (i) $132\,\mathrm{N}$ (ii) 0.635

4 $261\,\mathrm{N}$

5 $10\,\mathrm{m\,s^{-1}}$; $41.7\,\mathrm{m}$

6 (ii) $30\,\mathrm{m}$, $70\,\mathrm{m}$, $107.5\,\mathrm{m}$, $140\,\mathrm{m}$, $170\,\mathrm{m}$
(iv) $16\,\mathrm{N}$

7 $48\,\mathrm{m\,s^{-1}}$, $-8\,\mathrm{m\,s^{-1}}$; $1\,\mathrm{m\,s^{-1}}$; $x_B = -t^2 + 9t + 44$

Index

The page numbers refer to the first mention of each term, or the shaded box if there is one.

acceleration, 4, 160
    constant, equations for, 9, 166
    due to gravity, 31
    of free fall, 31
accelerometer, 39
air resistance, 19, 84
angle of friction, 151
average velocity, 14

coefficient of friction, 63
column vector, 137
component, of force, 128
conservation of momentum, 121
constant acceleration equations, 9, 166

deceleration, 5
displacement, 1
    –time graph, 2
dot notation, 167
driving force, 22

equilibrium, 24
    limiting, 60
external force, 109

force,
    air resistance, 19
    component of, 128
    diagram, 127
    driving, 22
    external, 109
    frictional, 20, 60
    internal, 109
    line of action of, 144
    normal contact, 36
    of gravity, 32
    polygon, 137
    resolved part, 44
    resultant, 126
    tension, 22, 102
    thrust, 102
free fall, acceleration of, 31
friction, 20, 60
    angle of, 151
    coefficient of, 63
    limiting, 60

g, 31, 106
gravity, acceleration due to, 31

impulse, 117
impulse–momentum equation, 118
initial velocity, 5
internal force, 109

limiting equilibrium, 60
limiting friction, 60
line of action, 144

mass, 20
model, 2
    air resistance, 85
    friction, 62
    inextensible string, 103
    light pulley, 104
    particle, 26
    rod, 102
    rough surfaces, 63
    smooth surfaces, 63
    strings, ropes, chains and cables, 102
momentum, 118
    conservation of, 121
multi-stage problems, 11

net force, 24
Newton's laws of motion, 19
    first law, 19
    second law, 21
    third law, 94
normal contact force, 36
normal reaction, 36

particle, 26
polygon, force, 137

reaction, 94
    normal, 36
resolved part, 44
resolving, 43
resultant force, 126
retardation, 5
rough surfaces, 63

scalar quantity, 126
SI, 2

smooth surfaces, 63
speed, 1
   terminal, 85
spring balance, 38

tension, 22, 102
terminal speed, 85
thrust, 102
total contact force, 151
triangle law, for combining forces, 127
triangle of forces, 144

unit vector, 138
units, 1
   consistent, 1
   kilogram, 20
   metre, 1
   newton, 21
   newton second, 117
   second, 1
   SI, 2

vector
   addition, 137
   column, 137
   quantity, 126
   unit, 138
velocity, 1, 160
   average, 14
   initial, 5
   –time graph, 3

weight, 32